# ERIC FISCHL LATE AMERICA

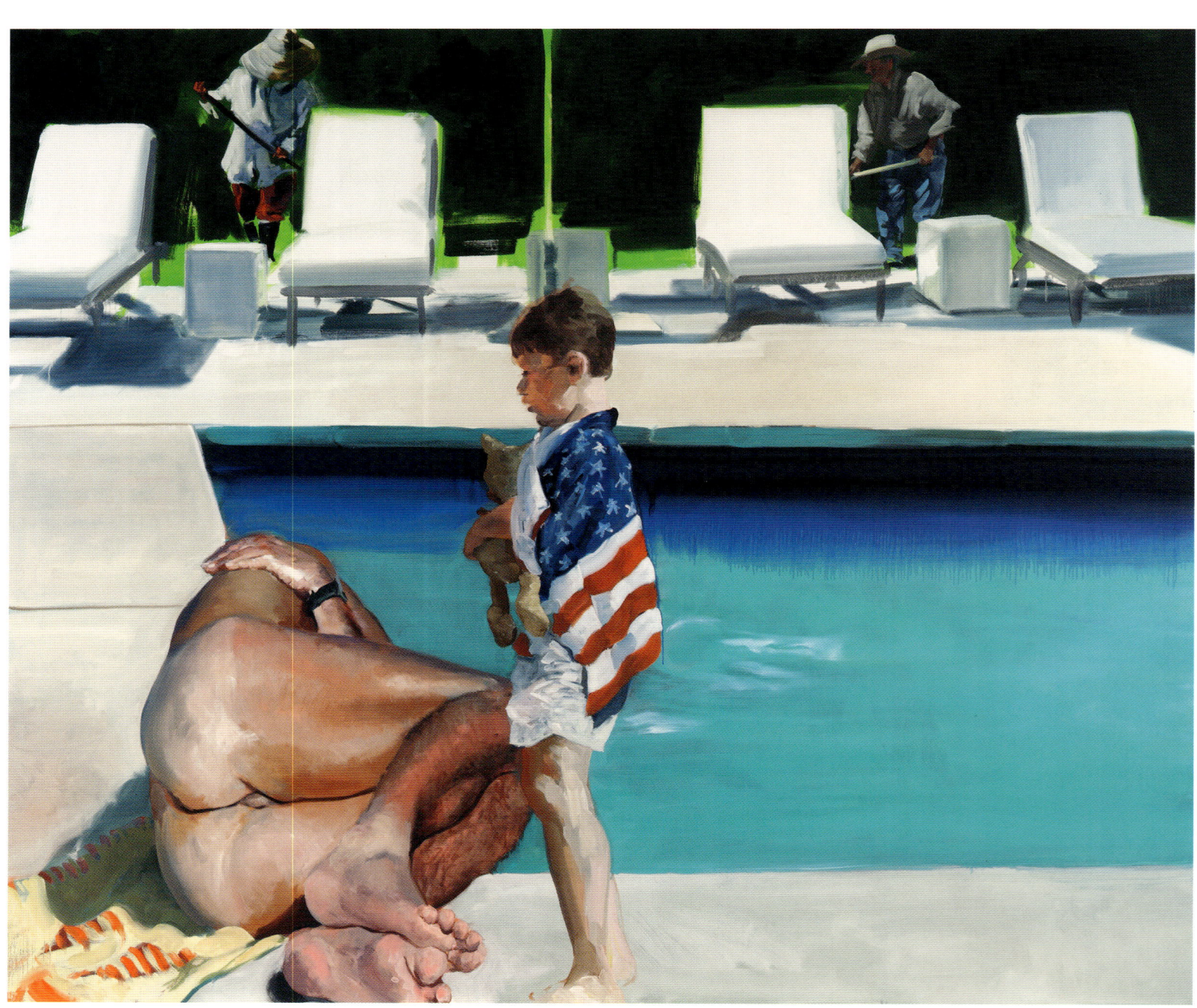

# ERIC FISCHL LATE AMERICA

EDITED BY HEATHER SEALY LINEBERRY

WITH CONTRIBUTIONS BY KATHRYN BROWN, ELEANOR HEARTNEY,
ELEANOR NAIRNE, DAWN BERG, ARCMANORO NILES, AND ERIC FISCHL

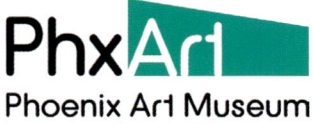
Phoenix Art Museum

IN ASSOCIATION WITH SCALA ARTS PUBLISHERS, INC.

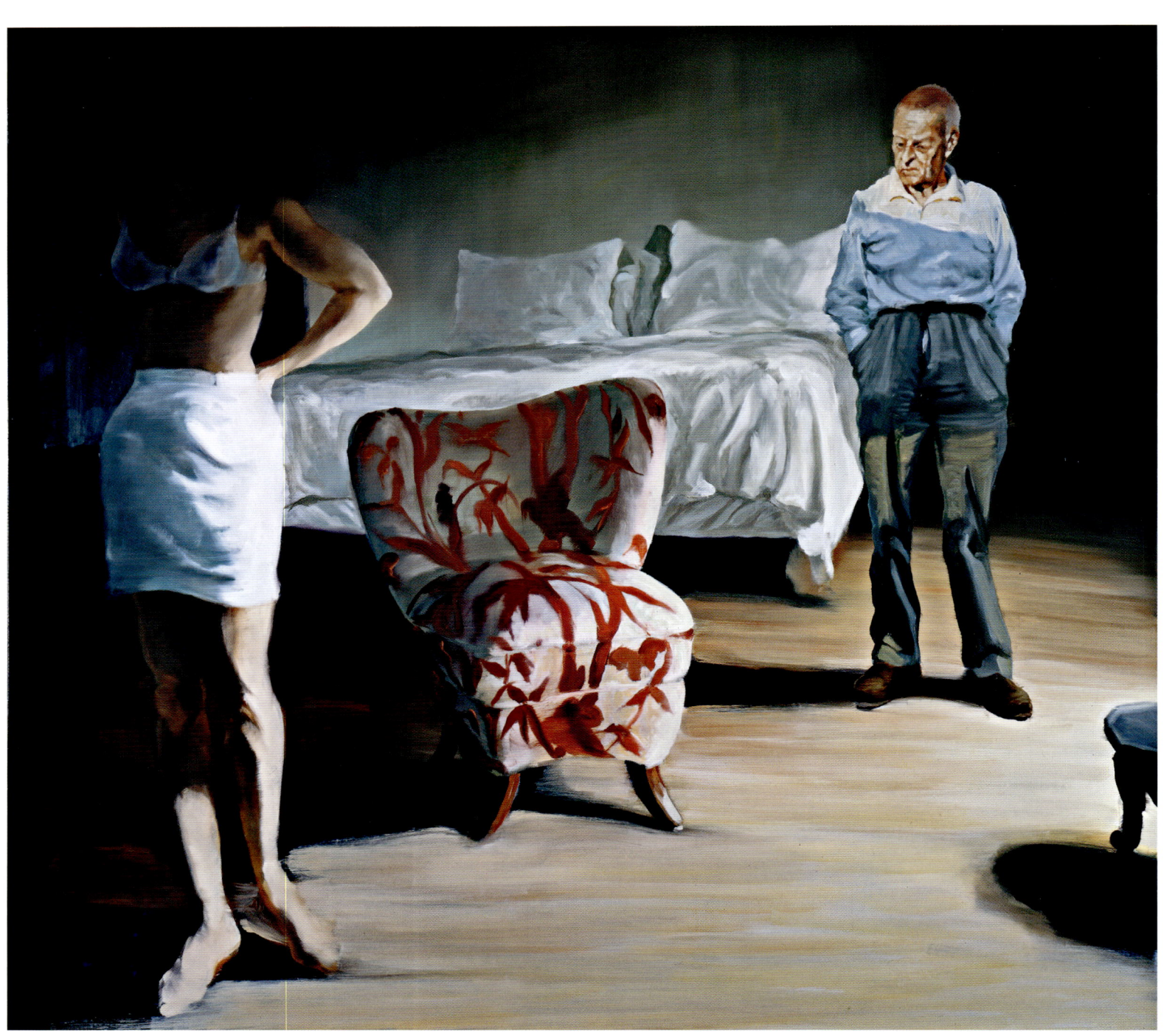

# CONTENTS

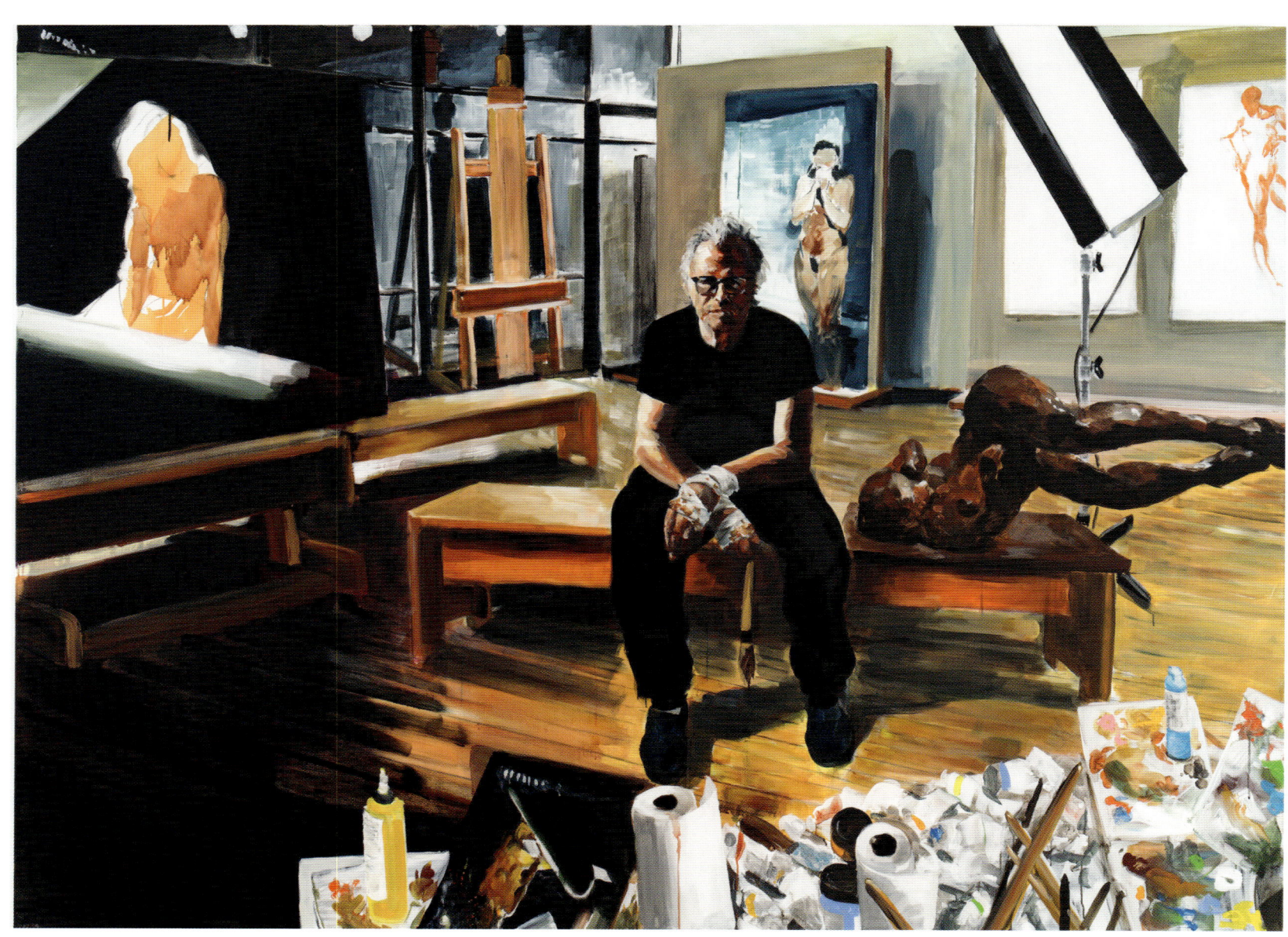

PLATE 1. *Broken Hallelujah*, 2023

# DIRECTOR'S FOREWORD

It is a tremendous honor for Phoenix Art Museum to serve as the organizing institution behind *Eric Fischl: Stories Told*. This major survey is the first in more than a decade to focus on the work of Eric Fischl, who has been largely absent from painting surveys for the past twenty years despite his position as one of the foremost American figurative painters of his generation. The exhibition is also a celebration of a true hometown hero who today maintains deep connections with the arts community in the Greater Phoenix metro region, the very place where his career as an artist was first nurtured.

Fischl (b. 1948) grew up in Long Island, New York, and Phoenix, Arizona. In the late 1960s, he attended Phoenix College, studying under contemporary landscape painter Merrill Mahaffey, and in 1972, he went on to graduate as part of the first class at California Institute of the Arts. His figurative paintings depicting memories of suburban life and the nuclear family of his childhood have long resonated with audiences and continue to do so in the context of the major social moments of our time.

Fischl's influence also extends deeply within the Phoenix arts community, primarily through numerous programs he's spearheaded at Phoenix College, the first place he says he was allowed to be an artist. This includes a gallery devoted to his name and an impactful scholarship program for students seeking an associate of arts degree with the goal of receiving a university transfer and earning a bachelor of arts.

Thank you to Men's Arts Council, the exhibition's lead sponsor, which continues to be a valued partner in supporting our exhibition and engagement programs, particularly those that mean so much to the Valley community. We are grateful to the Margaret T. Morris Foundation and to Steve Martin and Anne Stringfield for the generous contributions in support of the exhibition and public programs as well as the individual donors recognized on page 160 of this volume.

The Museum is deeply appreciative of Scala Arts Publishers and Jennifer Norman, Director of Publications, for their thoughtful collaboration, and Per Skarstedt and Alison Ward of Skarstedt Gallery, without whom this publication and project would not have been possible. I also extend my gratitude to contributors Dr. Kathryn Brown, Eleanor Heartney, Eleanor Nairne, Dawn Berg, and Arcmanoro Niles, whose conversation with Fischl on their commitment to contemporary figurative painting is inspiring. I offer my hearty congratulations to curator Heather Sealy Lineberry, who has worked tirelessly on this project for the past three years. Thank you to everyone at Phoenix Art Museum who dedicated tremendous time, attention, and efforts to this volume, particularly Olga Viso, the Selig Family Chief Curator; Dawn Berg, curatorial specialist; Katie Jones-Weinert, digital assets manager; and Charlotte Quinney, interpretation manager.

And lastly, we offer our deep thanks to Eric Fischl. We are humbled to share this exhibition and publication with wider audiences in tribute to an artist who has shared so much with the Valley of the Sun.

**JEREMY MIKOLAJCZAK**
The Sybil Harrington Director and CEO
Phoenix Art Museum

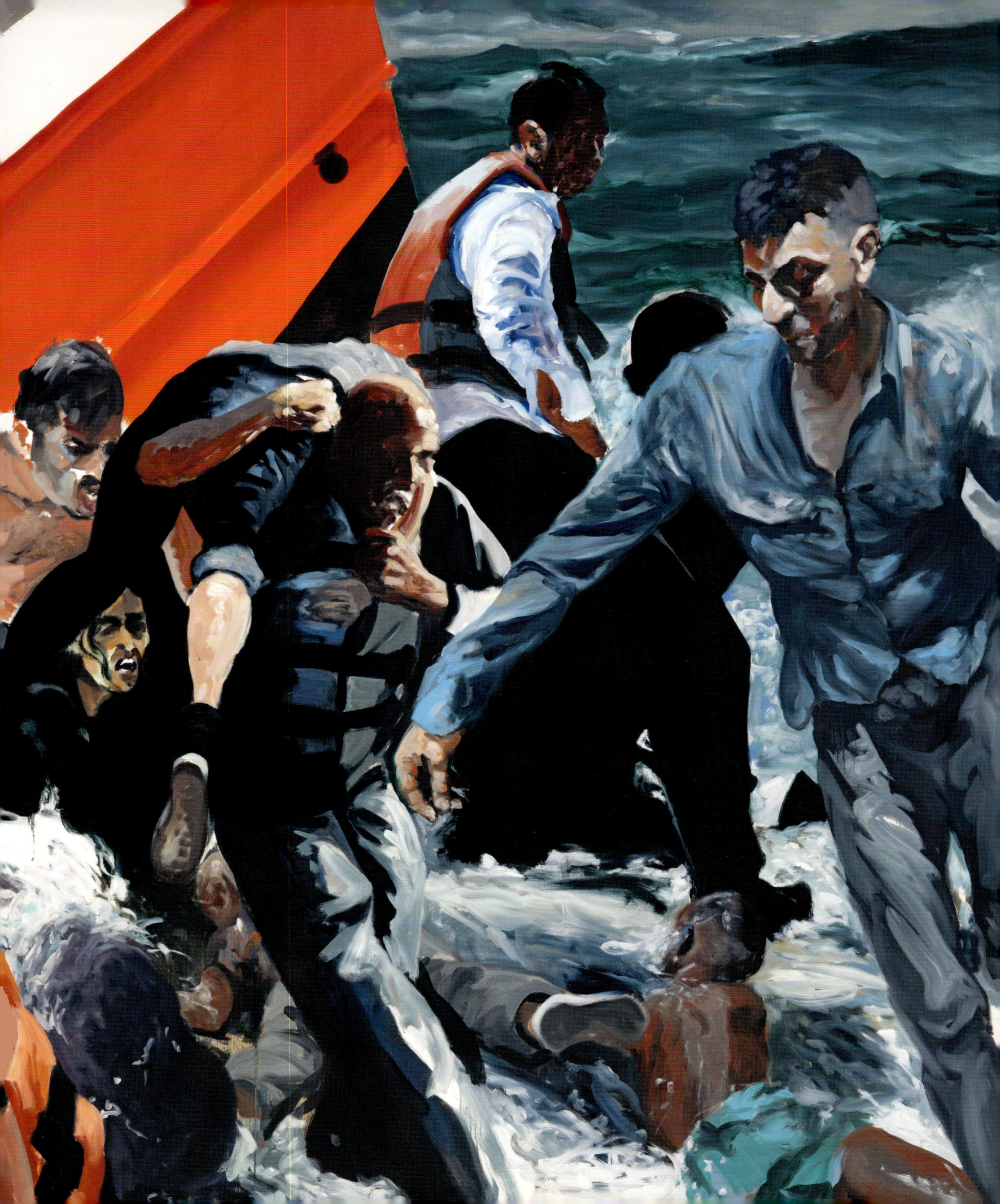

# HELLO FROM LATE AMERICA: AN INTRODUCTION
## HEATHER SEALY LINEBERRY

For more than forty-five years, Eric Fischl has been committed to painting the human form to investigate the central role of the body in individual and social experience. The exhibition *Eric Fischl: Stories Told* and this accompanying publication focus on his signature large-scale paintings in groupings defined by their key compositional element—figures—whether alone, in a couple, a family, or a crowd. These selections, which also include works on paper, cut across the decades from the late 1970s until today and reveal Fischl's constancy in exploring compositional strategies and recurring themes woven throughout his long career. The following essays examine some of these elements, including art historical influences, exploration of the American experience, use of the naked body, and painting practice.

Fischl (b. 1948) began working with recognizable and narrative content when it was out of favor in the art world, in contrast to today, when figurative painting has surged in prominence. His primary art education, in the mid-1970s, was in the painting department at the storied California Institute of the Arts (CalArts), where his abstract works were praised and any forays into representation were brutally criticized (FIG. 1).[1] As many artists before and after him, Fischl would

Detail of PLATE 38

later teach himself to paint by studying art history, particularly proto- and early modern European artists such as Edgar Degas, Édouard Manet, and Max Beckmann.

So, it may come as a surprise that a minimalist work by contemporary artist Elizabeth Murray was a key factor in Fischl's shift from abstraction to figuration. While teaching at Nova Scotia College of Art and Design—a hotbed of Minimalism, Conceptualism, and new media—after leaving art school, Fischl often visited New York to see galleries and exhibitions. On a 1976 trip, he saw a show of Murray's new work including a deceptively simple composition of a circle pushing against the confines of a square (FIG. 2). The metaphoric and formal subversion of allowing that circle to break from rigid geometries struck Fischl: "[Murray] had taken on a minimalist trope that was . . . very connected to a kind of elevated geometry of proportion and precision. She hand-painted it in a way that the circle didn't fit the square. It bulged. . . . It was one of those unexpected revelations . . . suddenly, I see the way forward."[2]

For Fischl, the encounter was the needed impetus to break from the prevalent style of the 1960s and 1970s and to innovate within an established tradition, which in his case was the daunting history of figurative

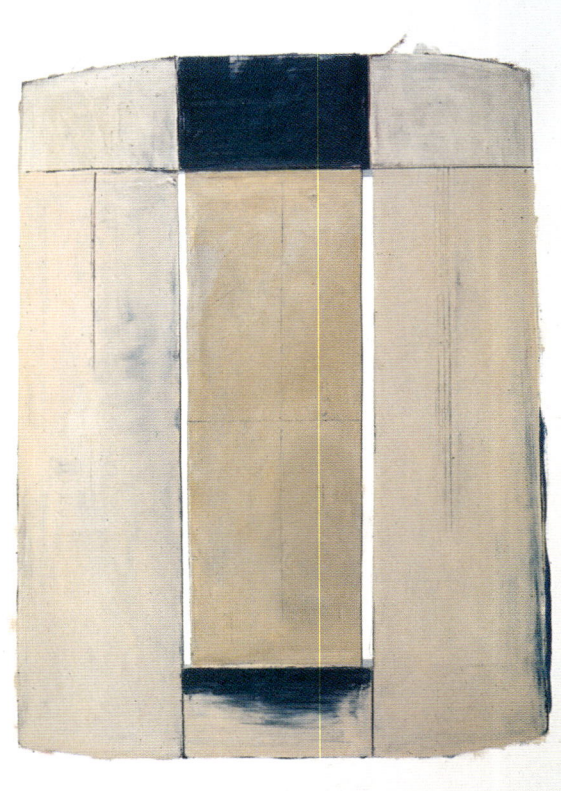

FIG. 1. **Eric Fischl**, *Shield*, **1975**. Oil and wax on paper. 22 × 30 in. (55.9 × 76.2 cm). Collection of the artist.

painting. He had been struggling to find a way to tell contemporary stories, to be more relevant. Western modernism was, for him, a stranglehold in its march to remove subjectivity and recognizable imagery from art.[3] Minimalist painters Frank Stella and Ellsworth Kelly had labeled the humanist content and compositional effects of historic European art as outdated and obsolete.[4] What Fischl saw as Murray's audacity was the push he needed to move fully into painting the figure, engaging with art history and finding his own space within it. Later that same year, he would start working with human forms on transparent sheets of glassine which he would layer and piece together in evocative combinations (FIG. 3; PLATES 34, 41).

A year later, in 1977, Fischl traveled to Europe for the first time and discovered the artists who would become his "guiding lights."[5] He is well-known for his unabashed interest in historic art, but not often noted is his attention to artists of his own time—largely ignored by the art world establishment—who were starting to use the figure to tell their stories. At CalArts he met Miriam Schapiro, who, with Judy Chicago, was running the Feminist Art Program.

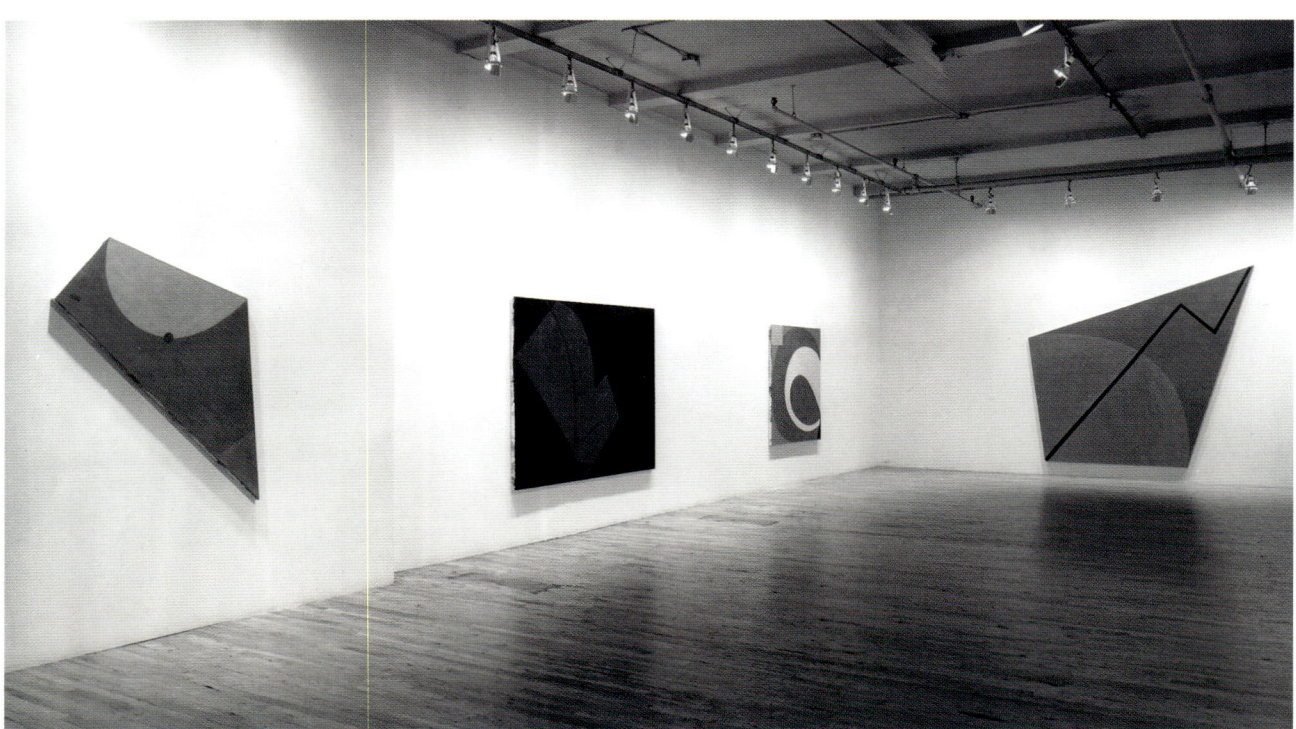

FIG. 2. Installation view of *Elizabeth Murray: Paintings* at Paula Cooper Gallery, New York, November 2–27, 1976.

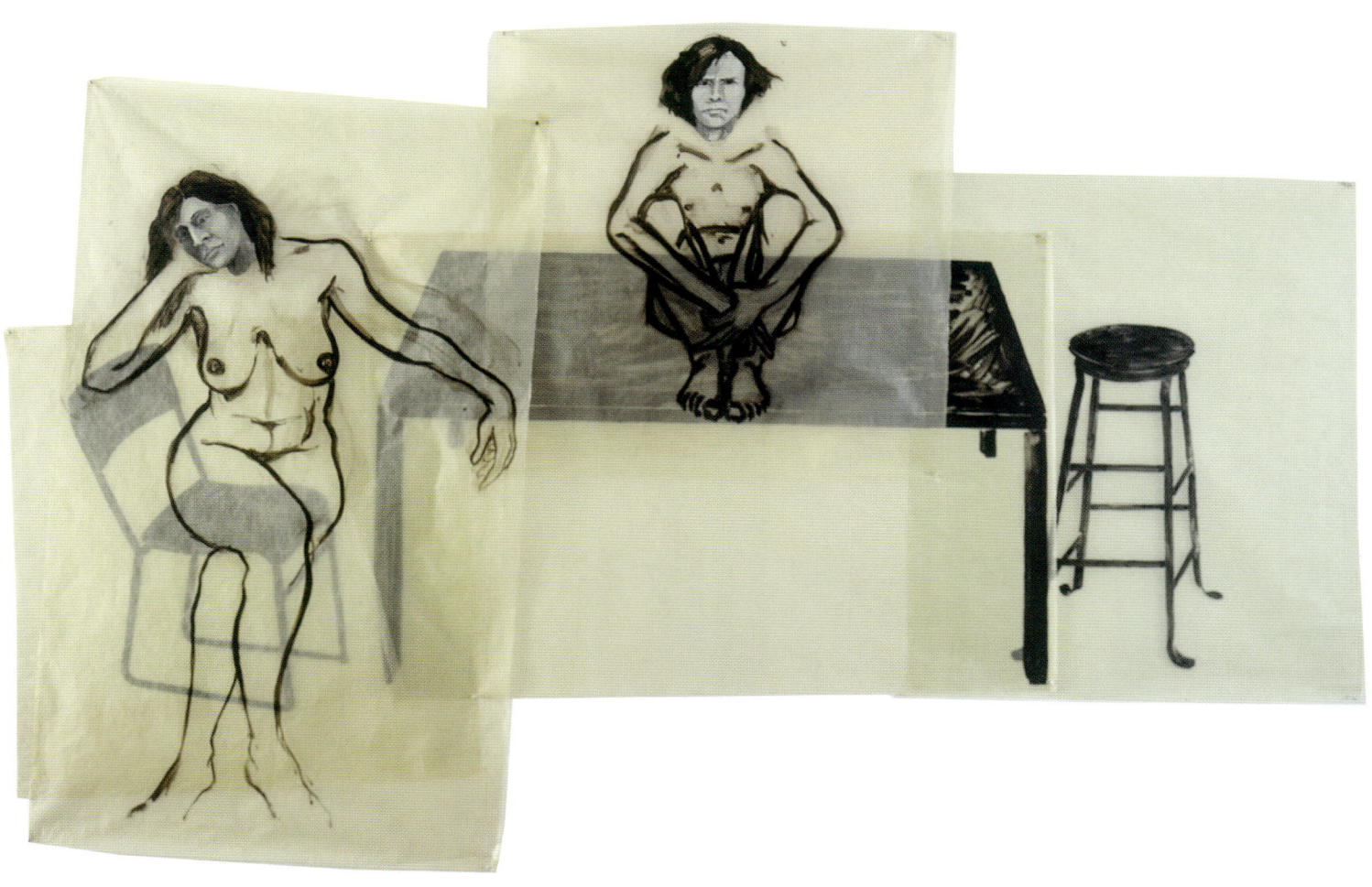

FIG. 3. **Eric Fischl,** *Mother and Son at Table,* **1978.** Oil on glassine.
76 × 121½ in. (193 × 308.6 cm). Private Collection.

When he moved to New York in 1978, feminist painters like Joan Semmel and Betty Tompkins were reclaiming sexualized images of the female body from popular culture and pornography to explore gender politics and the objectification of women. In a 1985 interview Fischl said, "I was fueled a lot by women artists who . . . were humanizing [painting]. There was definitely this sense in the women's work of content, personal content. I was getting something from this energy."[6]

Over the next few years, Fischl forged an analogous blend of contemporary themes and traditional figuration which quickly captured the art world's attention. He took as his subject matter what he knew from growing up in Long Island and Phoenix in the 1950s and 1960s—the aspirational white nuclear family at the center of post-WWII American ideals. He distinctively and persistently explored his subjective experience of American life, saying in 2014, "You must deal up front and openly with the emotional truths and psychological effects of your own life. That is the nature of art and the definition of authenticity."[7] From his earliest paintings, such as *Bad Boy* (1981; PLATE 15), with its bedroom setting and psychosexual tensions, or *Barbeque* (1982; PLATE 26), with its off-kilter backyard family gathering, he drew from and captured the disparities of his own background. His childhood was marked by trauma and dysfunction within the trappings of the suburbs, and by the contradictory values and exclusionary systems of the American Dream. His large paintings feature figures engaged in startling and unresolved exchanges in tract neighborhoods, bedrooms, backyards, and later beaches and hotels.[8]

In these early days in New York, Fischl would become associated with Neo-Expressionism, a loose movement of European and American painters who used exaggerated colors and brushwork to portray myths and personal imagery similar to the early twentieth-century German Expressionist artists.[9] Fischl, along with his friends David Salle and Julian Schnabel, was featured in a 1982 *Art in America* issue on "The Expressionism Question."[10] Critic Barbara Rose would later debunk Fischl's inclusion in this group, pointing out that his work is based on pre-Modern realism rather than Neo-Expressionist exaggeration and distortion of reality.[11] Yet, in Fischl's *Time for Bed* (1980; FIG. 4) and later work *Rift/Raft* (2016; PLATE 38) there is a bold use of color and shape which seems to draw upon the attenuated forms, dense design, and dark social commentaries of Ernst Ludwig Kirchner or Max Beckmann (FIG. 5; see FIG. 12). And throughout his work, Fischl has been more interested in conveying the complexities of human emotions with his paint handling than in realism.

Fischl gradually developed an active process wherein he builds photo collages—first analog and later digital—of figures frozen in motion. He uses his own photographs, usually taken in public spaces or of studio models who are given little direction. Then he adapts freehand the small collage to a large canvas, making changes along the way. Figures and objects get painted in and out and in again as the scene coalesces.[12] He has become more confident in this approach over time and, with increased digital capabilities, he often makes multiple collages which inform a single painting or series, as in the photocollages for *Scenes From Late Paradise* (2006–2007; FIGS. 7–9; PLATE 8).

Along the way there have also been shifts in his brushwork and explorations in printmaking, various media on paper, and sculpture. During the COVID-19 pandemic, Fischl switched from oil paint to acrylic for his evocatively titled series *Meditations on Melancholia* (2020) and *Towards the Ends of an Astonishing Beauty* (2022). He felt, as we all did, a sense of urgency and vulnerability and wanted the immediacy afforded by quick-drying acrylic. This mirrored a spontaneity he earlier found with his watercolors on paper, such as *Untitled* (1989; PLATE 12).

*The Parade Returns* (2022), which depicts a group of Halloween revelers in Sag Harbor, New York, Fischl's current hometown, has this looser paint handling and darker palette (PLATE 39). A boy in a Revolutionary

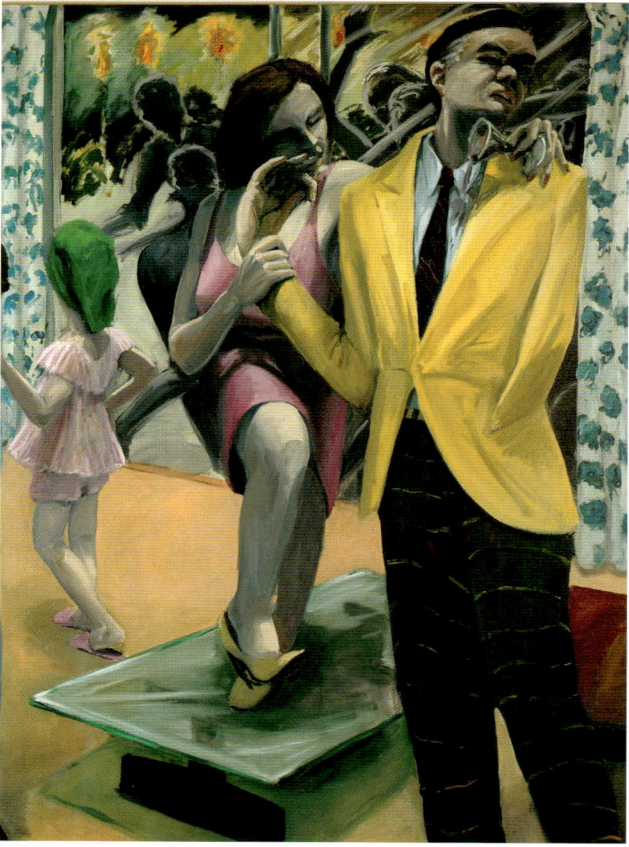

FIG. 4. **Eric Fischl**, *Time for Bed* (detail), **1980**. Oil on canvas. 72 × 96 in. (182.9 × 243.8 cm). Private collection of David Geffen, Los Angeles. PLATE 24

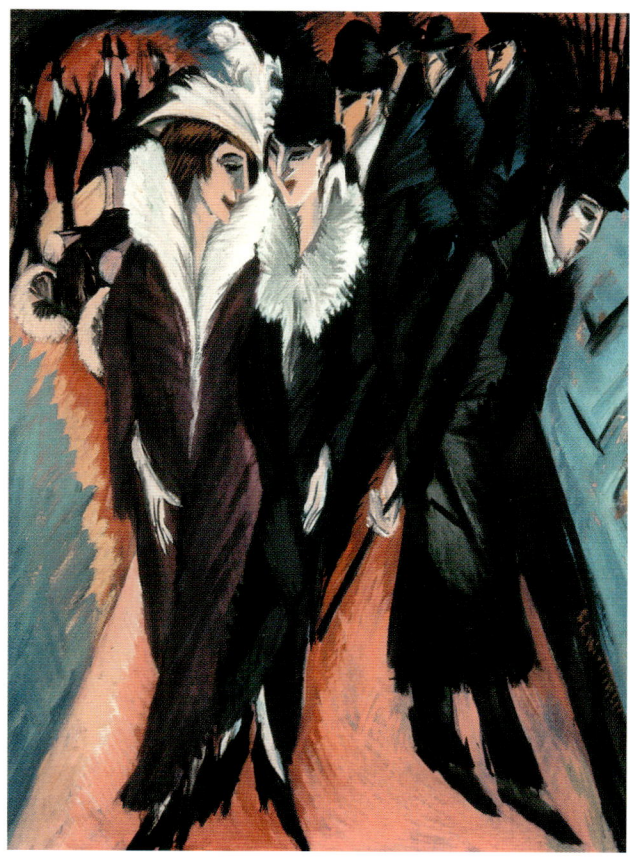

FIG. 5. **Ernst Ludwig Kirchner** (German, 1880–1938), *Street, Berlin*, **1913**. Oil on canvas. 47½ × 35⅞ in. (120.6 × 91.1 cm). Museum of Modern Art (MoMA), New York.

War costume attempts to lead a group—a surprising number of them using crutches and canes—including a few costumed children and an older man veering off on his own. What should be a fun community event instead feels chaotic and unsettling. The painting captures Fischl's remarkable ability to frame the ambiguous moment and to generate, rather than resolve, questions. His subjects are depicted mid-gesture, rarely at rest or at peace, and their poses trigger multiple associations. He has said, "There are moments when the body becomes awkward and difficult and betrays your internal life. I'm interested in things that look like one thing and then become something else and flip back and forth."[13]

This ability to pose multiple perspectives is at the center of Fischl's work, whether his figures are part of a parade or alone. In *Master Bedroom (Her Master's Voice)* (1983), a topless young woman kneels on a rumpled king-size bed hugging a Newfoundland dog (PLATE 5). The deceptively casual brushstrokes build the scene with varying degrees of description. Her body language, the objects in the room, the construction of space, the dramatic lighting, the selectively painted details, and the title offer a variety of possible interpretations: Who is she looking at? Why are her lips smudged? Is she hugging the dog for joy or for comfort or protection? We are given competing visual information and invited to consider various connections between the painting's elements.[14] We slip back and forth between objectivity and subjectivity, between observer and participant as we bring our own perceptions to completing the narrative. Fischl intentionally allows for an often-uncomfortable triangulation of the image, the viewer, and the artist.

Critic Jackson Arn has recently said that Fischl's paintings are "a risky combination of the overdetermined and the underdeveloped, the insisted upon and the gestured at."[15] This insight can be applied to the way Fischl paints and constructs his compositions, leaving some areas abstract and others concrete, but more pointedly it describes his provocative staging of social and political critiques. Take the painting, *Untitled* (1982), where two unabashedly nude women, seemingly lovers, are posed in a comfortable bedroom with a wide lawn outside the window (PLATE 16). Staring out at the viewer, one luxuriates on the bed while the other towels herself off as if after a shower. On closer examination, a television plays a baseball game. Fischl uses loaded objects to inform or obfuscate, and they lurk throughout his paintings from the strange bowl of fish in *Barbeque* to the American flag pool towel in *Late America* (2016; PLATE 28). Here the TV could add to the scene's leisure or refer to the American fixation with mass media, or it could suggest and assert the male gaze and the problematics of female nudes by male artists. Are the women resigned and resentful, rather than relaxed and bold? We are forcefully reminded of the objectification of women throughout Western art history and popular culture and of the artist's positionality and complicity as well as our own. Fischl builds a dynamic, unstable space where all these interpretations are imaginable and as relevant today as in 1982.

Alongside issues of gender, age is a recurring element throughout Fischl's paintings—not surprising considering the span of his career and emphasis on the body. In *Best Western* (1983), a white adolescent boy tosses oranges at toy cowboys and Indians (PLATE 2). The twilight scene with large swimming pool could be his backyard or the motel chain from the title. The composition wittily refers to multiple tropes of the American West: the heroic history of white settlers, the family road trip, sun-bleached suburban life (particularly in Phoenix, known for its orange trees), and classic Western films with prescribed good and bad guys. All these threads, familiar to Fischl's childhood, swirl around and inform the boy and ultimately the man.

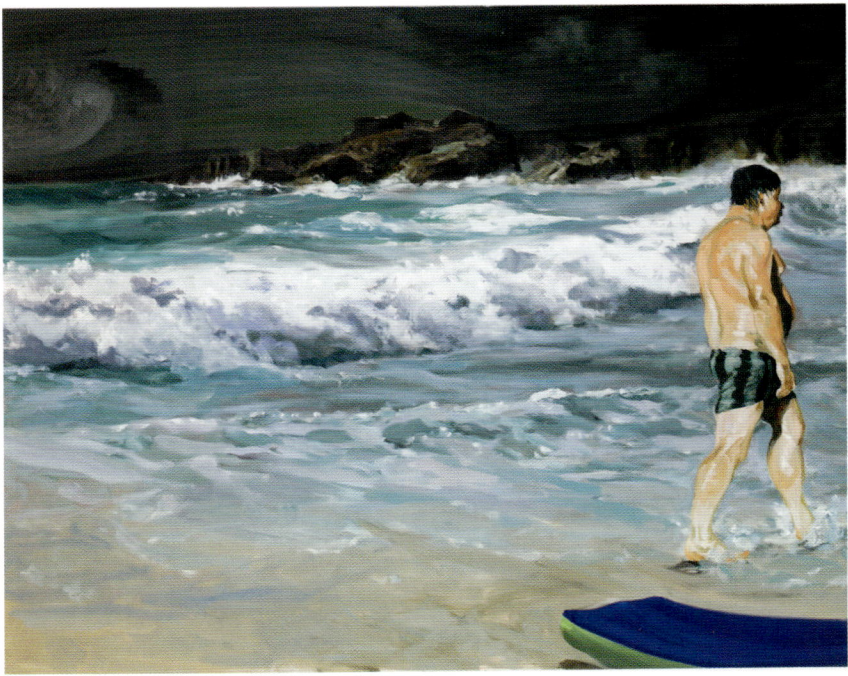

FIG. 6. **Eric Fischl,** *Scenes From Late Paradise: Stupidity*, **2007.** Oil on linen. 84 × 108 in. (213.36 × 274.32 cm). Hall Art Foundation. PLATE 8

*Best Western* contrasts starkly with later works of single men, such as *Scenes From Late Paradise: Stupidity*, where a paunchy, middle-aged, white man slumps across a beach. Or *Frailty is a Moment of Self-Reflection* (1996) with an elderly male figure naked and stumbling in an unadorned hallway (PLATE 7). Traditional American ideals of masculinity and the privileges that come with it are unable to save these men from the indignities of aging bodies and minds. The latter work was painted while Fischl was mourning the loss of his own father and contemplating the white, middle-class aversion to body morbidity.

Another consistent dynamic in Fischl's painting is the exploration of public versus private spaces and actions, and the uncomfortable moments when they are blurred. Nude figures are often vulnerable and exposed in public, as in *My Old Neighborhood: Private Property* (2021), where a woman is confronted by police in front of a yellow house with a white picket fence (PLATE 33). The scene is drawn from Fischl's memories of his alcoholic mother and his neighborhood on Long Island. The two police officers are

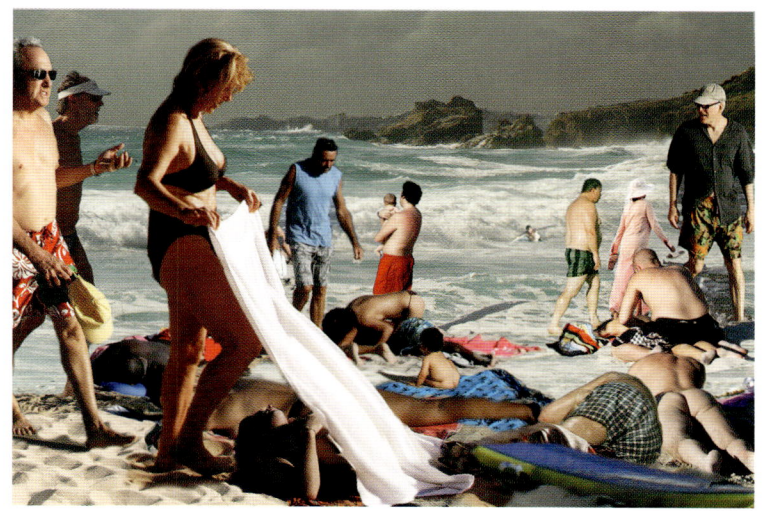

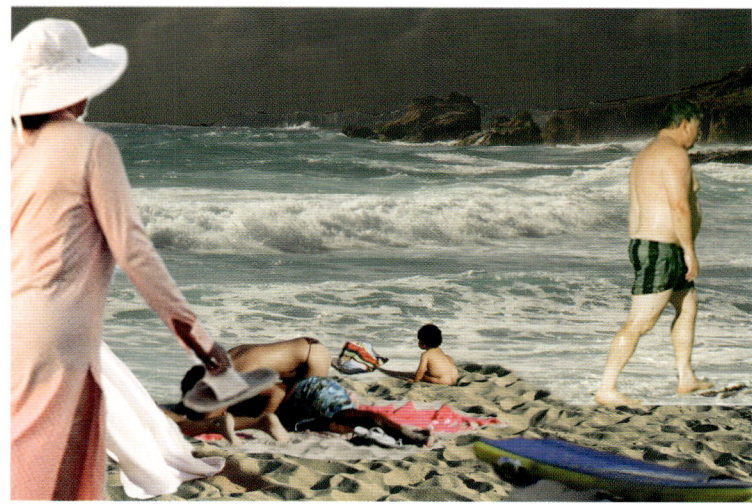

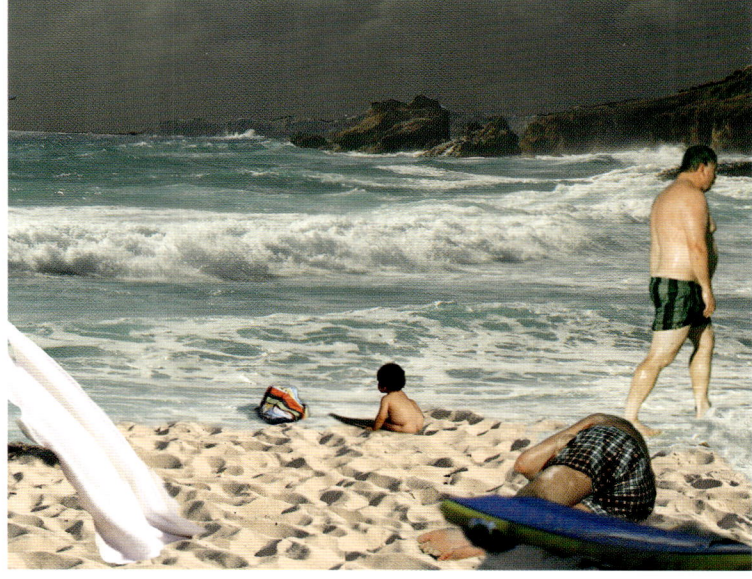

FIGS. 7–9. Eric Fischl, *Scenes From Late Paradise: Stupidity Studies #1, #2, and #3, 2007.* Digital collages. Collection of the artist.

focused on apprehending the woman with her hands in the air, whose crime seems to be her nakedness. The officers display no concern for the bystander, a sullen youth with a semiautomatic rifle on his T-shirt. The four darkly shadowed people stand at the edges of the canvas, directing the eye to the sunny facade of the suburban house. Throughout his career, Fischl has contemplated the realities hidden within privileged, predominantly white enclaves, where social taboos of the naked body seem to be more concerning than issues of gun culture and violence or the state of policing.

In the most recent series of paintings, *Hotel Stories*, the narratives are similarly grounded in current events with long and systemic histories. In *October 7: Heading Out* (2023), a white woman—who has appeared in other Fischl paintings—stands in the public/private space of her hotel room transfixed by the TV screen (PLATE 9). The title tells us that she's watching news coverage on October 7, 2023, when the Palestinian militant group Hamas attacked Israel. Her outfit is that of the quintessential late-twentieth-century professional working woman, and a laptop and mouse are visible on the desk. Perhaps she has just returned from a long day at work and is now ready to go out for the evening; she is framed by an abstract nighttime cityscape beyond the window. Yet the world has irrevocably changed. The path forward is uncertain—with many alarming potentialities for her, the artist, and the viewer.

Fischl started painting the human form when it was out of favor, but in the twenty-first century there has been a significant reconsideration of figure painting.[16] A number of recent survey exhibitions have focused on a new generation of international artists—including artists of color, women, and queer artists—who paint their communities, spaces, and everyday lives

to address "the politics of seeing and being seen."[17] Arcmanoro Niles is part of this younger generation. As he records in the conversation in this book, he was drawn as a student to Fischl's work for its use of the figure and his investigation of the realities of suburban life—the artist's own life. Fischl's work can be considered both predecessor and parallel to Niles's painting and to that of this younger generation.

Fittingly, *Eric Fischl: Stories Told* is presented in Phoenix, a place that since the 1950s has been defined by its suburban and exurban sprawl and the promises of the American Dream. It is also where Fischl first started painting. The exhibition examines his decades-long career from our current art historical and social context. The essays in this book focus on dominant themes that weave in and out of his works over the years. Dr. Kathryn Brown traces how Fischl draws from the past to reveal the present. Eleanor Nairne reconsiders his intentional use of the naked, sexualized body. Touching on both his personal and shared experiences, Eleanor Heartney surveys Fischl's ongoing exploration of American life. Niles hosts a conversation on their painting practices, comparing and contrasting their generational, social, and cultural positions. Closing the volume is an illustrated and annotated chronology of Fischl's life and work, the most comprehensive among his many publications.

Fischl paints his stories with empathy and disdain, gravity and irreverence, the psychological and the sensual. His works encompass the possibilities and promises as well as disparities and contradictions of his late America. He allows for shifting perspectives, building a space which recognizes the positionality of the artist and the viewer and their roles in meaning making.[18] And always, with the vulnerable human body at the center. ■

## Notes

1     Before CalArts, Fischl attended Phoenix College and Arizona State University; see the Artist Chronology in this volume. Fischl talks about the positive responses to his early abstract paintings and dismissal of his attempts to incorporate representational images in Eric Fischl and Michael Stone, *Bad Boy: My Life On and Off the Canvas* (Crown, 2012). Although other art forms and innovative approaches were being explored elsewhere on campus, Fischl was firmly located in the painting department.

2     Eric Fischl, interview with the author, June 17, 2024. Murray was an established abstract painter whose biomorphic shapes would become recognizable images in the 1980s. For more information on this 1976 exhibition, see "From the Archive: 40 Yrs Ago This Month EM Opened First Solo Show in NYC," Elizabeth Murray (website), November 5, 2016, https:// elizabethmurrayart.org/archive/2016/11/5/from-the-archives -from-the-archives-40-yrs-ago-this-month-em-opened-her -first-solo-show-in-nyc. John Russell called the show at Paula Cooper Gallery "puzzling" and described Murray's colors and lines as "awkward and grouchy" in *The New York Times*. John Russell, "Art: New Collages by William Dole," *New York Times*, November 12, 1976, https://www.nytimes.com/1976/11/12/ archives/art-new-collages-by-william-dole.html.

3     "I felt like I had to leap a hundred years back in time in order to find a way to paint, that all of the modernist stuff had removed the figure from painting and had removed it in a way that was hard to know how to get it back." Fischl, interview with the author, June 17, 2024. Fischl further discusses the impact of modernism on representational painting in "A Meditation on the Death of Painting," in Merrill Falkenberg and Eric Fischl, *All the More Real: Portrayals of Intimacy and Empathy* (Parrish Art Museum, 2007), published in conjunction with an exhibition of the same title, August 12–October 14, 2007, pp. 22–28.

4     Tony Godfrey, *Painting Today* (Phaidon, 2009), p. 14. See Godfrey on the impact of modernism on contemporary painting.

5     Fischl, interview with the author, June 17, 2024.

6     Gerald Marzorati, "I Will Not Think Bad Thoughts: An Interview with Eric Fischl," *Parkett* 5 (1985): 15, https://static1 .squarespace.com/static/5e614fa6565bfc04478be7be/t/5ea00 51d18019900d18a4d87/1587545385321/Parkett+5+Fischl+Eric .pdf. For discussion of feminist painters as precursors to the Neo-Expressionists, see Alina Cohen, "The Bad Boy Artists of the 1980s Owe a Debt to their Feminist Predecessors," *Artsy*, February 28, 2019, https://www.artsy.net/article/artsy -editorial-bad-boy-artists-1980s-owe-debt-feminist -predecessors.

7     Fischl, quoted in "Drawing the Figure: Eric Fischl in an Interview with Lawrence Weschler" in *Eric Fischl—Friends, Lovers and other Constellations*, ed. Klaus Albrecht Schröder and Elsy Lahner (Verlag für Moderne Kunst, 2014), published in conjunction with an exhibition of the same title at the Albertina Museum, Vienna, February 13–May 18, 2014, p. 27.

8     American art critic Barbara Rose quipped in a 1985 *Vogue* article that conservative critics were calling for "a return to realism, hoping for the rational social order that realism implies. But who could have predicted that 'reality' would be what Fischl envisions." Barbara Rose, "Fischl," *Vogue*, November 1, 1985, pp. 402–405, 462.

9     The movement was codified in 1981 by the survey exhibition *A New Spirit in Painting* curated by Norman Rosenthal at the Royal Academy, London.

10     Fischl's work was also featured in *American Neo-Expressionists* at the Aldrich Contemporary Art Museum, Ridgefield, Connecticut, in 1984, the first US museum exhibition on the movement.

11     Rose, "Fischl," 403.

12     See the conversation between Fischl and artist Arcmanoro Niles in this volume.

13     Robert Enright, "Fischl on Fischl," in Arthur C. Danto, Robert Enright, and Steve Martin, *Eric Fischl 1970–2007* (Monacelli Press, 2008), p. 245.

14     Ralph Rugoff, *Mixing It Up: Painting Today* (Hayward Gallery, 2021), p. 6. In considering painting today, Rugoff describes the medium as the most relevant "technology" for making art today, because "the ongoing exchange between paint and image, materiality and representation, allows it to formulate provocative uncertainties in what we are seeing and the ways that we are looking." He goes on to say that contemporary figurative painting moves between "depiction, invention and allegory." Godfrey similarly talks about the relevance of painting: "In the age of mass visual media, painting is distinguished by its variety and flexibility, its rich past, its collective memory and our apparently innate hunger for it." Godfrey, *Painting Today*, 8.

15     Jackson Arn, "All-American Angst," *Art in America*, March 22, 2021, https://www.artnews.com/art-in-america/aia-reviews /eric-fischl-meditations-on-melancholia-skarstedt-1234587435/.

16     One stellar example was *When We See Us: A Century of Black Figuration in Painting*, organized by Koyo Kouoh for the Zeitz Museum of Contemporary Art Africa, Cape Town, South Africa, November 20, 2022–September 3, 2023, which also traveled to Kunstmuseum Basel, Switzerland. Kouoh says in her introduction to the catalog and exhibition, "One of the most enduring features of the human condition is the inexhaustible desire to see oneself through visual culture and storytelling." Kouoh, *When We See Us: A Century of Black Figuration in Painting* (Thames & Hudson, 2023), p. 9.

17     One such exhibition, which included Niles's work, was *A Place for Me: Figurative Painting Now* at the Institute of Contemporary Art Boston, March 31–September 5, 2022, https://www.icaboston.org/exhibitions/place-me -figurative-painting-now/.

18     Rugoff, *Mixing It Up*, 10.

SINGLE & ALONE

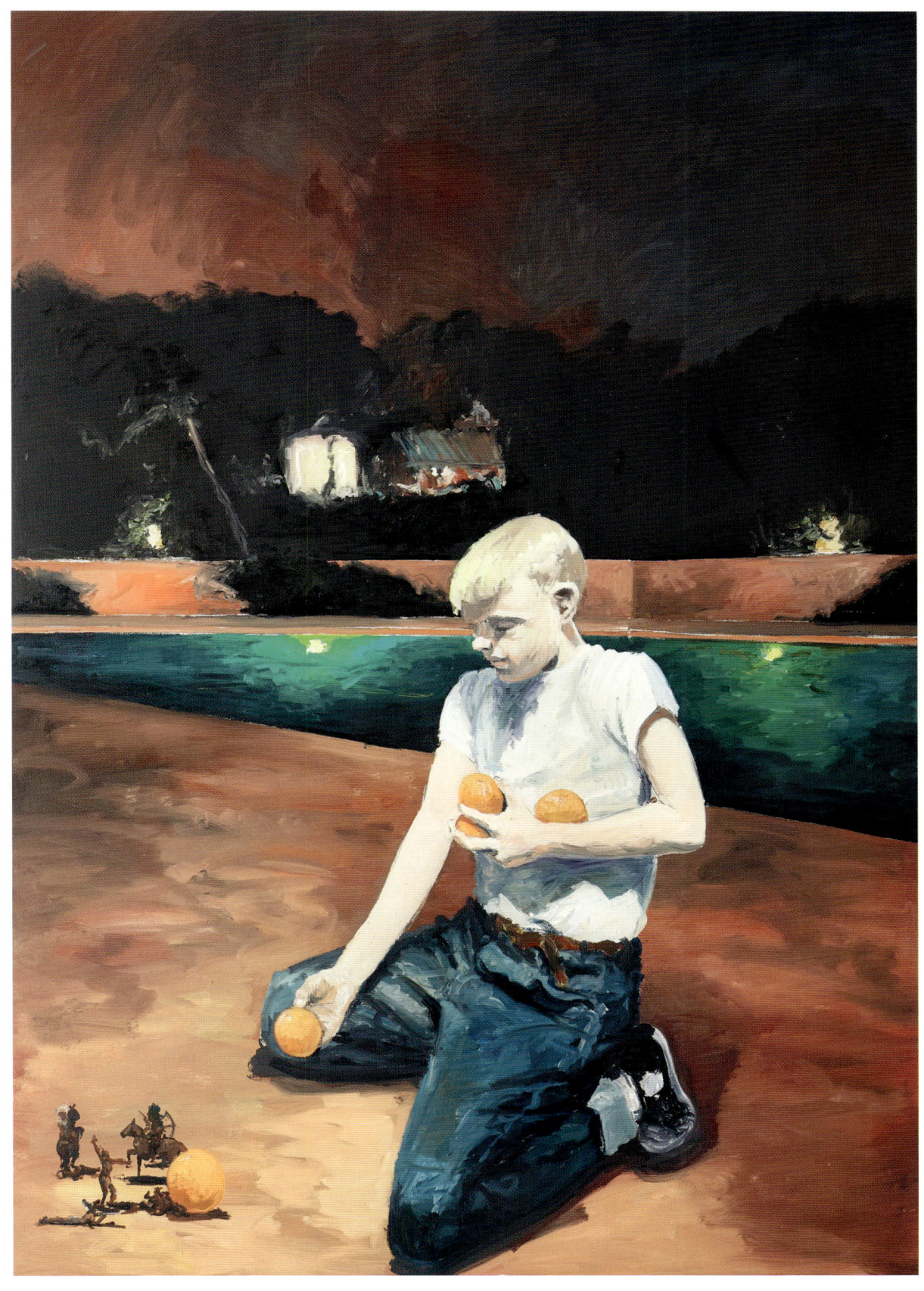

PLATE 2. *Best Western*, 1983

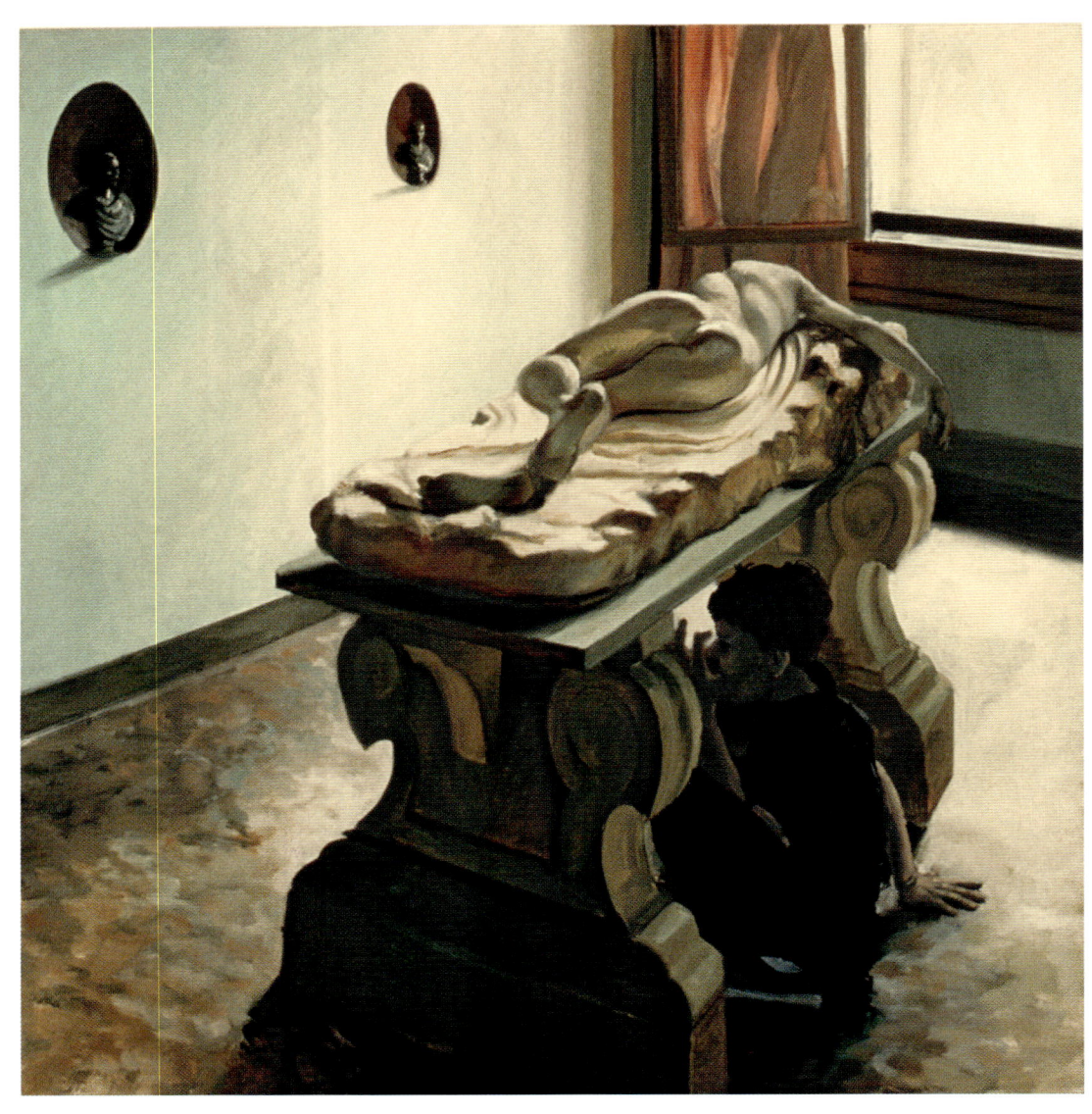

PLATE 3. *The Sheer Weight of History,* 1982

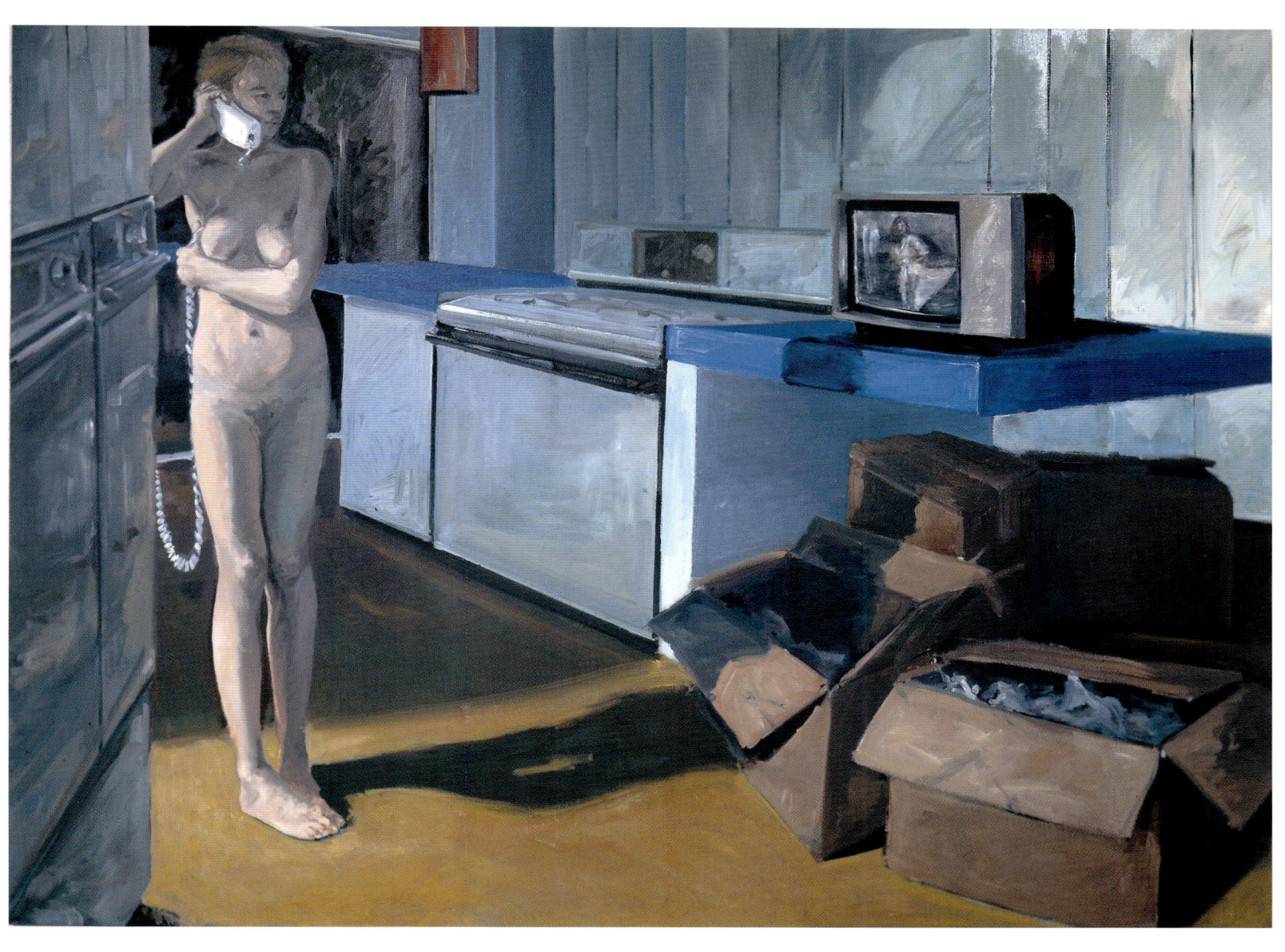

PLATE 4. *New House*, 1982

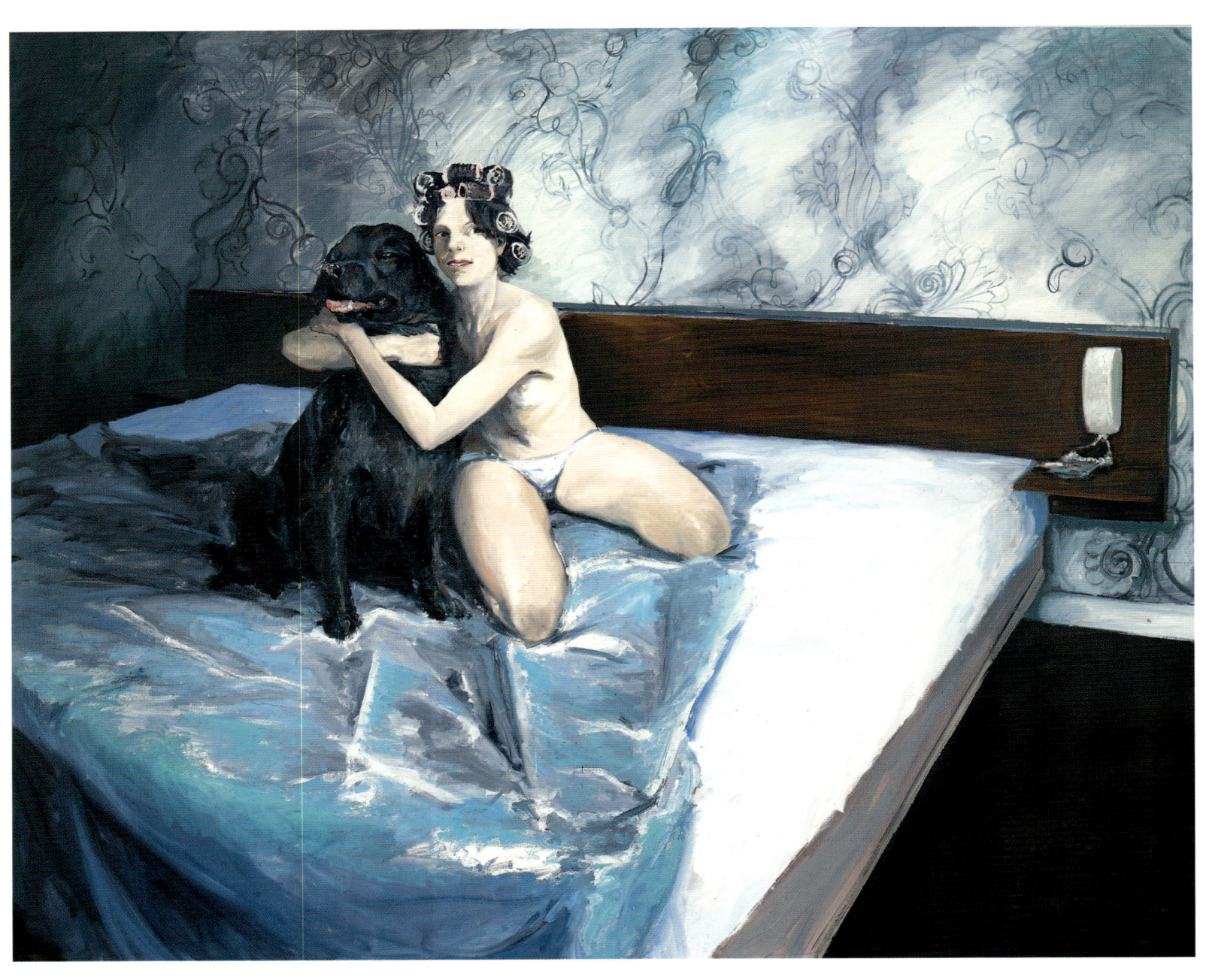

PLATE 5. *Master Bedroom (Her Master's Voice),* 1983

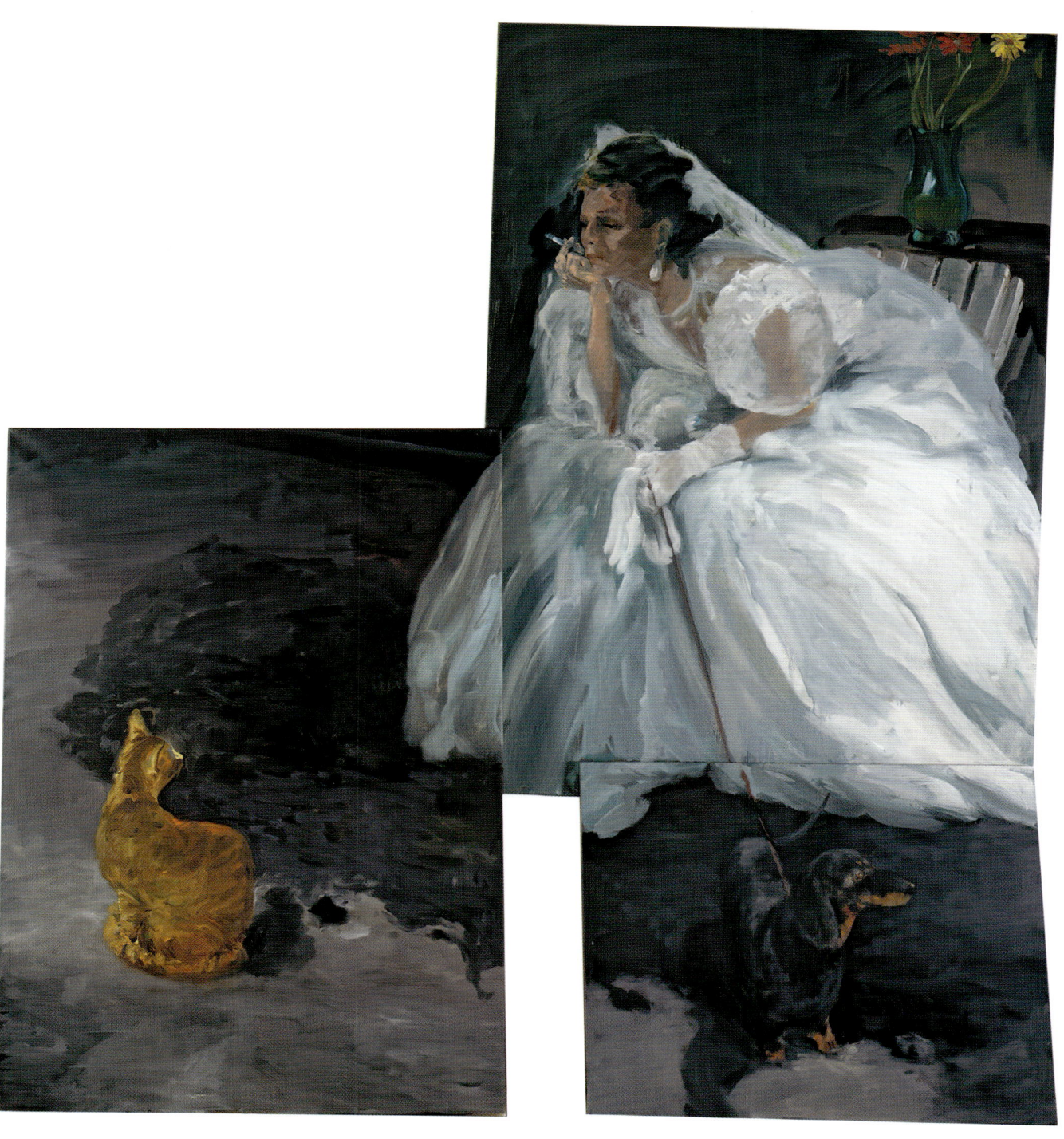

PLATE 6. *Scarsdale*, 1986

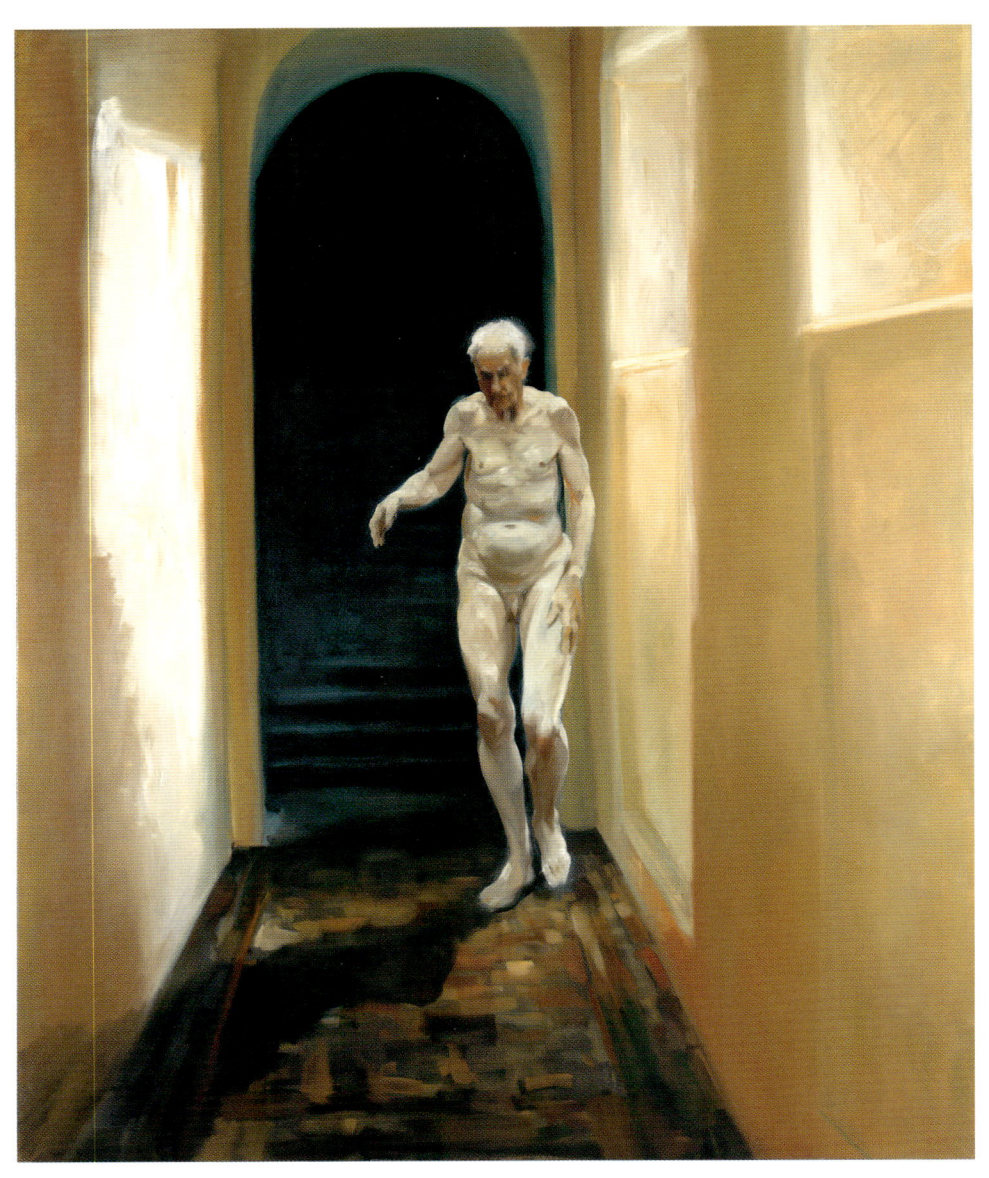

PLATE 7. *Frailty is a Moment of Self-Reflection,* 1996

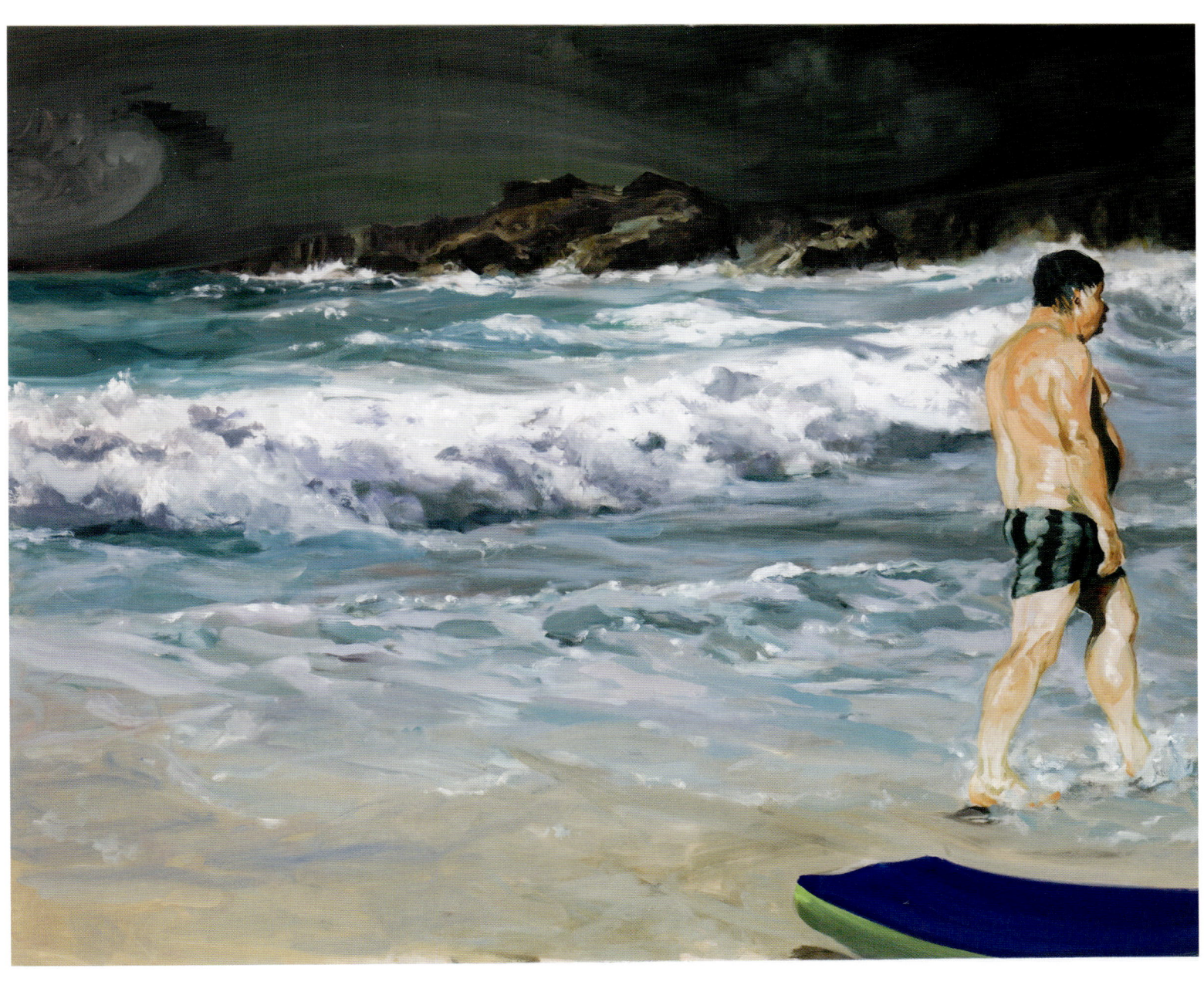

PLATE 8. *Scenes From Late Paradise: Stupidity*, 2007

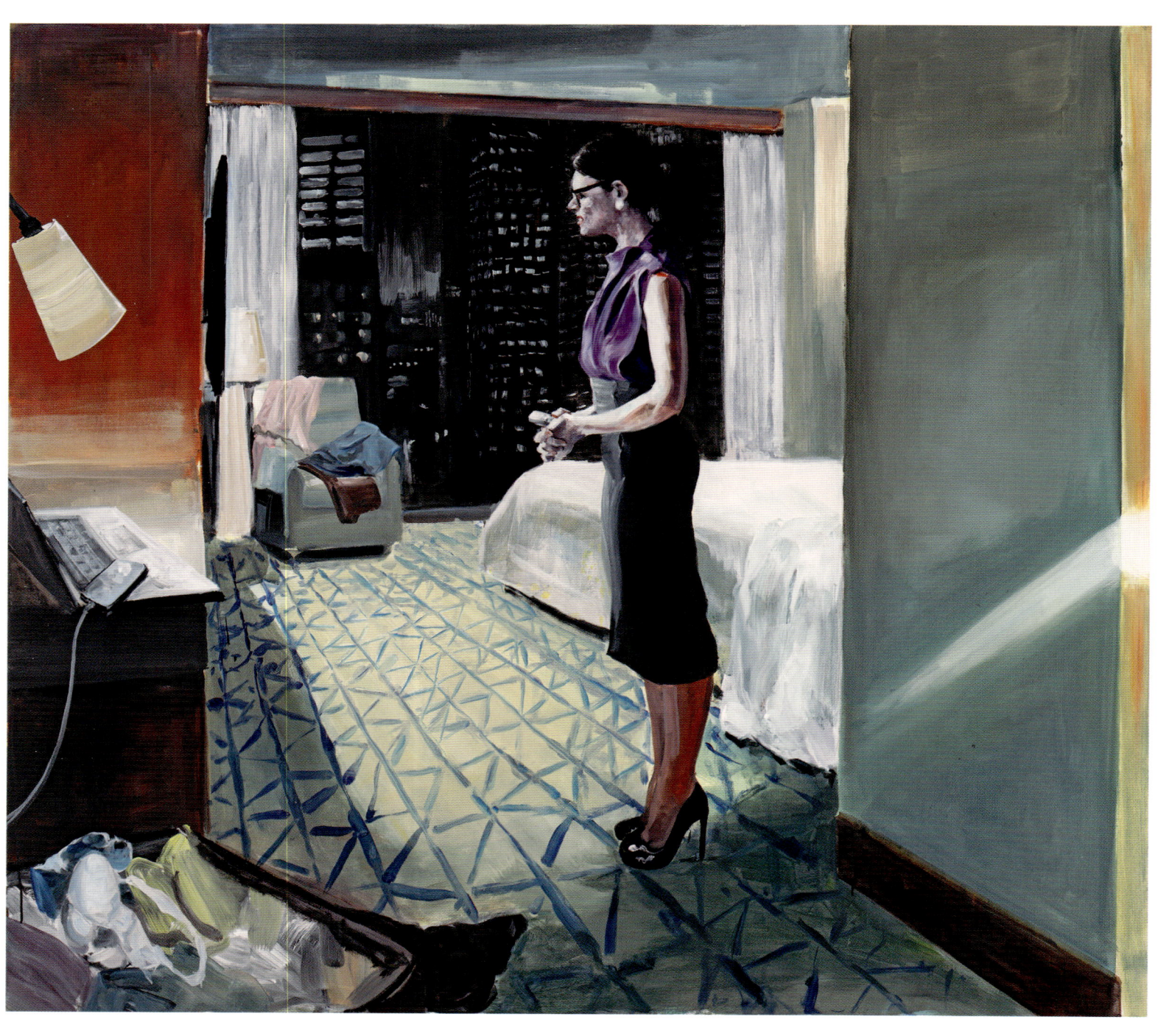

PLATE 9. *October 7: Heading Out*, 2023

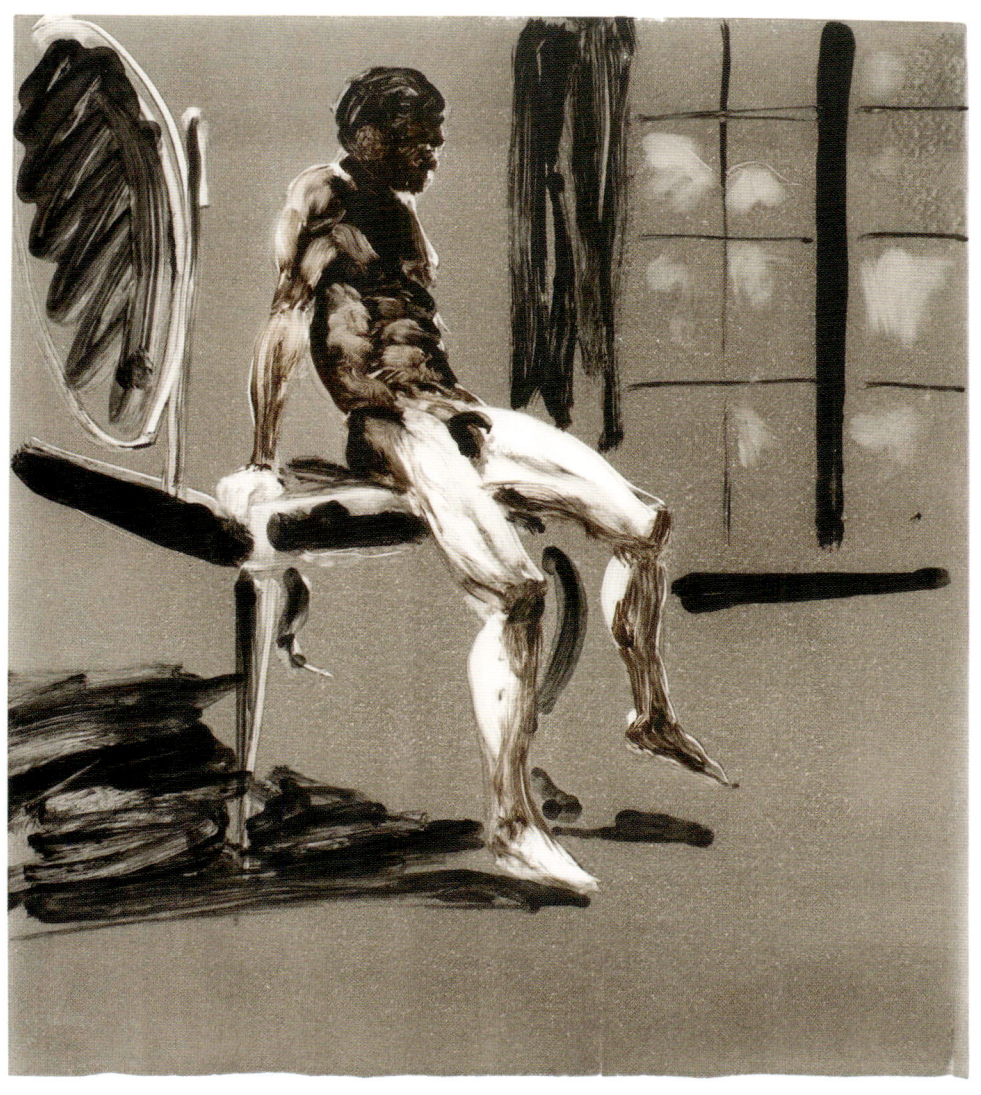

PLATE 10. *Scenes and Sequences: Man,* 1986

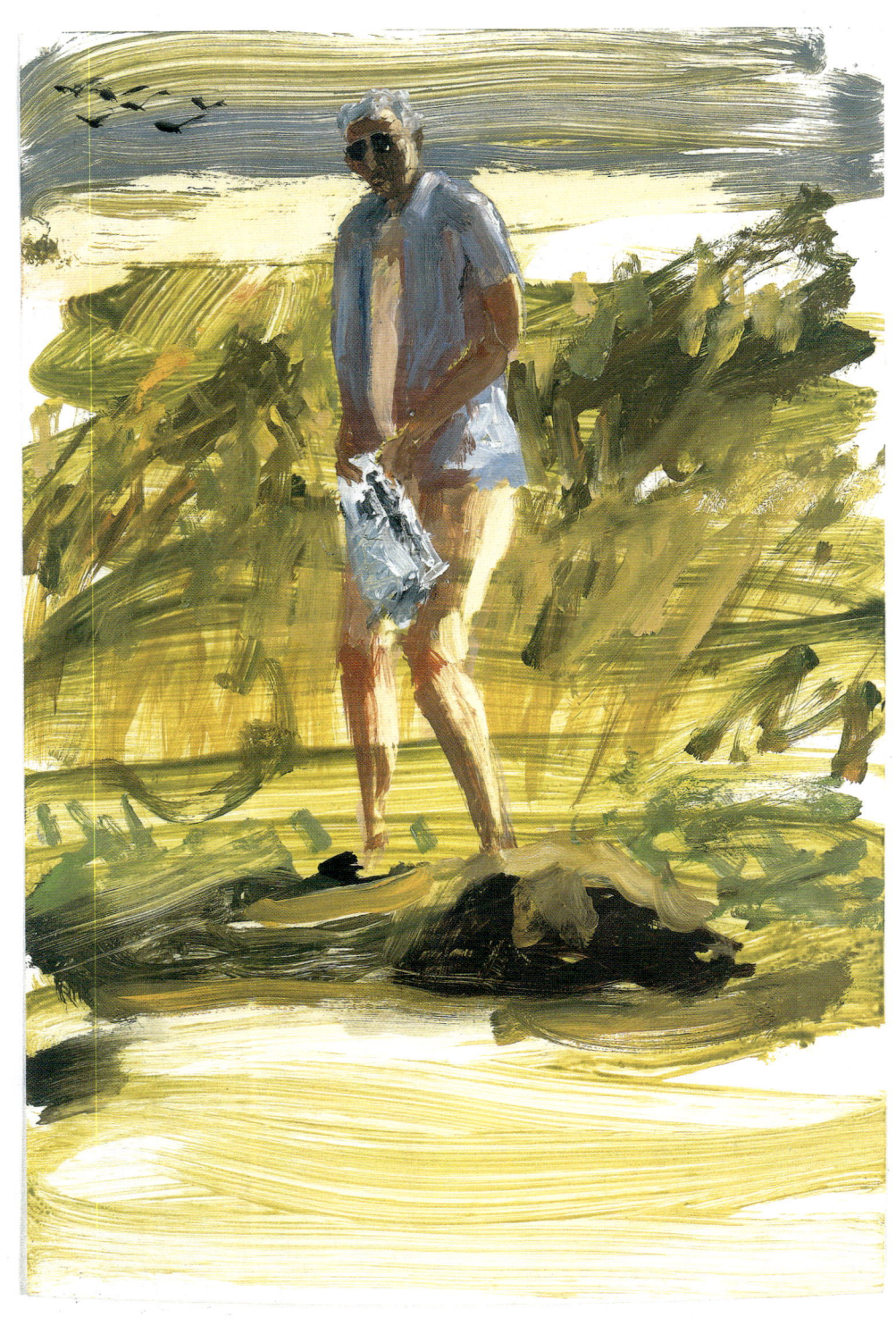

PLATE 11. *Study for Portrait of the Artist as an Old Man*, 1985

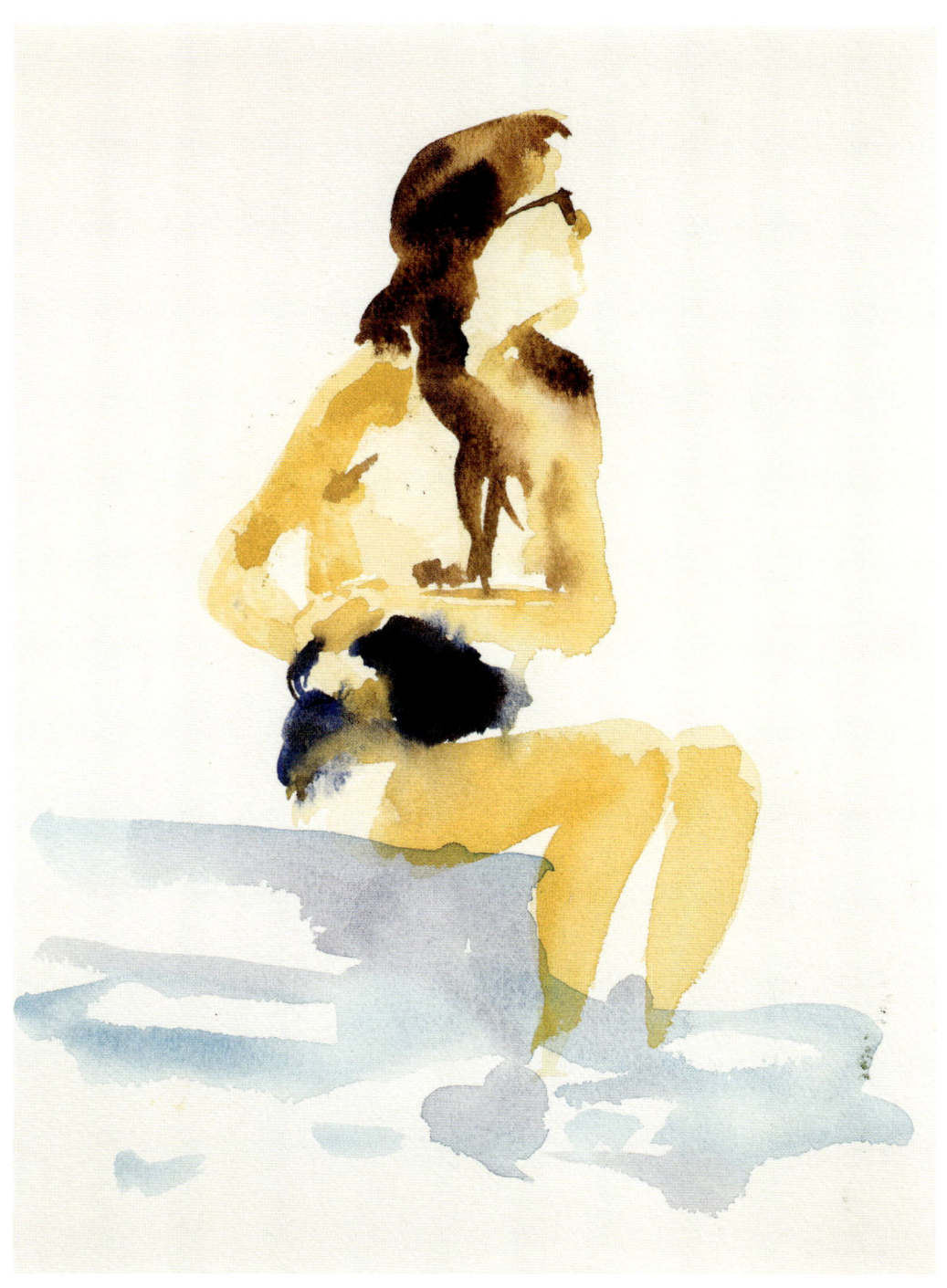

PLATE 12. *Untitled*, 1989

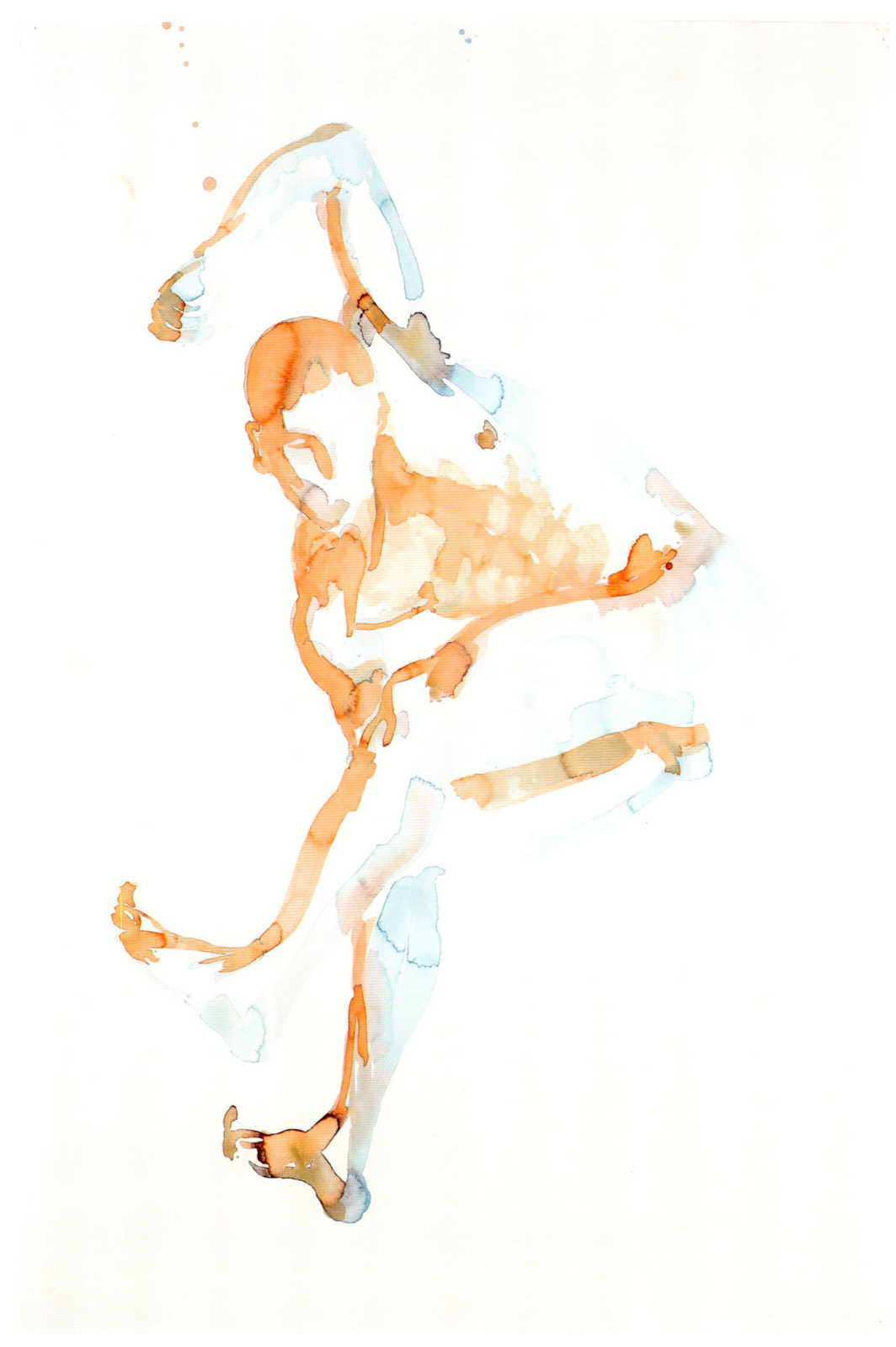

PLATE 13. *Falling Figure #6*, 2001

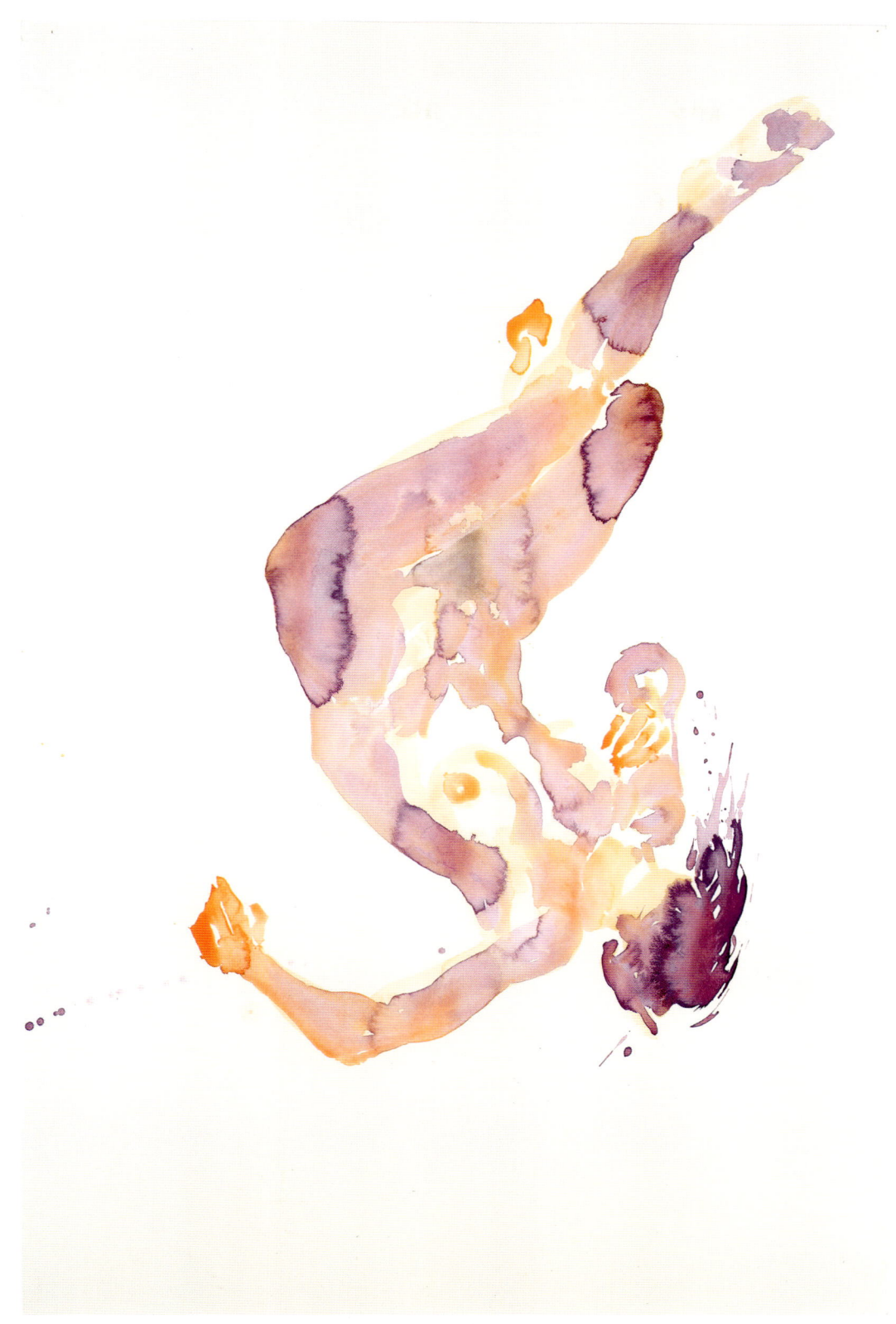

PLATE 14. *Falling Figure #7*, 2001

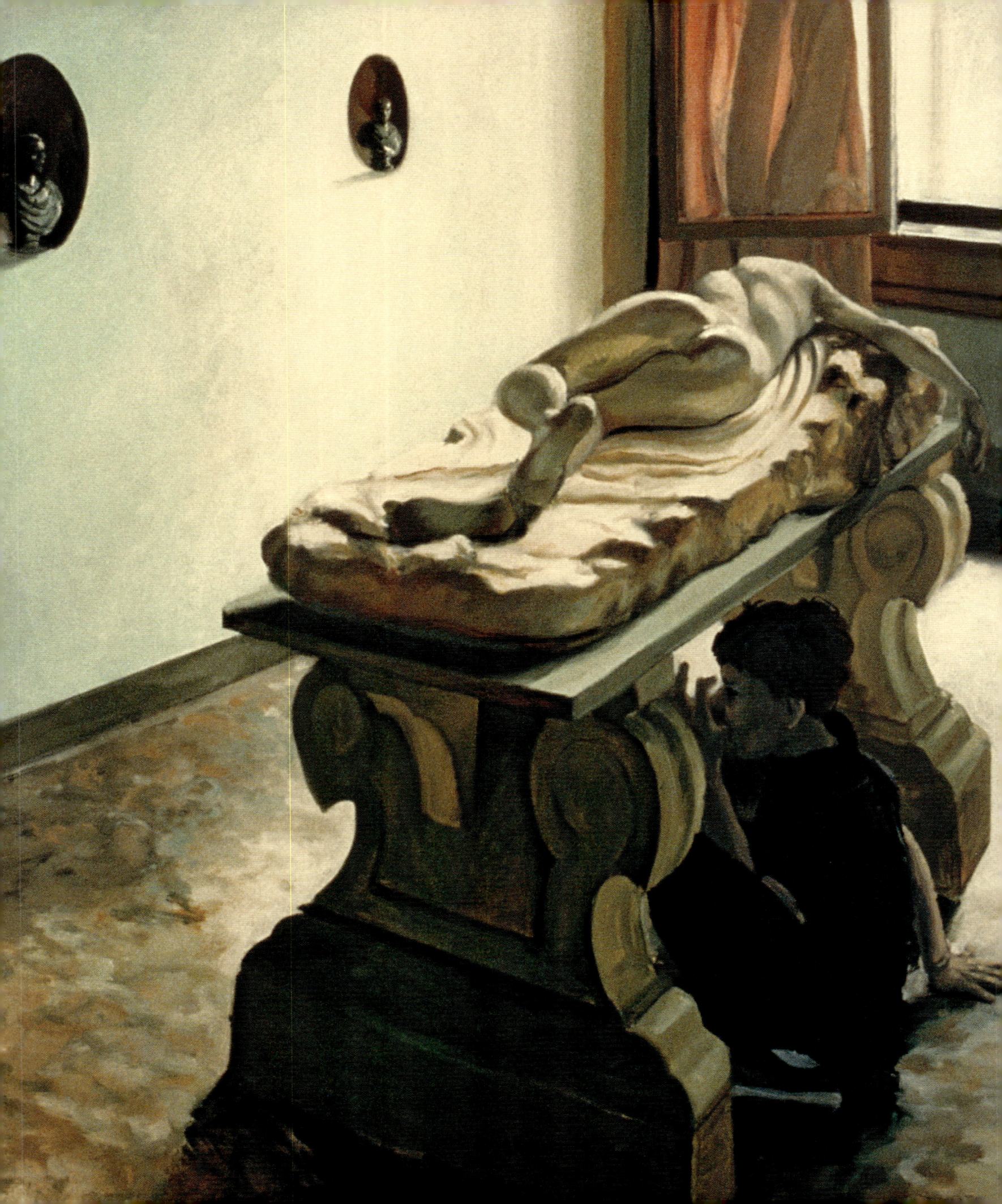

# NAVIGATING THE WEIGHT OF HISTORY
## KATHRYN BROWN

Painting is a very difficult thing.

MAX BECKMANN, "ON MY PAINTING," 1938[1]

In 1982 Eric Fischl created a painting titled *The Sheer Weight of History* (PLATE 3). As is typical of the artist's everyday scenes, this work is simultaneously mundane and uncanny: A classical marble sculpture lies atop a chiseled plinth in a quiet museum interior. The gender of the outstretched figure is unclear, and it is only by reading Fischl's writings that the identity and context of the depicted artwork become apparent. The sculpture portrays the mythological character Hermaphroditus and was created in the second century AD. Fischl encountered the work on a trip to the Uffizi Galleries in Florence and, thinking later about its fusion of male and female bodies, began exploring ways in which contemporary individuals might engage with it.[2]

In Fischl's painting, a boy crouches beneath the sculpture, his alert expression contrasting with the repose of the body above him. We may be witness to an innocent game of hide-and-seek, but Fischl imbues the setup with an erotic charge. The boy sucks his thumb and focuses intently on something or someone. An outstretched arm of the sculpture hangs tantalizingly off the edge of the support and reaches towards the young protagonist. Echoing Fischl's

Detail of PLATE 3

controversial painting of 1981, *Bad Boy*, the nakedness of the sculpture brings the motivations of the boy into question, and a childish game opens onto the uncertainties of adolescent sexuality (PLATE 15). The boy hides but remains subject to the gaze of two Roman senators—symbols of legal authority—whose busts are embedded in adjacent architectural niches.

*The Sheer Weight of History* imagines the past in physical and psychological terms for the purpose of creating a complex pictorial narrative. Yet the *idea* of history also plays an important role throughout Fischl's output. In his autobiography, Fischl notes that many of his contemporaries turned their backs on the past in their quest for new expressive idioms. How could the works of earlier artists—particularly those drawn from European traditions—be relevant to an American, twentieth-century art world that prized abstraction, sweeping institutional change, and rupture with conventions of seeing and making? During his student days at CalArts in the 1970s, Fischl experienced the full force of this emphasis on radical creative freedom. Here was an environment, he recalls, that "turned its back on the canon" and focused, instead, on devising strategies for "freeing up and redefining art."[3] In this case, history was a weight to be thrown off and discarded.

Yet Fischl never fully subscribed to an absolute break with the past. Through the influence of Bill Swaim, one of his teachers at Arizona State University, Fischl was encouraged to think about the history of European modernism and to reflect more closely on works by artists including Paul Cézanne, Edgar Degas, Édouard Manet, and Pablo Picasso. He increasingly found that arts of the past offered a means of stimulating new creative trajectories. The following discussion focuses on just a few of the artists with whom Fischl has engaged or competed. When navigating the weight of history, how does an artist decide what is useful and what should be discarded in the pursuit of originality?

## *A Split*

For Fischl, histories of art have served not simply as a source of inspiration, but also as a means of self-definition. Two artists were central to the development of his early work: Degas and Max Beckmann. Belonging to art worlds separated by both time and geography—nineteenth-century France in the case of Degas, and Weimar Germany, the Netherlands, and the US in the case of Beckmann—these individuals appear to have little in common either personally or creatively. As Fischl himself puts it: Degas's paintings contain a "cool, voyeuristic space" and "detailed intimacy." By contrast, Beckmann's works are full of "powerful emotions—his anger, outrage, passion."[4] These differing approaches to the communicative potential of painting awakened opposing tendencies in Fischl's creative persona of the early 1980s. Yet one thing that unites all three artists is a deep interest in depicting the human figure.

Degas was renowned for his relentless study of the body, and he developed innovative techniques in pastel, paint, and sculpture to render the complexities of pose and movement. In the words of another twentieth-century American painter, R.B. Kitaj, Degas's art seemed to "owe its very *permission* to the human figure."[5] It was precisely this aspect of Degas's art, however, that made his work seem irrelevant to many twentieth-century modernists. By the 1940s, Degas's

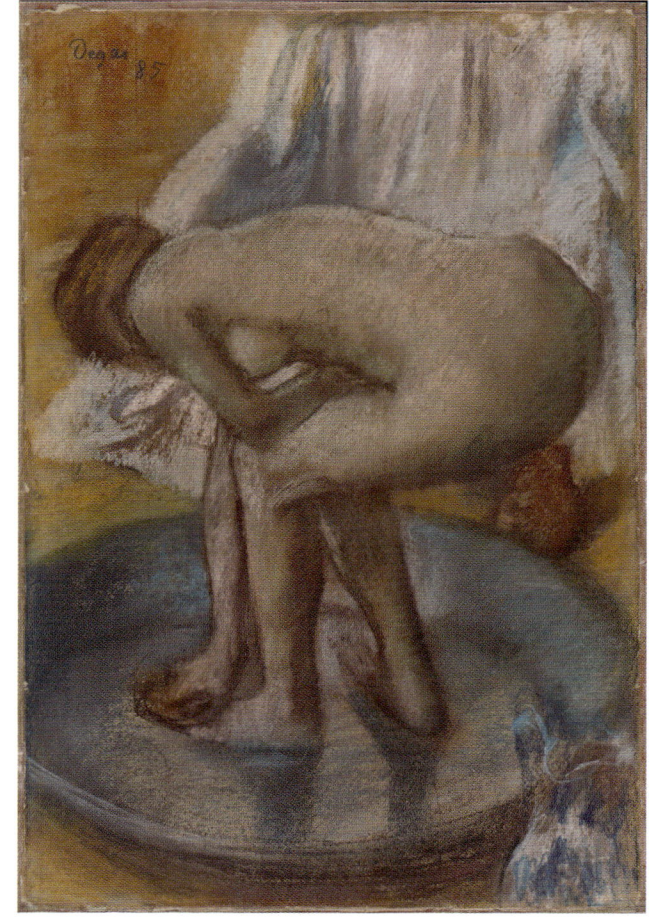

FIG. 10. **Edgar Degas** (French,1834–1917), *Woman Bathing in a Shallow Tub*, **1885.** Charcoal and pastel on light green wove paper. 32 × 22⅛ in. (81.3 × 56.2 cm). The Metropolitan Museum of Art, New York, H. O. Havemeyer Collection, Bequest of Mrs. H. O. Havemeyer, 1929 (29.100.41).

art had, according to some commentators, been left behind by practitioners of Fauvism, Cubism, and Abstraction.[6]

For Fischl, however, there was much to respond to in Degas's output—even at the risk of aligning himself with an apparently outmoded tradition of figurative art. This is particularly clear in connections between Fischl's portrayals of the female nude and the experimental pastels that Degas produced and exhibited a century earlier. For both artists, the challenge of depicting the nude was an impetus to pictorial innovation and a means of posing important questions about the relationship between the viewer and potentially transgressive images.

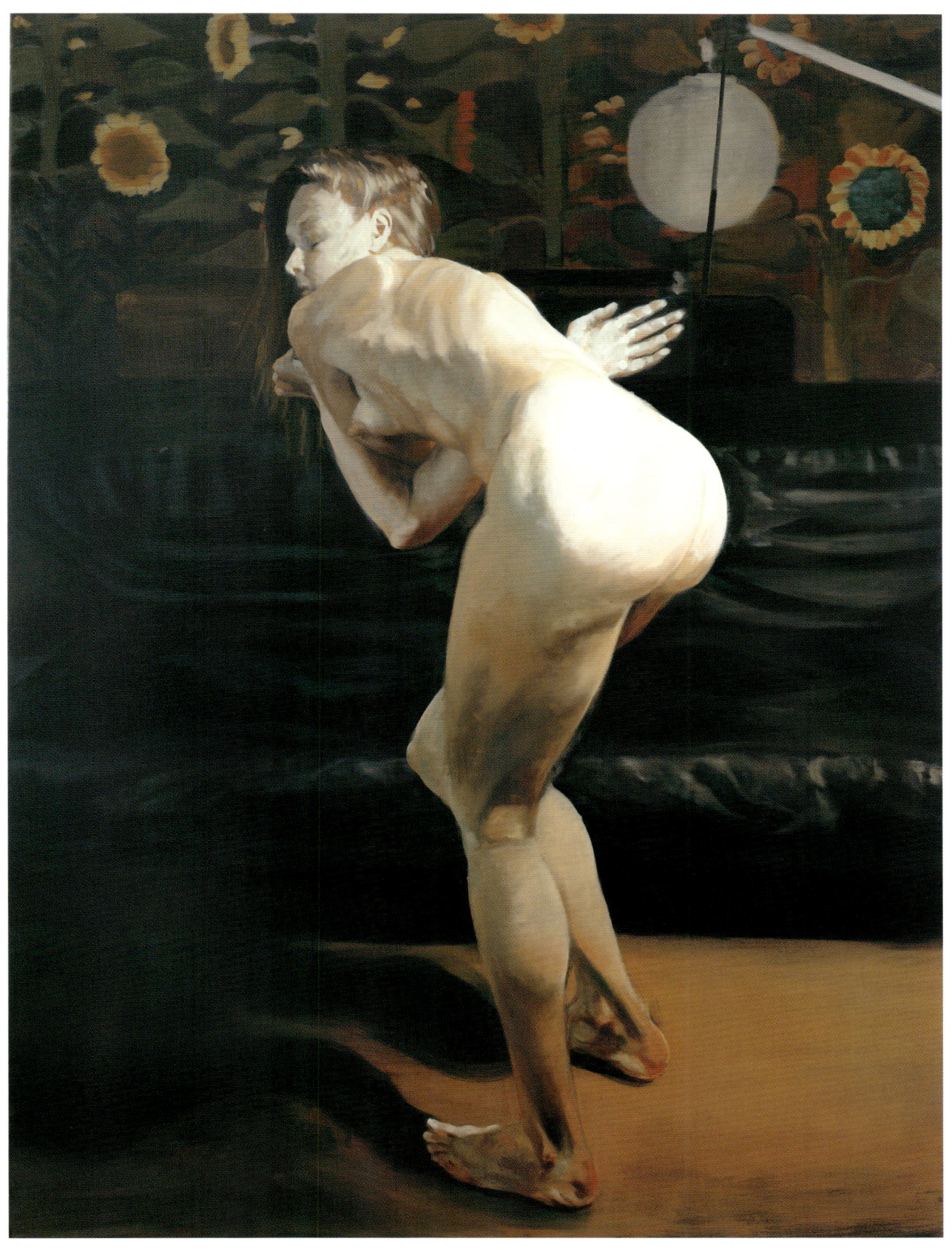

FIG. 11. **Eric Fischl**, *Questionable Pleasure II*, **1994**. Oil on linen.
70 × 54 in. (177.8 × 137.2 cm). Collection unknown.

When Degas exhibited a suite of pastels depicting female bathers at the eighth Impressionist exhibition in 1886, critics declared that the works were "cruel" and that the artist had debased his subjects.[7] The idea that Degas created art that infringed on private moments swiftly became a mainstay of critical responses to his work.[8] In similar fashion, Fischl's portrayals of women dressing, undressing, bathing, or lounging by swimming pools have been found provocative by some viewers.[9] It is undoubtedly the case that both Degas and Fischl toy with their audiences by depicting intimacies to which viewers would not—or should not—ordinarily have access. Yet focusing simply on the works' potential to confront misses key elements of their composition, including the idea that the viewer is, in fact, excluded from some of these fictional scenes.

A comparison between Degas's *Woman Bathing in a Shallow Tub* (1885) and Fischl's *Questionable Pleasure II* (1994) illustrates this point (FIGS. 10, 11). Fischl comments that Degas was capable of painting (and one might add drawing) in a way that imbues the scene with a degree of objectivity, "thus absenting himself" from the action.[10] Fischl captures an important aspect of Degas's experimentation with the complexities of spectatorship. I have argued elsewhere that Degas's *Bather* pastels can be divided into two groups that contain contrasting spectatorial gazes: observed-subject works and solitary-subject works.[11] In the case of observed-subject works, an implied viewpoint is constructed through the inclusion of structural motifs such as open doors, curtains, and other devices that suggest the presence of another person. By accepting the invitation to perform this role, the viewer becomes complicit with the content of the work and engages directly with the troubling moral, psychological, and sexual themes of the scene.

By contrast, Degas's solitary-subject works contain no internal viewpoint that is relevant to the fictional content of the composition. The radical foregrounding of the depicted bodies and absence of a clear narrative framework reduce the works' voyeuristic potential. In consequence, these pastels stage a kind of

"impersonal imagining," which has a point of view but not one that belongs to a particular person.[12] Whereas Degas's observed-subject *Bather* pastels experiment with an aesthetics of presence, his solitary subject works in the same series do not.

Fischl appreciates this contrast in Degas's oeuvre and develops it further in his own art. Many of his works featuring nudes contain a character that watches the other person—*Bad Boy* being one of the most powerful examples of this structure. Other works implicate the viewer by creating a role that is internal to the scene. Several of the paintings from *Krefeld Redux* (2004–2006), for example, use doorways and frames to position viewers and to implicate them in the action. By contrast, the lone female protagonist of *Questionable Pleasure II* can be understood as enjoying her nakedness and physical movement simply for herself.[13] Like many of Fischl's paintings from the mid-1990s, it adopts the structure of Degas's solitary-subject compositions and subverts the performance of voyeurism.

When the viewer's absence from the scene is admitted, it becomes possible to focus on other aspects of the depicted bodies and the ways in which they are positioned in their respective interiors. In the cases of *Questionable Pleasure II* and *Woman Bathing in a Shallow Tub*, we become more alert to the dramatic articulation of limbs, twist of the torso, ninety-degree angle of the left arm, and precarious balance of the pose. By exploring continuities with Degas's solitary bathers, Fischl opens fresh opportunities for interrogating the rhythms of human gesture. He rightly notes that Degas created a "new kind of visual language," one in which "foregrounds were distorted, figures were cropped awkwardly or silhouetted, and depth of focus felt more haphazard."[14] For both artists, depicting the nude was not simply a means of posing complex questions about looking at bodies, but also a way of reinventing space around those bodies.

This is not to suggest, however, that Fischl employs a purely forensic gaze in his art. Indeed, it was the

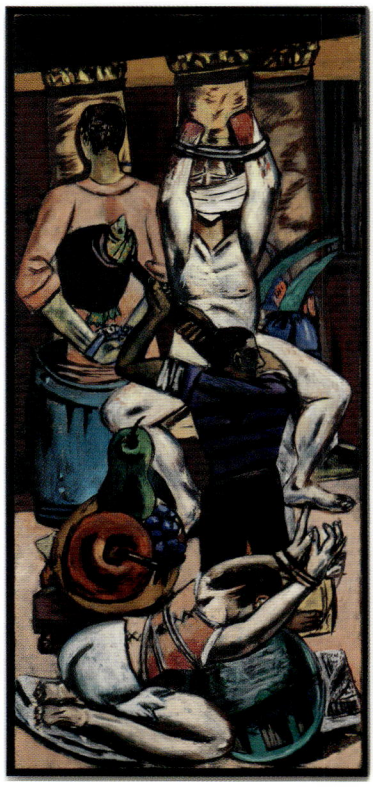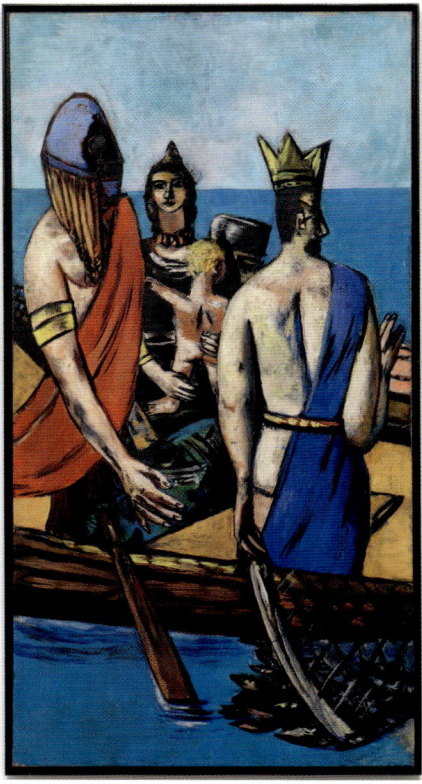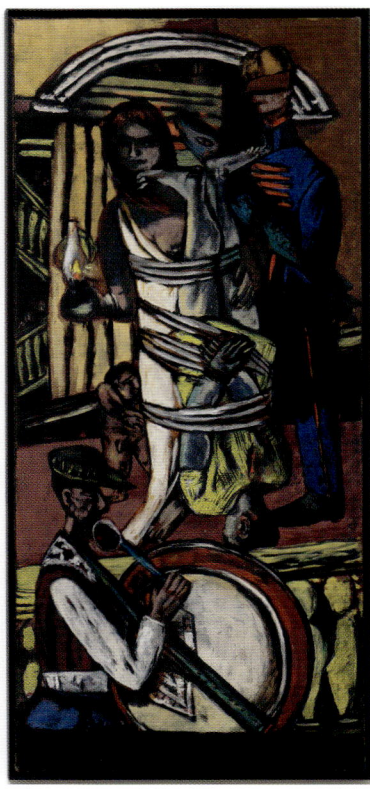

FIG. 12. **Max Beckmann** (German, 1884–1950), *Departure*, **Frankfurt 1932, Berlin 1933–35**. Oil on canvas, three panels. Side panels 84¾ × 39¼ in. (215.3 × 99.7 cm), center panel 84¾ × 45⅝ in. (215.3 × 115.2 cm). The Museum of Modern Art, New York, Given anonymously (by exchange).

need to test more visceral reactions to imagery that spurred his enthusiasm for Max Beckmann's works. While Beckmann is celebrated for his figurative painting, it was his ability to capture "psychological necessity through the physical language of painting" that seized Fischl's imagination.[15] One work that exemplifies this intensity is *Departure*, a triptych that Beckmann painted in the early to mid-1930s before he fled Nazi Germany (FIG. 12). The central panel of the piece depicts a king and queen embarking on a sea voyage; these characters are flanked by images of imprisonment and brutal torture. Are the king and queen responsible for these events, or have they been captured? Do they abdicate political authority or symbolize the hope of attaining a new and better world? The panels do not offer an easy interpretation. The element of the work that sparked Fischl's interest, however, was neither the action nor the relationship between the characters, but rather the fishing net in

the left hand of the king and the ambiguous directions in which the fish swim. Do they move into or out of the net? Fischl understands this detail as key to the work as a whole, a double entendre that exemplifies the uncertainty of the story and its meaning.

Fischl describes his simultaneous attraction to Degas and Beckmann as representing an early split in his artistic personality.[16] In the 1980s, this navigation of history helped Fischl to understand the kind of artist he wanted to be: a figurative painter, swimming against the tide and striving to build complex narratives that could test the viewer's expectations about the role of painting in the twentieth century.

### History as Memory

While history is typically understood as a systematic analysis of past actions and events, Fischl often uses it to explore more personal terrain. In the mid-1990s, shortly after the death of his father, he traveled to Rome. With its combination of ancient ruins and urban modernity, the city became a staging ground for interweaving collective history and private memory. In this atmospheric setting, the artist found

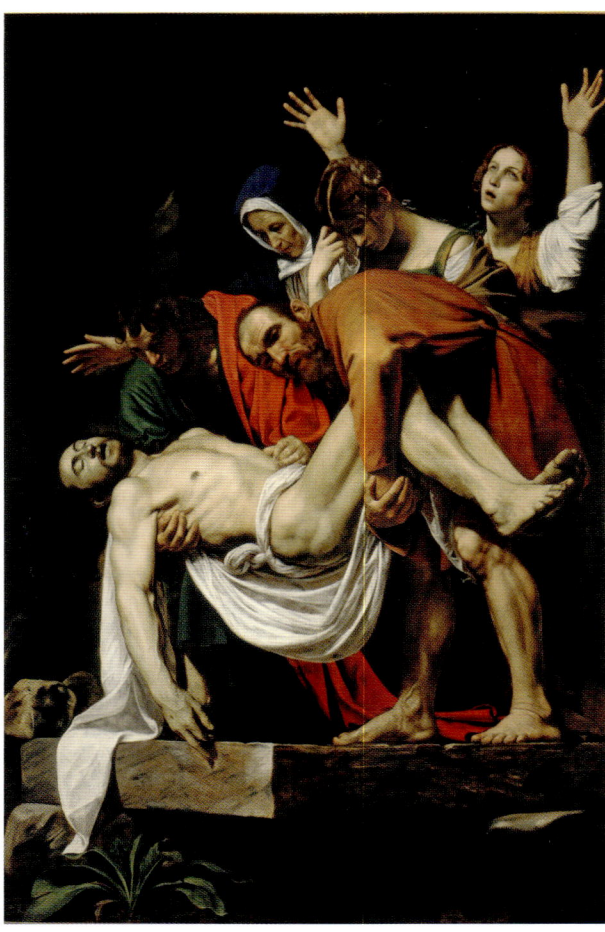

FIG. 13. **Caravaggio (Michelangelo Merisi da)** (Italian, 1571–1610), *The Deposition*, c. 1600–1604. Oil on canvas. 118 × 80 in. (300 × 203 cm). Pinacoteca, Vatican Museums, Vatican State.

himself thinking about Italian Baroque painting and architecture, including works by Caravaggio, Bernardo Strozzi, and Francesco Borromini. The theme of light recurs in Fischl's recollections of the city. On his visit to the Basilica of San Giovanni in Laterano, renovated by Borromini in the mid-seventeenth century, Fischl was struck by the effect of sunlight on the sculptures. White marble was suddenly illuminated, giving the impression that the figures had "been awakened."[17]

While the effects of natural light could bring sculptural forms eerily to life, it was Caravaggio's juxtaposition of light and shade in painting that offered Fischl a new set of ideas about his own work in this medium. Caravaggio had the uncanny ability to create, Fischl suggests, a "third light, an umber glow of a

netherworld inhabited by our thoughts and emotions, sparked by the events we're witnessing."[18] A work such as *The Deposition* (1600–1604), depicting the entombment of Christ, in the collection of the Vatican illustrates the point (FIG. 13). The mourners' dramatic hand gestures contrast with Christ's lifeless arm that droops to the ground. The spirituality of the scene has a counterpoint in the dramatic physicality and stark illumination of the mortal body. If Degas experimented with techniques for excluding the viewer in his nudes, Caravaggio brings his audience dramatically into the scene by staging an encounter with the direct gaze of John the Evangelist.

Upon his return to New York, Fischl drew together the inspirations he had taken from Rome and produced a series of paintings set in cathedrals and ruins. *Once Where We Looked to Put Down our Dead* (1996) captures the synthesis of history and memory that Fischl had been pondering during his travels (FIG. 14). Like the naturally occurring spotlights the artist had witnessed in the Basilica of San Giovanni or the dramatic contrasts of Caravaggio's painting, Fischl's canvas illuminates two human figures in an otherwise somber and empty cathedral interior. A man carries what appears to be the lifeless body of a woman in a dramatic laying to rest. Echoing the position of Christ in Caravaggio's painting, the woman's arm droops to the floor, symbolizing loss as a combined physical weight and psychological burden. If monumental edifices were constructed in seventeenth-century Rome to mourn the dead, is there an effective means—other than through art—to erect such memorials in the present? The past tense in the title of Fischl's painting leaves the point moot.[19]

While the setup and theme of the painting echo the influences of religious art, Fischl brought these historical touchstones into a secular and distinctly American remit. The poses and nakedness of the man and woman are derived from an 1885 photograph by the realist painter Thomas Eakins. By basing the positions of his figures on this image, Fischl pays homage to one of the most important figurative painters and teachers

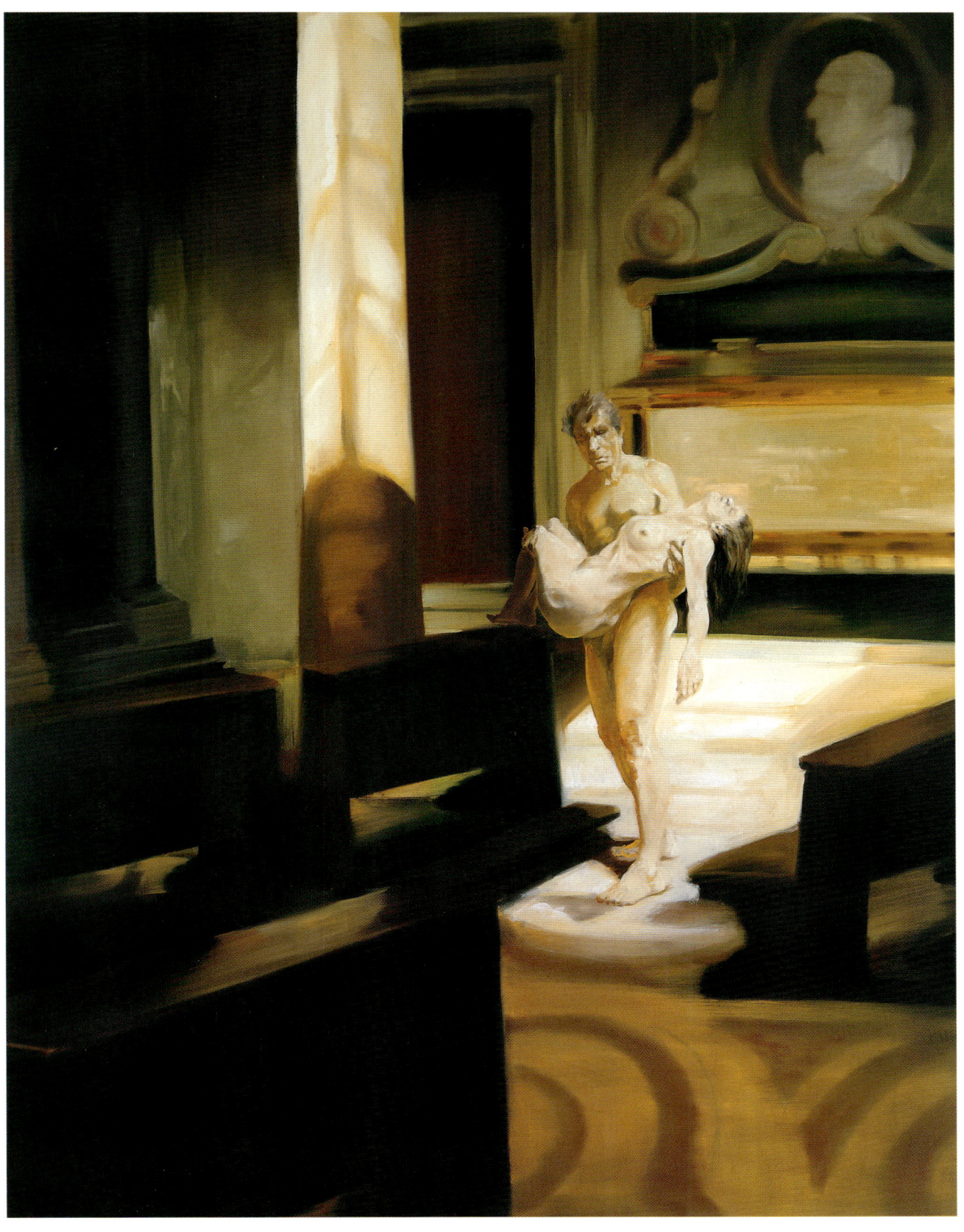

FIG. 14. **Eric Fischl**, *Once Where We Looked to Put Down our Dead*, **1996.** Oil on linen. 98 × 80 in. (248.9 × 203.2 cm). The Eli and Edythe L. Broad Collection.

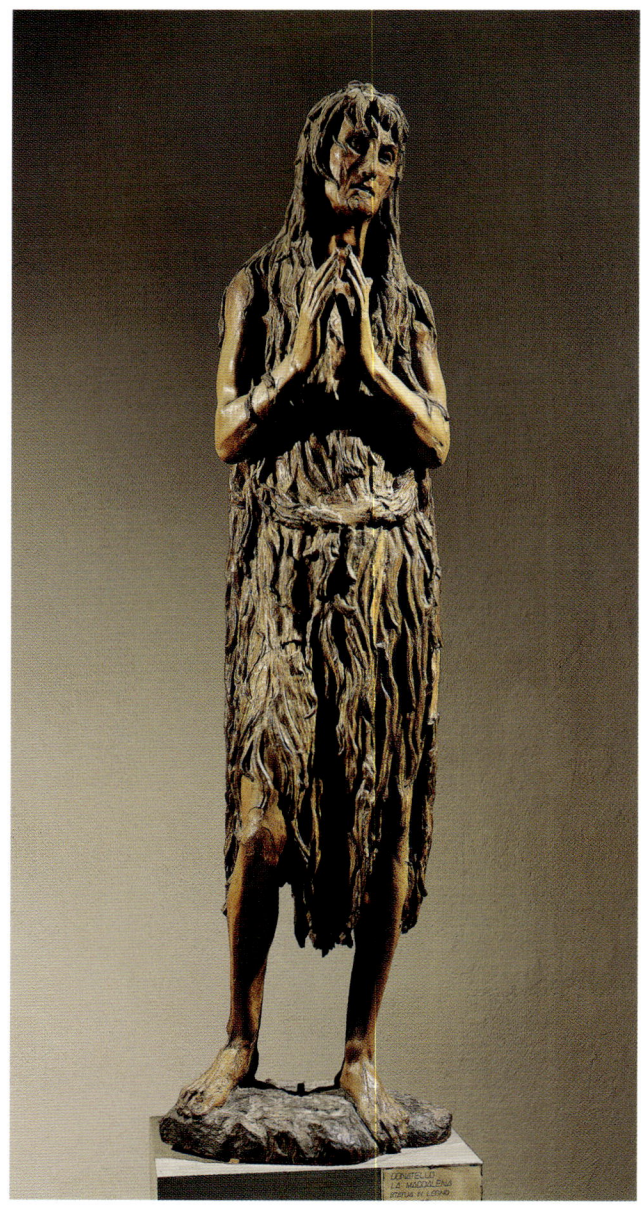

FIG. 15. **Donatello** (Italian, 1386–1466), *Penitent Magdalene*, **c. 1453–55.** Wood. 72¾ × 20 × 17¾ in. (185 × 51 × 45 cm). Museo dell'Opera di Santa Maria del Fiore (Duomo), Florence, Tuscany, Italy.

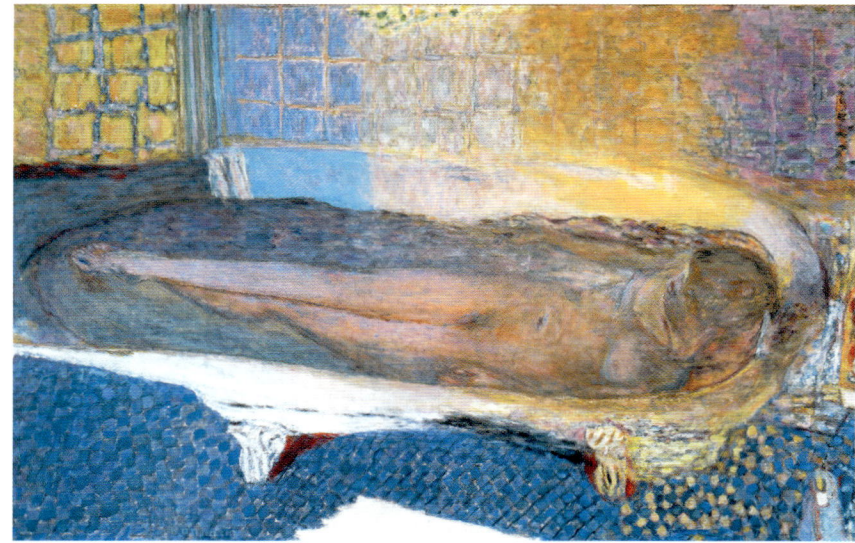

FIG. 16. **Pierre Bonnard** (French, 1867–1947), *Nude in the Bathtub*, **1936.** Oil on canvas. 36⅝ × 57¾ in. (93 × 147 cm). Musée d'Art Moderne, Paris, France, Purchased from the artist in 1937.

in the history of American art. Eakins's willingness to depict the human body in its frank nakedness—all the better for demonstrating the ways in which limbs move through space—attracted as much controversy in the nineteenth century as Fischl's works have in the twentieth and twenty-first centuries. In both cases, that controversy has been sparked not just by depictions of women but also by portrayals of the male nude. While Eakins's paintings featuring naked male swimmers and wrestlers challenged prevailing social

conventions, Fischl's sculpture in Flushing Meadows Corona Park in Queens, New York, celebrating the great American tennis player Arthur Ashe (2000), brought to light similar tensions about the public visibility of the naked male body a century later.[20]

In *Once Where We Looked to Put Down our Dead*, as in many of Fischl's other paintings from the Rome series, histories of art serve as counterweights to the artist's personal present. Fischl has written, for example, about his difficult relationship with his father while growing up and the problems he encountered when determining how to mourn the latter's death. The paintings that developed from the Rome sojourn were a way for Fischl to come to terms with this loss. Whether through the brushstrokes of Caravaggio, the architecture of Borromini, or the photographic lens of Eakins, travel to Rome suggested that the combination of history and memory was a weight to be carried and gently set down in the quiet seclusion of pictorial space.

### The Space Between

Reminiscing about one of his early trips to Europe, Fischl recalls the impact that Renaissance art produced on him: "Through Michelangelo I began to understand how exaggeration expresses truth and

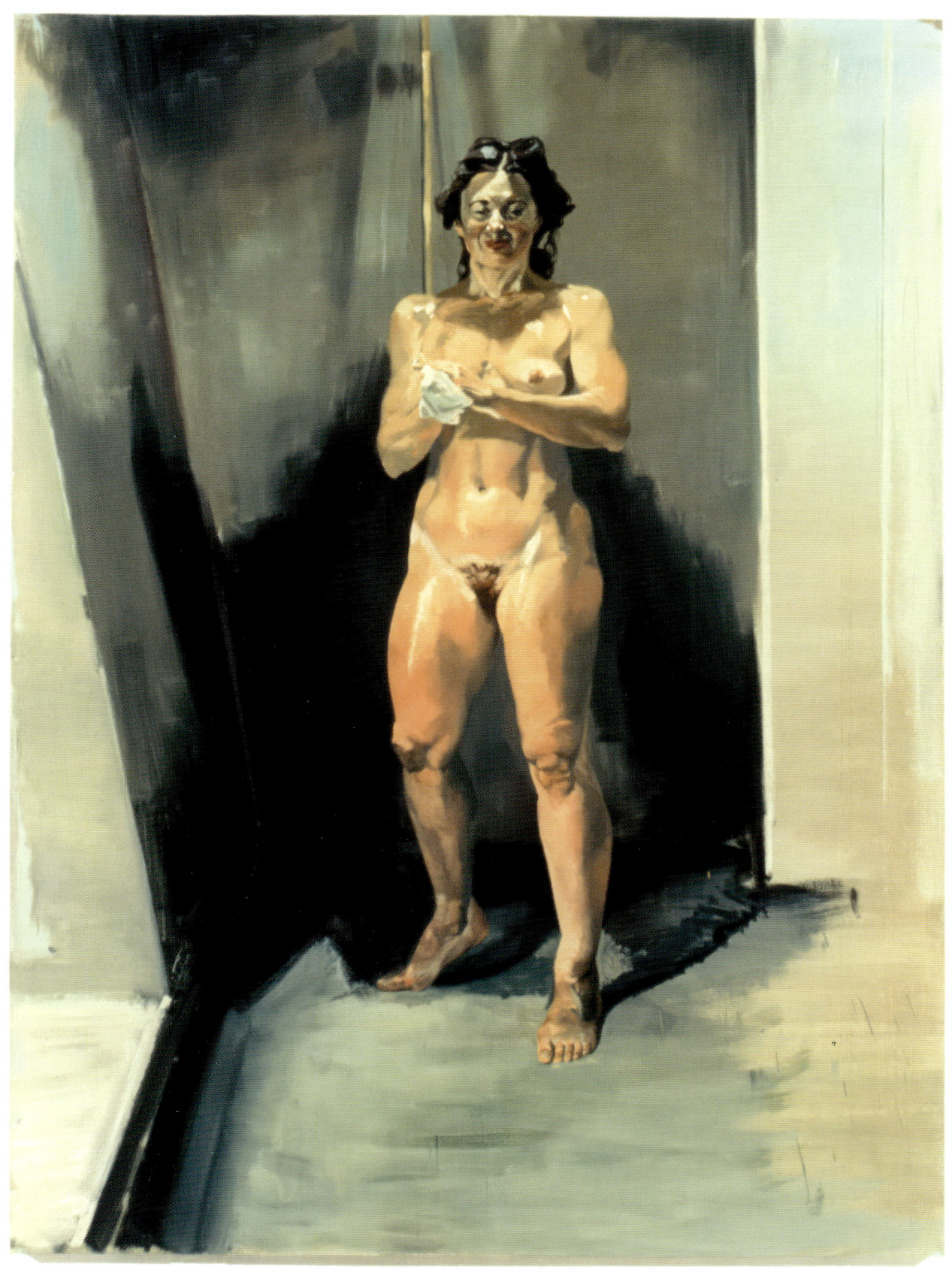

FIG. 17. **Eric Fischl,** *April in the Shower,* **1991.** Oil on linen. 98 × 74 in. (248.92 × 187.96 cm). Collection unknown.

how the body carries multiple and simultaneous meanings. Through Donatello, I began to understand the importance of knowing where to stop time."[21] For Fischl, the idea that art was capable of arresting time came powerfully to the fore in Donatello's sculpture titled *Penitent Magdalene* created around 1455 (FIG. 15). This wooden sculpture is a harrowing work. Anticipating the painfully angular bodies in Beckmann's painting discussed above, Donatello imagines Mary Magdalene as an emaciated figure, her clothes in rags, her eye sockets enlarged, her feet bare. This is a human form stripped to its elements.

Yet Fischl was once again attracted by an aspect of the work that audiences might typically overlook, namely, the space between the figure's hands as they come together in a gesture of prayer.[22] This small gap imbues a static work with dynamism while also demarcating a space of grace. Extending beyond narrowly religious symbolism, however, the space signals the point at which a person becomes unknowable and psychologically inaccessible to the viewer. Donatello creates a recognizable figurative sculpture, but one that resists conventions of understanding.

Art's capacity to identify and problematize the distance between people is central to Fischl's creativity. While this is a theme that runs throughout the works discussed above, it is most clear in Fischl's depictions of the individuals who are closest to him, notably, those featuring his wife, the landscape painter April Gornik. In his comments about portraying Gornik over the course of their long relationship, Fischl draws a connection between his art and that of the French Post-Impressionist painter Pierre Bonnard.

Known for the shimmering palette of his paintings, Bonnard spent much of his career depicting his wife, Marthe, bathing and dressing. He turned to closed interiors such as bedrooms and bathrooms to explore the optical effects of water and reflections as well as the psychological realities of spaces shared by two individuals. On the highly patterned surfaces of Bonnard's canvases, Marthe's figure asserts itself as a

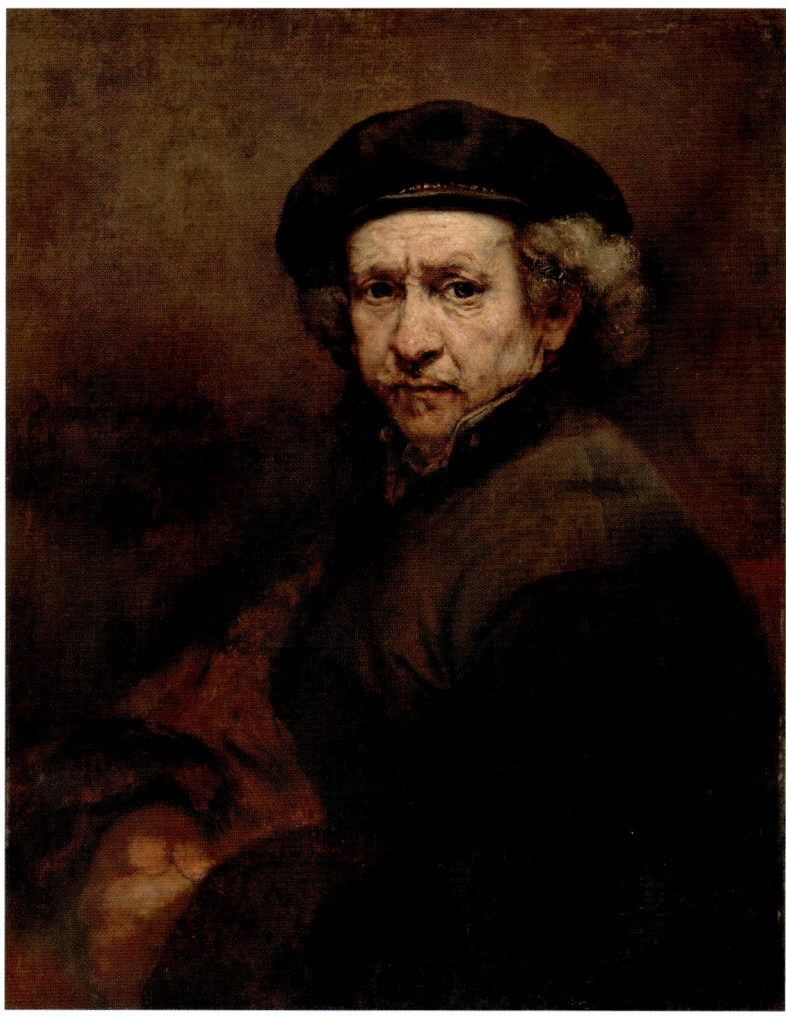

FIG. 18. **Rembrandt van Rijn** (Dutch, 1606–1669), *Self-Portrait*, **1659.** Oil on canvas. 33¼ × 26 in. (84.5 × 66 cm). National Gallery of Art, Washington, DC, Andrew W. Mellon Collection (1937.1.72).

luminous, coloristic presence. In *Nude in the Bathtub* (1936), as in many of Bonnard's other works featuring Marthe, the body absorbs and reflects the radiant colours of the surroundings but never disintegrates into them (FIG. 16). In a comment that anticipates Fischl's commitment to figurative painting, Bonnard stated that it is always necessary for painting to have "a subject," thus maintaining contact "with the world of beings and things."[23]

Fischl imagines the pleasure that Bonnard took in observing Marthe in these closed settings and equates this to his own delight in watching and depicting Gornik: "I'd watch her as a way of measuring the space between us, hoping to define myself

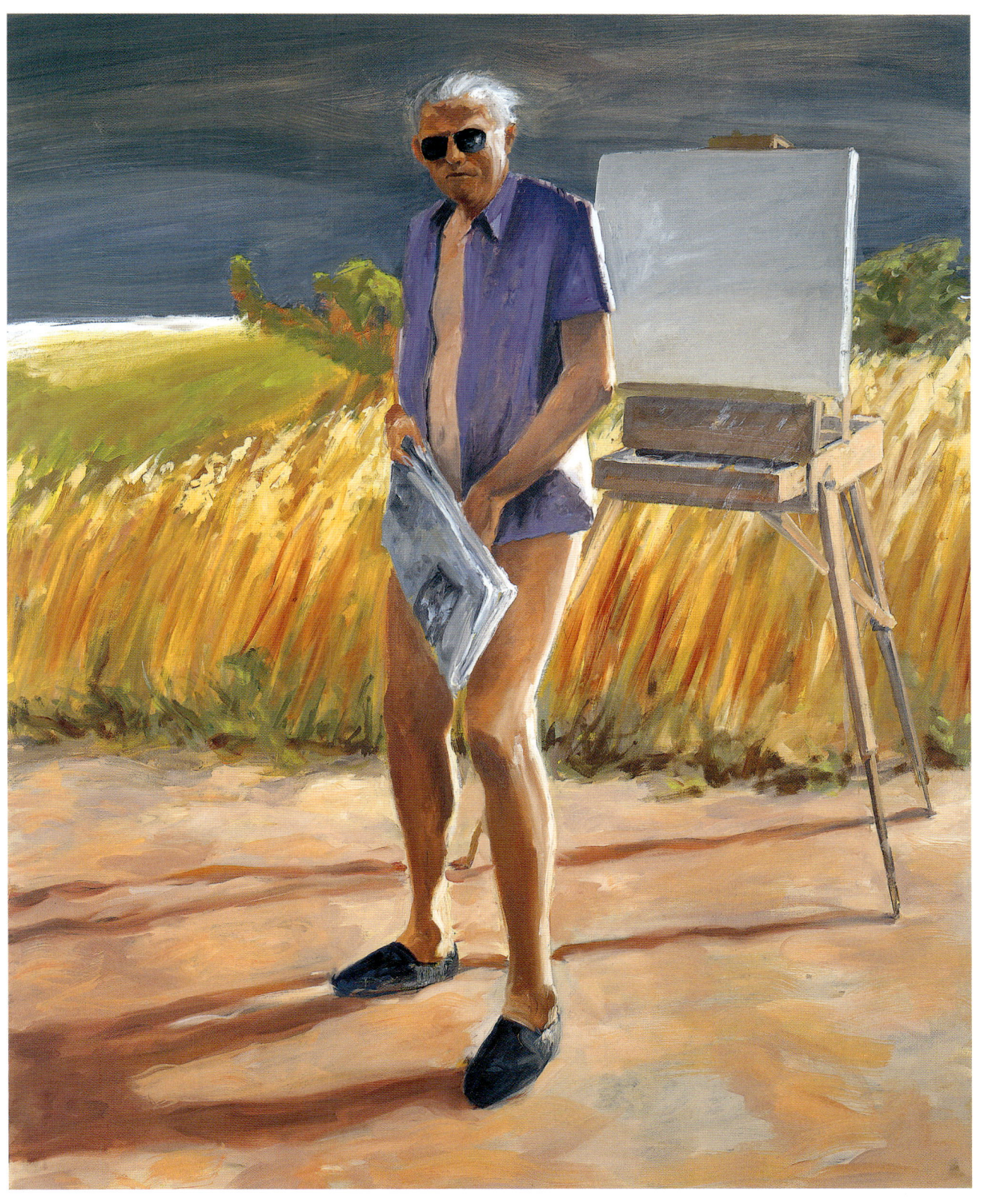

FIG. 19. **Eric Fischl,** *Portrait of the Artist as an Old Man,* **1984.** Oil on canvas, 85 × 70 in. (215.9 × 177.8 cm). SFMOMA, Gift of Collectors Forum in honor of the 50th Anniversary.

more precisely by it" (FIG. 17).[24] Interestingly, Fischl's remark is not simply about looking or even painting. Rather—echoing his observation about Donatello's sculpture—it concerns a charged physical, psychological, and imaginative space between two people. Far from turning an objectifying or prurient gaze on another person, Fischl envisages his depictions of Gornik as a necessary part of his own creative world and articulation of self.

His writings on this subject also awaken ideas about temporal space and how bodies inhabit time. Whereas Bonnard depicted Marthe with a permanently youthful body, Fischl uses portraiture to confront and depict the realities of age and its associated physical changes. In this case, art becomes a tool for expressing personal histories and navigating the shifting spaces between two individuals who share a life and a commitment to depicting the world in paint.

These explorations of spaces between things, states, and people also come to the fore when Fischl turns his painterly gaze on his own person. Here too history plays a role. He discusses his passion for self-portraits by Bonnard and Beckmann but reserves special praise for those of the aging Rembrandt (FIG. 18). In a painting of 1659, Rembrandt captures a moment in his life when, despite having achieved international fame, he suffered financial failure and had been forced to sell his house and possessions to satisfy the demands of his creditors. The painting turns an unflinching gaze on the artist's older self but is uncompromising in its direct confrontation with the viewer. Fischl makes the point that throughout Rembrandt's late self-portraits, there is a combination of strength and vulnerability, a willingness to acknowledge the realities of being human and depicting them in paint.[25]

Fischl's *Portrait of the Artist as an Old Man* (1984) takes up Rembrandt's challenge by staging a complex reflection on age, family, and creativity (FIG. 19). Produced in the mid-1980s when Fischl was not yet forty, the painting is of a much older man—the artist's combined self-portrait and depiction of his father. In this case, memory of another person stimulates an involuntary

transformation of the self. As in Rembrandt's painting, the work is a mixture of heroism and vulnerability. The depicted figure is caught off guard in an embarrassing position and hides his nakedness behind a newspaper just as he hides his eyes behind dark sunglasses. If Donatello's sculpture queries what we can know about another person, Fischl's self-portrait asks what we can know about the self.[26]

In the shift from a preliminary study to the work's final realisation, Fischl adds a blank canvas on an easel to the background of the composition. Does the stooped, hesitant individual have the strength and self-possession to start—let alone complete—a new work? The easel mimics the fragility of the man's body: The elongated shadows of the two forms merge in the foreground and the paint box juts forward as a suggestively phallic presence. Through a combined engagement with history and personal memory, the painting envisages the artist's future self as an accumulation of past images and associations. Fischl has commented that a successful portrait is one in which the subject "is there."[27] In this painting, by contrast, the artist is and is not present. Physicality is a metaphor for the simultaneous exposure and concealment of the artistic self, and the blank canvas symbolizes the combination of courage and dread inherent in the practice of creativity.

Throughout his career, Fischl has engaged closely with history for the purpose of extending his own expressive repertoire, finding sources of inspiration, and placing his art in genealogies of making and thinking. Yet there is also a sense in which these encounters with the past have a more fundamental significance. This concerns art's capacity to articulate the things that unite people as human beings across different times, cultures, and geographies. As a visual storyteller and figurative painter, Fischl uses his creativity to reveal often uncomfortable truths about "what it is we share, what we have in common on the most intimate levels of our being."[28] Turning to art's histories is a powerful means of bringing those points of connection vividly into the present. ▪

Notes

1  Max Beckmann, *On My Painting*, ed. George Scrivani (Hanuman Books, 1988), p. 11. © 2025 Artists Rights Society (ARS), New York.

2  Robert Enright, "Fischl on Fischl," in Arthur C. Danto, Robin Enright, and Steve Martin, *Eric Fischl 1970–2007* (Monacelli Press, 2008), p. 77.

3  Eric Fischl and Michael Stone, *Bad Boy: My Life On and Off the Canvas* (Arcade, 2016), p. 47.

4  Fischl and Stone, *Bad Boy*, 140.

5  R.B. Kitaj, "Introduction," in *The Artist's Eye: An Exhibition Selected by R.B. Kitaj at the National Gallery London* (National Gallery, 1980), published in conjunction with an exhibition of the same title, May 21–July 21, 1980, n.p.

6  See, for example, Maurice de Vlaminck, *Portraits avant décès* (Flammarion, 1943), p. 142.

7  Georges Jeanniot, *Souvenirs sur Degas* (L'Échoppe, 2017), p. 44; Joris-Karl Huysmans, *Certains* (Tresse & Stock, 1889), p. 23. For further discussion see Kathryn Brown, *Dialogues with Degas: Influence and Antagonism in Contemporary Art* (Bloomsbury, 2023), pp. 48–50.

8  For a critique of this approach see Norma Broude, "Degas's 'Misogyny,'" *Art Bulletin* 59:1 (1977), pp. 95–107.

9  See Arthur C. Danto, "Formation, Success, and Mastery: Eric Fischl Decade by Decade" in Danto, Enright, and Martin, *Eric Fischl*, 16.

10  Fischl and Stone, *Bad Boy*, 140.

11  Kathryn Brown, "The Aesthetics of Presence: Looking at Degas's Bathers," *Journal of Aesthetics and Art Criticism* 68, no. 4 (November 2010), p. 334.

12  On the notion of "impersonal imagining," see Gregory Currie, *Image and Mind: Film, Philosophy, and Cognitive Science* (Cambridge University Press, 1995), p. 179.

13  See also Robert Rosenblum, "Eric Fischl: The Krefeld Project" in *Eric Fischl: The Krefeld Project*, ed. Martin Hentschel (Kerber, 2003), published in conjunction with an exhibition at Museum Haus Esters, Krefeld, Germany, October 12, 2003–January 25, 2004, p. 11.

14  Fischl and Stone, *Bad Boy*, 140. See also Carol Armstrong's discussion of Degas's compositional techniques for "ousting" the viewer from the scenes. Carol Armstrong, *Odd Man Out: Readings of the Work and Reputation of Edgar Degas* (University of Chicago Press, 1991), p. 166.

15  Fischl and Stone, *Bad Boy*, 141.

16  Fischl and Stone, *Bad Boy*, 141.

17  Fischl and Stone, *Bad Boy*, 291.

18  Fischl and Stone, *Bad Boy*, 291.

19  On Fischl's works from this period, see also Victoria Fleming, "Narratives of the Sacred: An American in Rome," in *Eric Fischl: Paintings and Drawings 1979–2001*, ed. Annelie Lütgens (Hatje Cantz, 2003), published in conjunction with an exhibition of the same title at the Kunstmuseum Wolfsburg, Germany, September 13, 2003–January 25, 2004, pp. 115–122.

20  See, for example, J. A. Adande, "It's Art, but It's Sure Not Arthur," *Los Angeles Times*, August 30, 2000, https://www.latimes.com/archives/la-xpm-2000-aug-30-sp-12485-story.html.

21  Fischl and Stone, *Bad Boy*, 104.

22  Fischl and Stone, *Bad Boy*, 104.

23  Pierre Bonnard, "Pour et contre l'art abstrait," in Pierre Bonnard, *Un sentiment qui tient le mur: Notes, propos et entretiens*, preface by Alain Lévêque, ed. François-Marie Deyrolle (L'Atelier Contemporain, 2023), p. 81.

24  Fischl and Stone, *Bad Boy*, 311.

25  Fischl and Stone, *Bad Boy*, 342.

26  For further discussion of this self-portrait, see Eleanor Nairne in this volume.

27  Fischl and Stone, *Bad Boy*, 265.

28  Fischl and Stone, *Bad Boy*, 321.

COUPLES & PAIRS

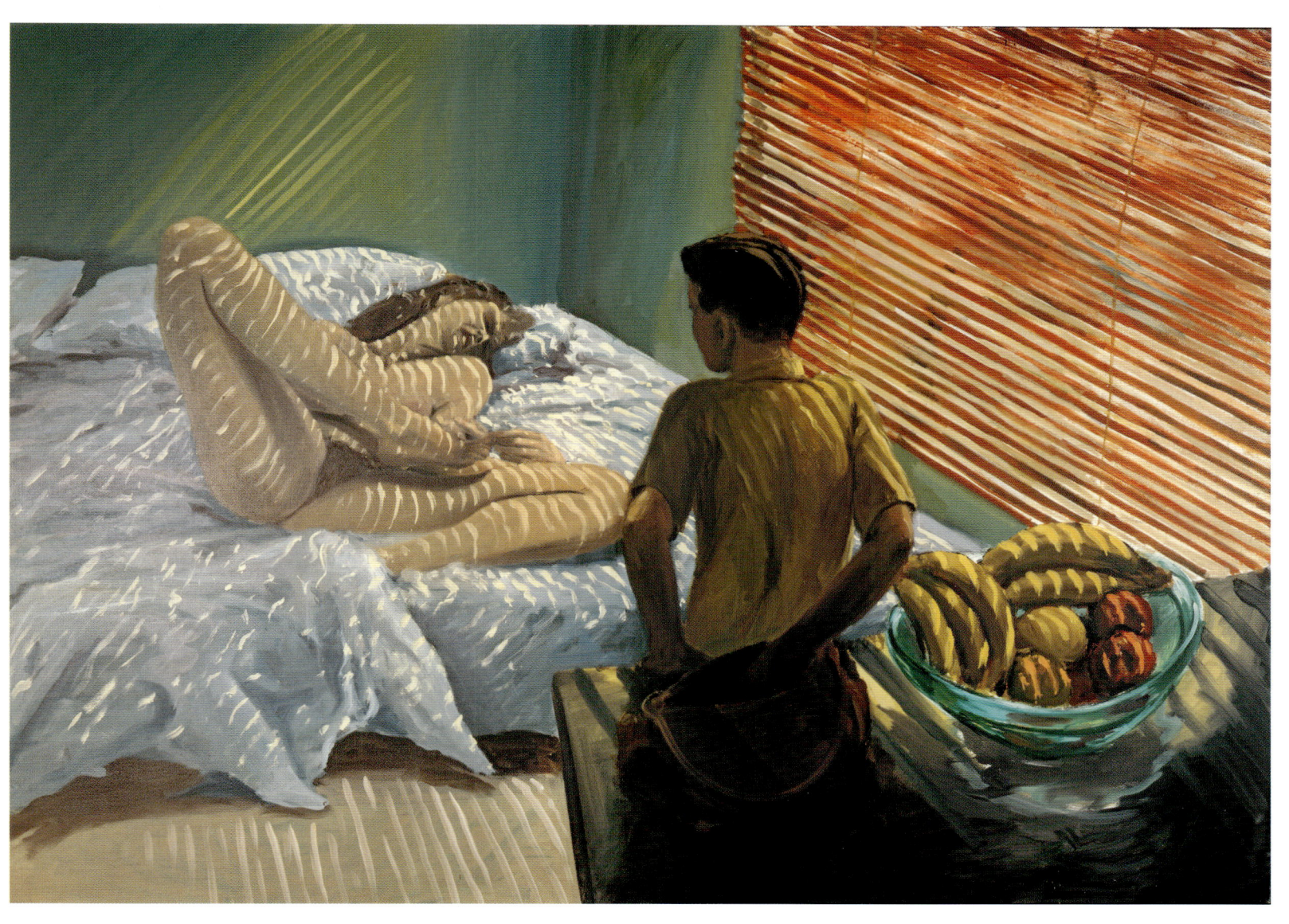

PLATE 15. *Bad Boy*, 1981

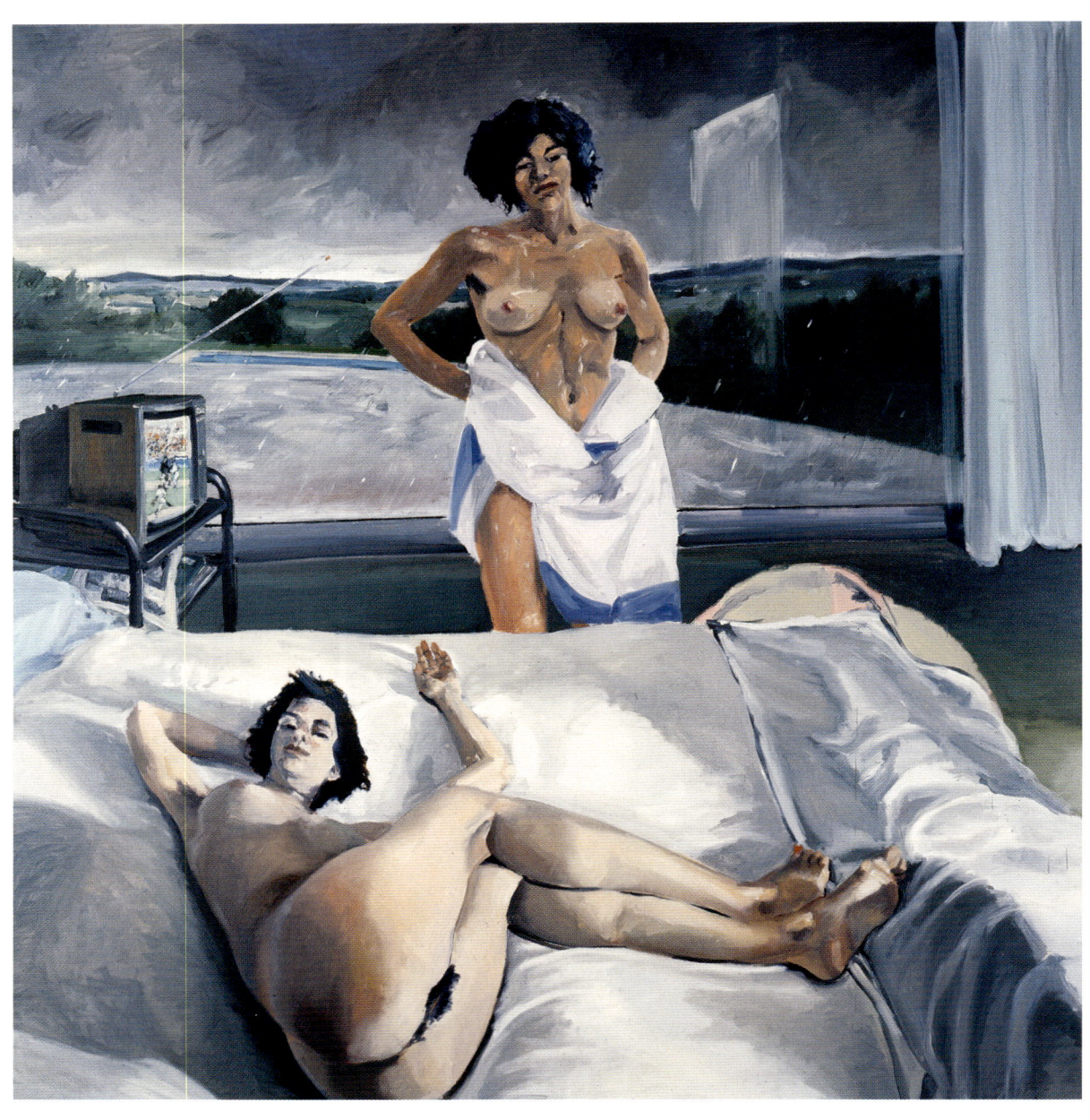

PLATE 16. *Untitled*, 1982

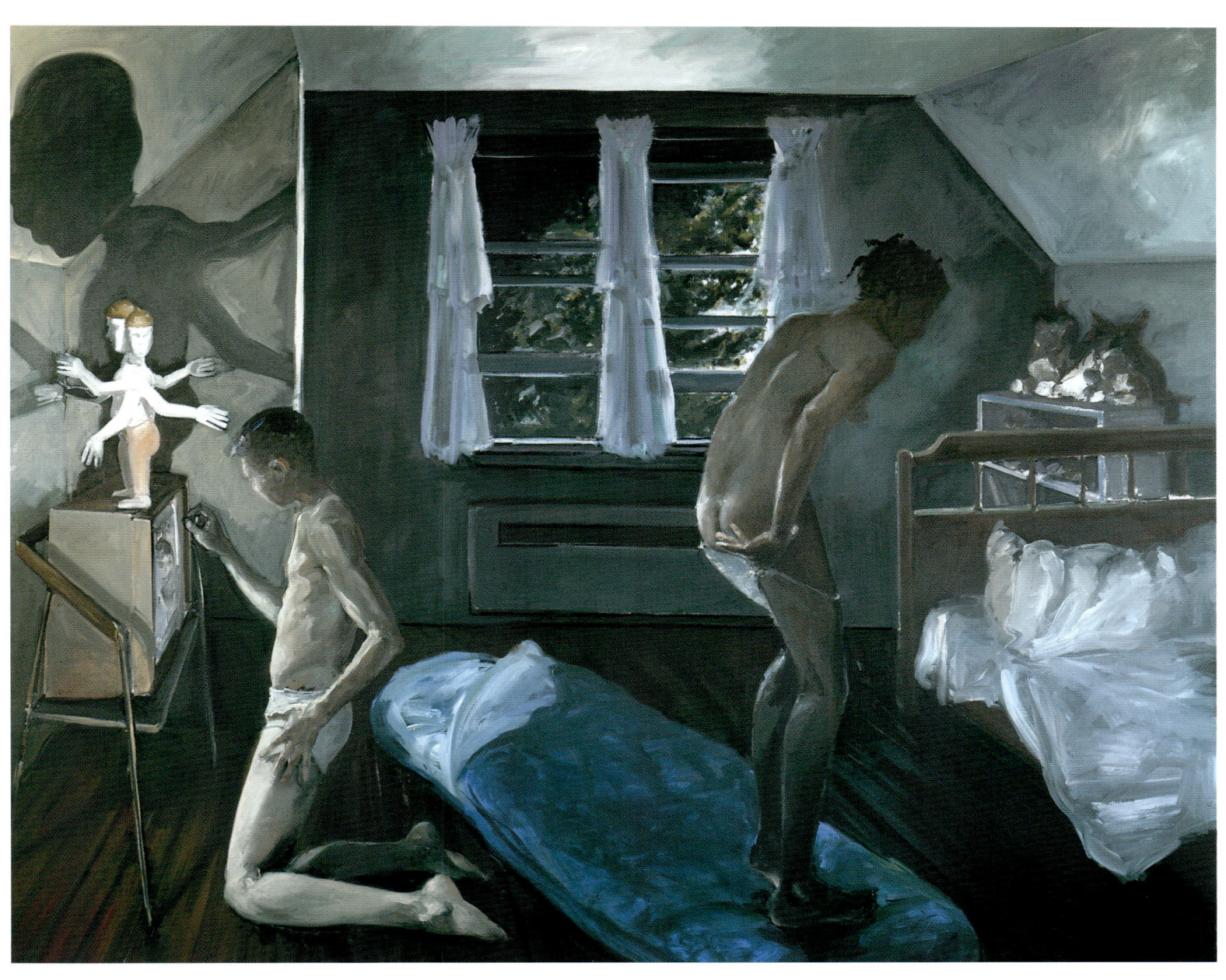

PLATE 17. *Slumber Party*, 1983

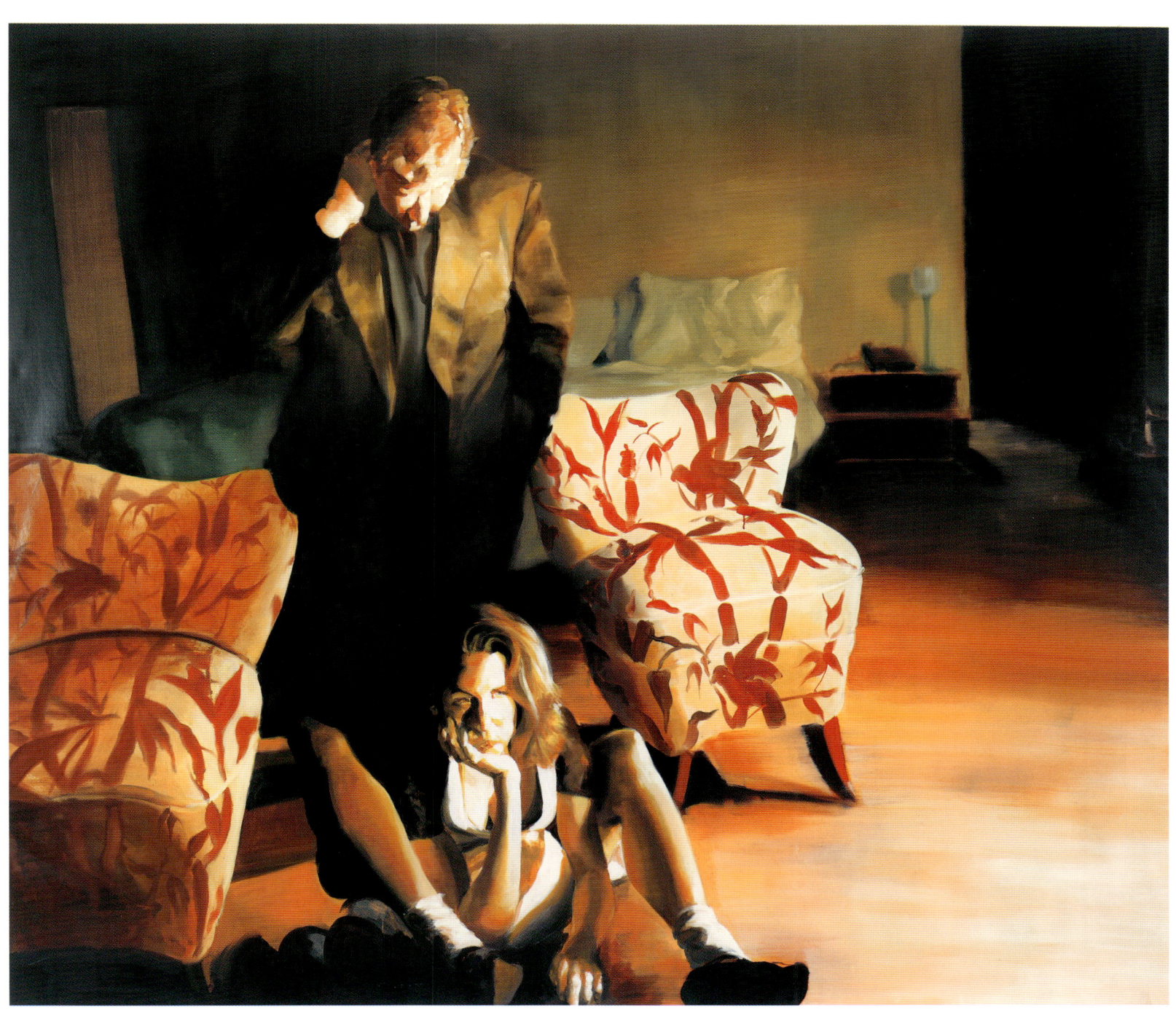

PLATE 18. *The Bed, The Chair, The Sitter,* 1999

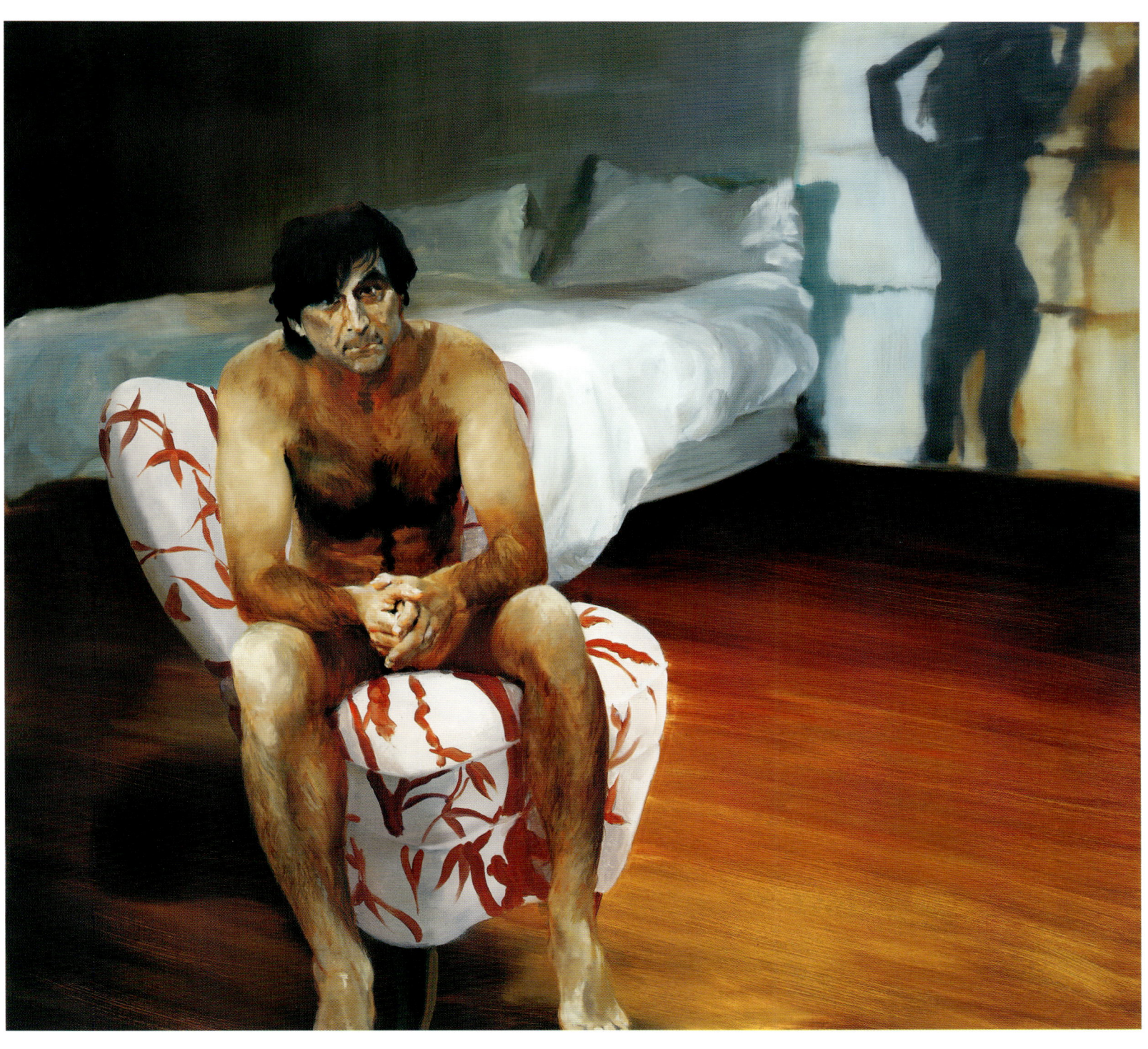

PLATE 19. *The Bed, The Chair, Dancing, Watching*, 2000

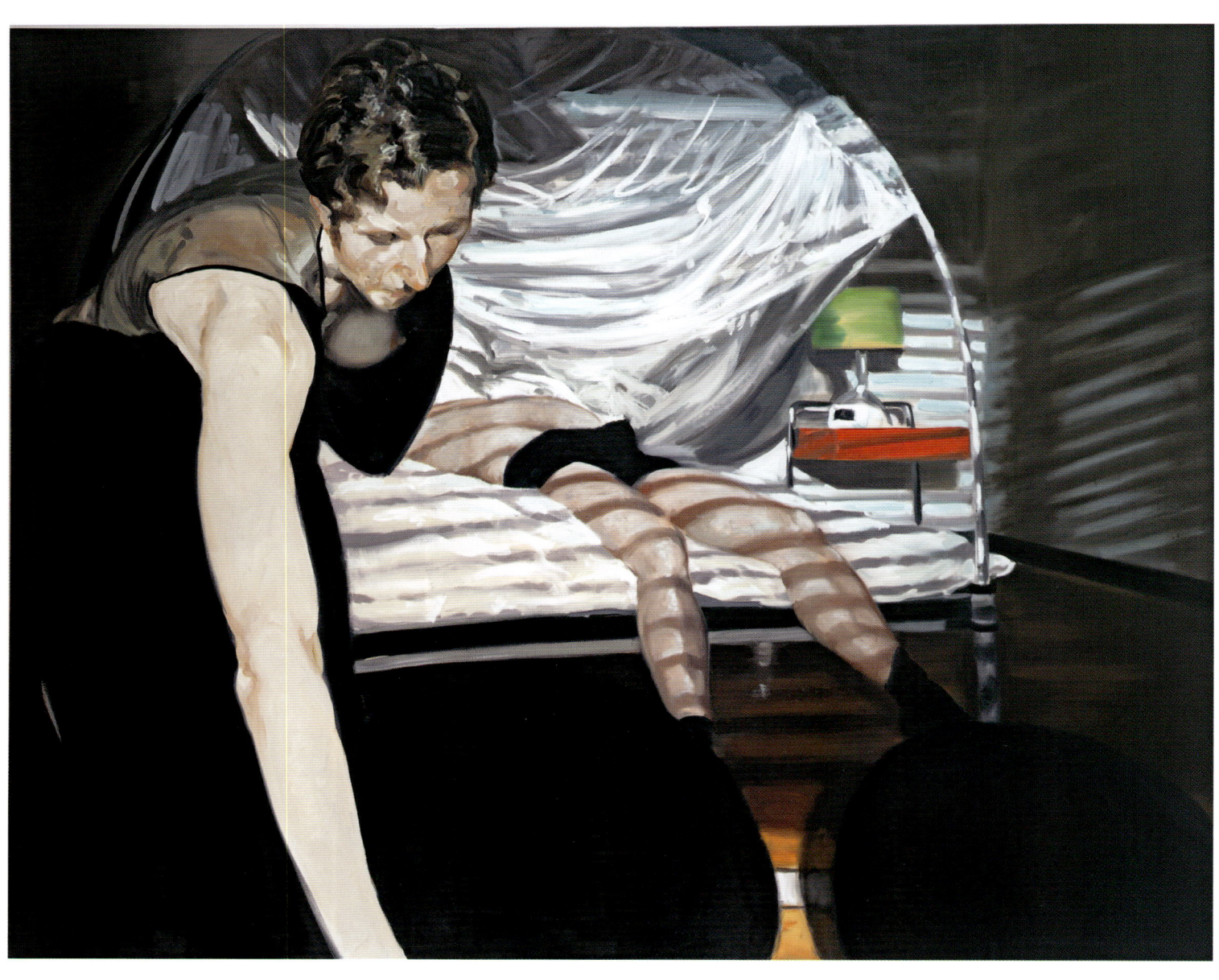

PLATE 20. *Bedroom, Scene #3, Mistakes Mistakes! Everything Shakes
from All the Mistakes,* 2004

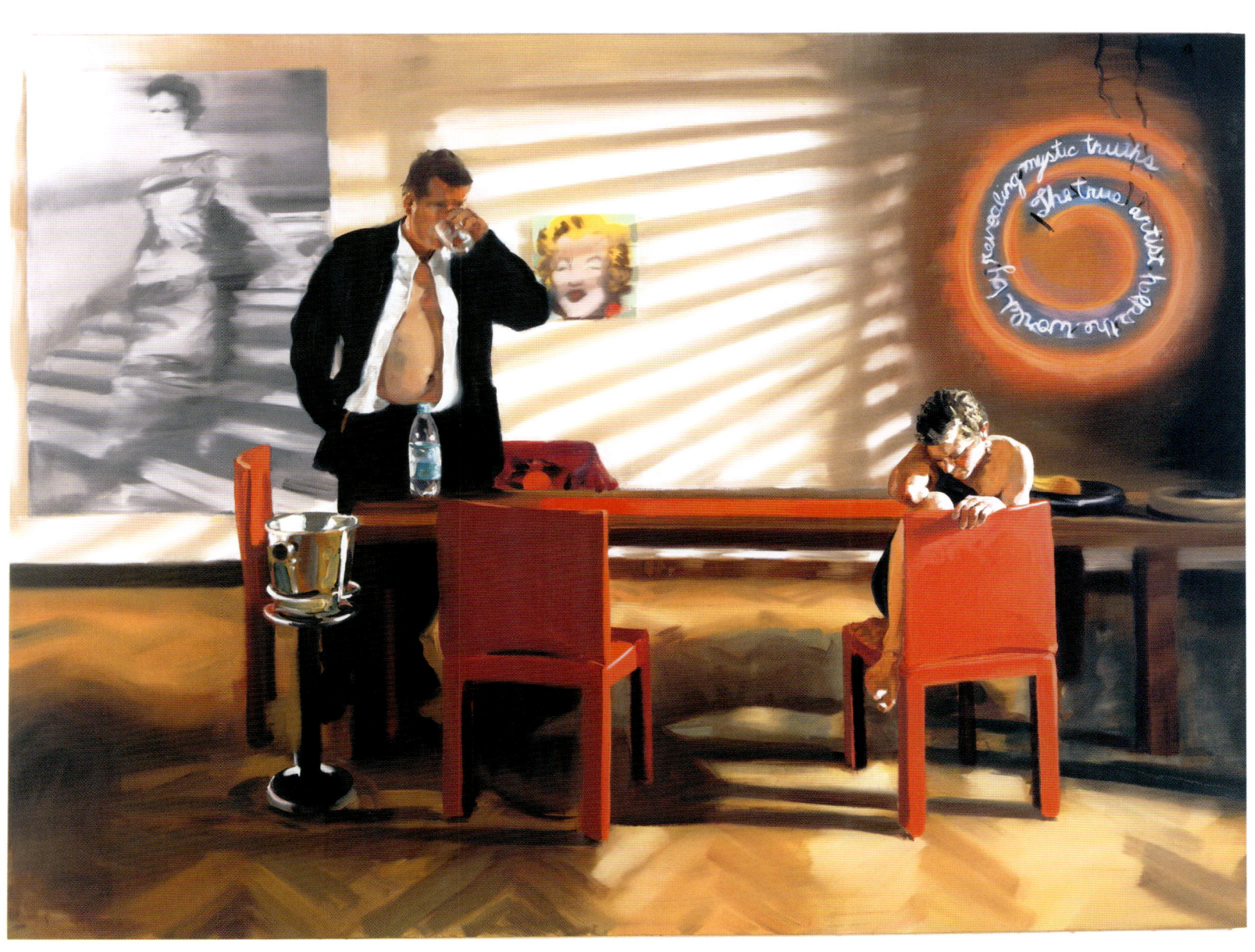

PLATE 21. *Krefeld Project; Dining Room, Scene #2*, 2003

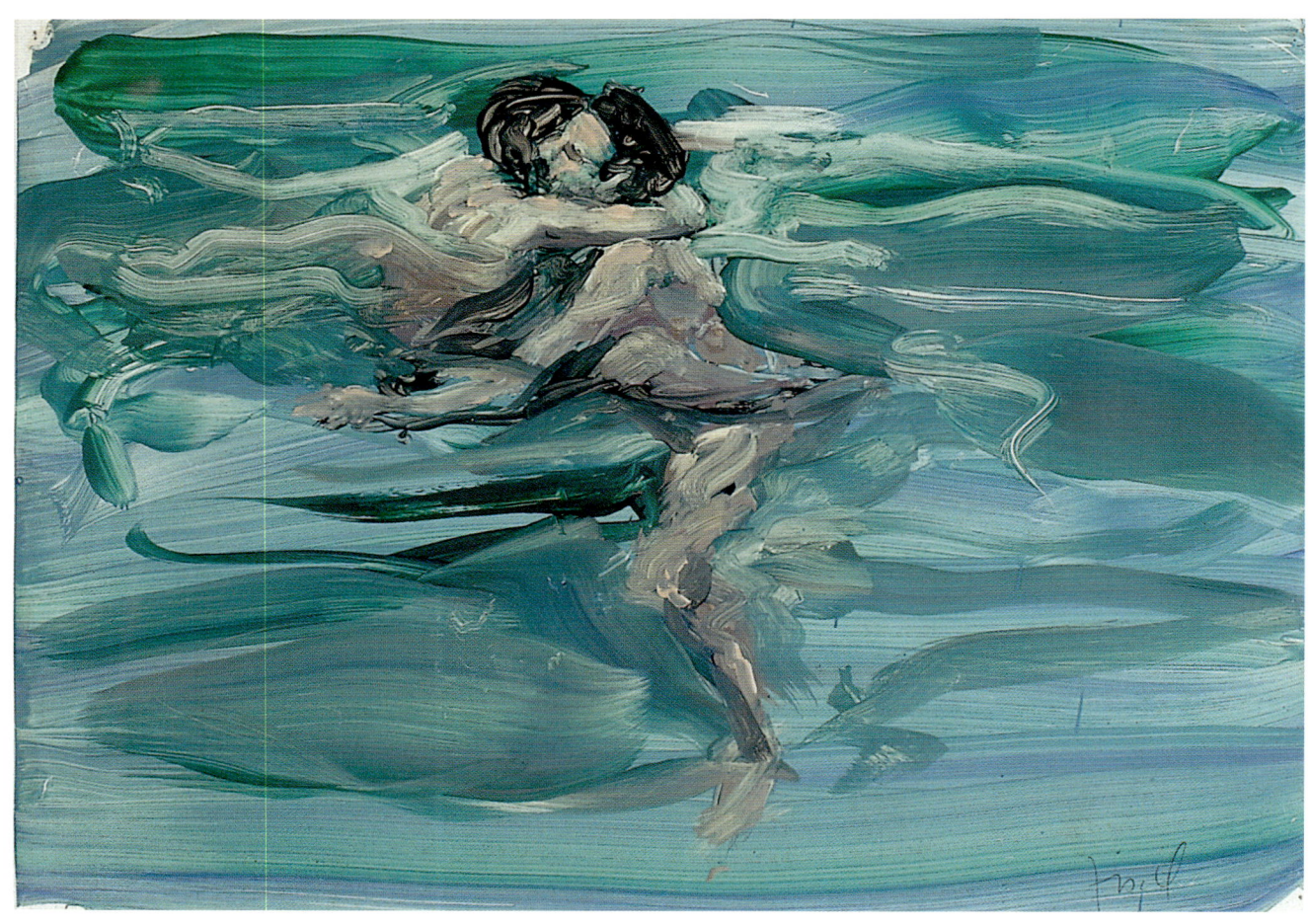

PLATE 22. *Swimming Lovers*, 1984

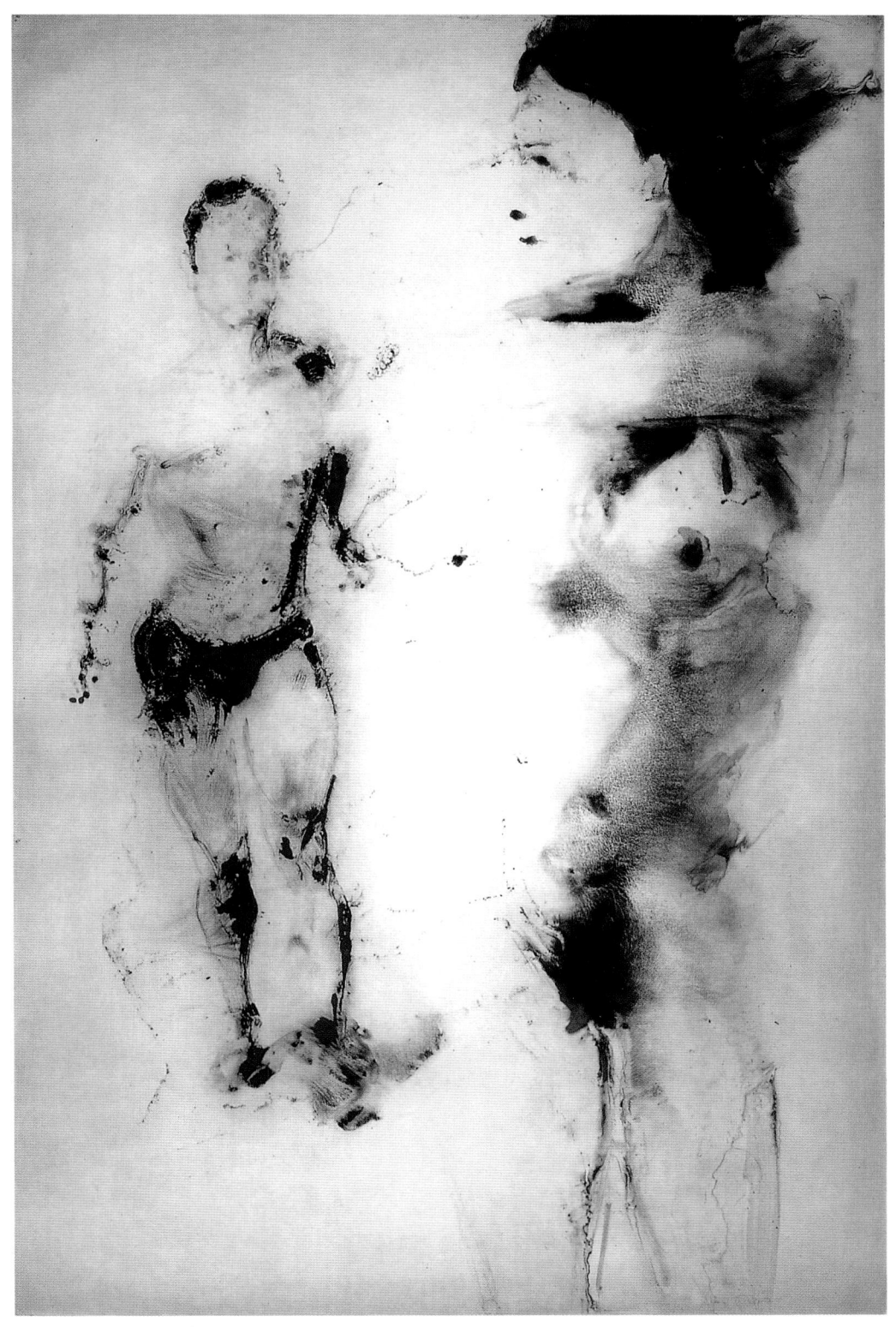

PLATE 23. *Untitled (Two Figures)*, 2006

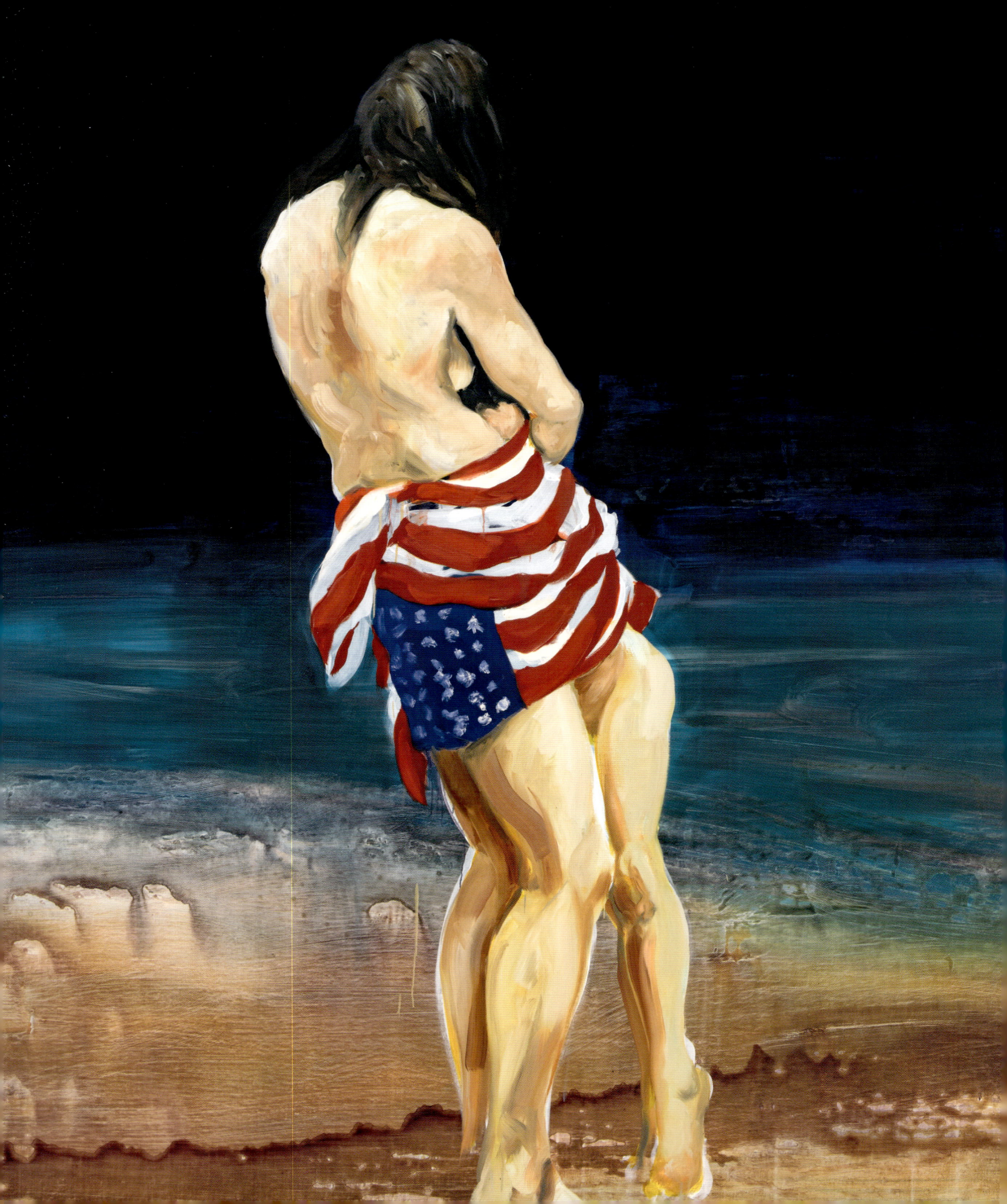

"Having grown up in Eden before the Fall, I had first-hand experience with how fragile the illusion of Paradise is, how devastating its loss."

ERIC FISCHL [1]

The title of this volume, *Late America*, comes from a 2016 painting by Eric Fischl (PLATE 28). In this work, a small boy wrapped in an American flag towel stands over a naked middle-aged man curled in the fetal position at the edge of a suburban backyard pool. In the background, partially obscured by a row of empty beach chairs, two faceless gardeners toil on the grounds. The foreground character types—an overweight white man and a confused-looking boy—have appeared frequently in Fischl's paintings. So has the setting, with all its associations of carefree leisure and economic privilege. As is so often the case in Fischl's work, the cheerful ambience of this sun-drenched suburban backyard is undermined by disturbing psychological undercurrents. Why is this flabby man so unresponsive to the boy who hovers over him? What does the boy want from him, and why is he swaddled in a flag? How should we understand their obliviousness to the laborers who maintain their picture-perfect world? And what does the title *Late America* mean?

The title lifts the painting out of the territory of psychosexual drama and into the realm of allegory. The phrase "Late America" can be read a variety of ways: it encompasses the idea of aging, a reminder that America is no longer a young country; it carries the

specter of decline, senescence, and even death in the way we apply the adjective "late" to those who have passed on; it could be a reminder of missed opportunities and possibilities. One critic has even suggested that the series to which this work belongs might be titled "Too Late, America."[2]

Fischl reports that he painted this work in the aftermath of the 2016 election. While *Late America* embodies his fears for America following the election of Donald Trump, it also connects to the loss of innocence that has long been a theme in his work. Beginning with his early explorations of the complicated dynamics of growing up in a dysfunctional family, Fischl has presented characters whose hopes and fantasies cannot be satisfied by the empty materialism, unfulfilling hedonism, and missed connections that characterize contemporary American life. This theme has taken on an ever more social dimension in his work since the catastrophe of September 11, 2001. Fischl remarks, "9/11 set us on this intractable path. For a lot of Americans, our myths exploded in an instant. It became clear we weren't invulnerable; we weren't the most loved nation. . . . It was a dream we couldn't sustain, and we haven't figured out how to replace it."[3]

In *Late America*, Fischl created an indelible image of impotence and isolation. Four years later, in the midst

Detail of PLATE 29

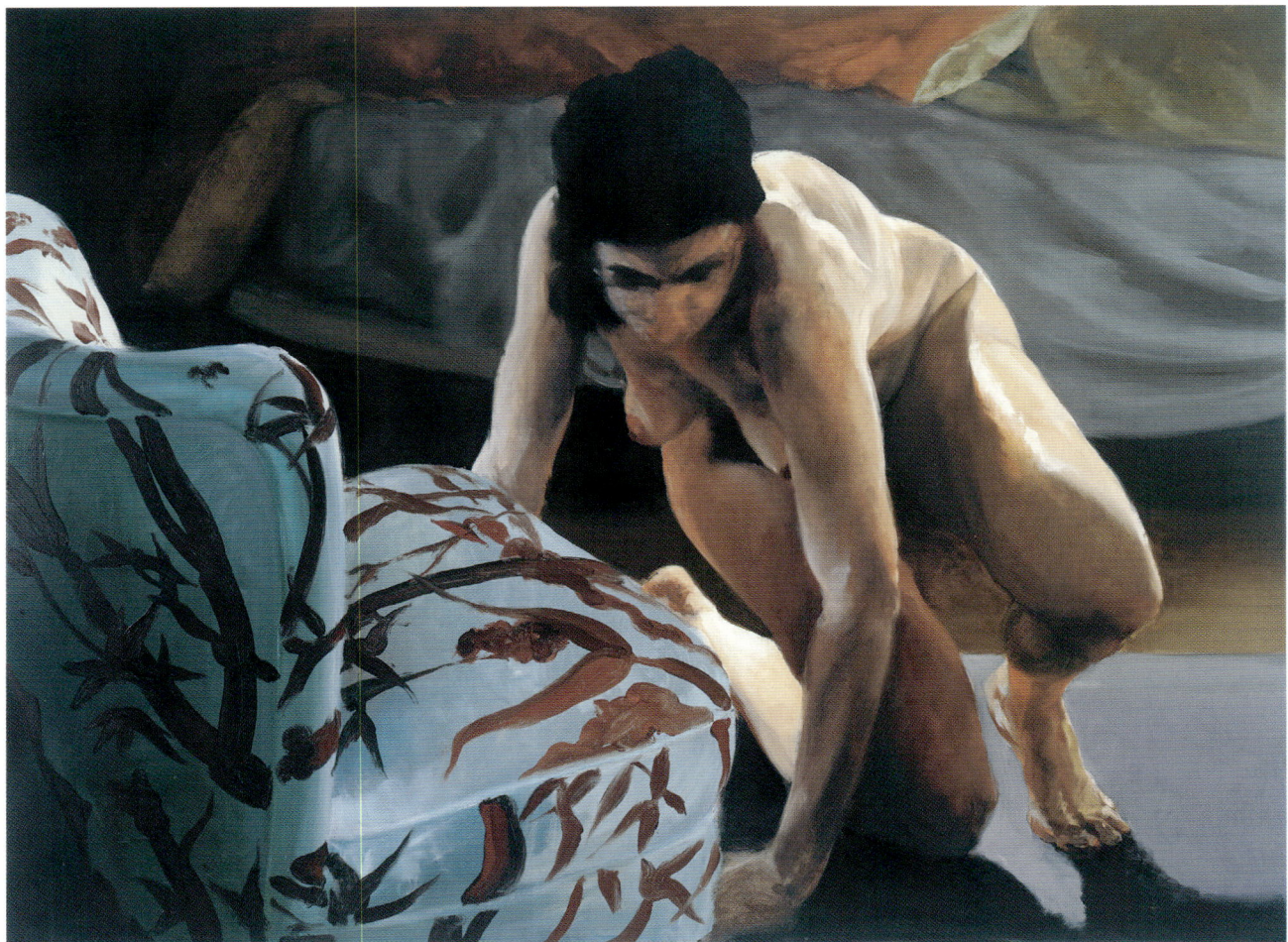

FIG. 20. **Eric Fischl**, *The Bed, The Chair; Hiding*, **2001**. Oil on linen. 38 × 52 in. (96.52 × 132.08 cm). Collection of Katherine Harrison in honor of Stephen Harrison.

of the COVID-19 pandemic, he painted a new iteration of this idea. Titled *Late America 2*, it depicts a woman, her back turned to us, binding a child to her body with an American flag (PLATE 29). The two are outlined against a turbulent, near-black sky that rises above roiling surf. While the setting is far more ominous, the woman's protective gesture is in stark contrast to the man's paralysis in the earlier painting. The apocalyptic overtones of *Late America 2* offer a potent metaphor for the sense of doom that enveloped humanity as the pandemic spread across the globe.

As a symbol, the American flag operates differently in these two works. In *Late America,* it separates the two figures: one naked, and the other wrapped in the stars and stripes. It hints at aspirations to which the young boy still clings but that have been abandoned by the man. In *Late America 2*, the flag connects the two figures, protecting them, however ineffectually, against

the storm. These differing treatments of the flag point to Fischl's own ambivalence toward the idea of America. As a place of lofty ideals that it too often fails to honor, America, like the family unit that is the basis of much of Fischl's work, is rife with contradictions.

Fischl insists his work is not political, at least in the conventional sense of the word. Throughout, his career has been informed by the traumas and pathologies that infect contemporary reality. He digs into his own history, life, and experiences to create scenarios that express the conflicts that shaped both his personal history and that of society at large. While he has traveled widely, he reports that his adventures abroad have served to heighten his realization of his own Americanness. In his compelling memoir, *Bad Boy: My Life On and Off the Canvas,* he remarks that this particularly came to the fore the first time he visited the beaches of southern France. He notes, "The experience of being on a beach in St. Tropez [*sic*] and seeing nude men and women interacting socially was both an inspiration and an assault on my puritanical American background." He adds, "There was also a racial element to it. You had these African men combing the beach, hawking baubles and approaching wealthy, fancy white women lying naked in the sun. . . . The dynamic becomes different, more complicated because of how Americans have mythologized the potency of black men."[4] The tension he felt was a factor of his own prudery but also a reflection of a discomfort with the body and sexuality rooted in the American puritan tradition. He has explored this tension to great effect in paintings of beach and poolside scenes where nudity is at once nonchalant and subtly nauseating.

And in fact, the great subject of Fischl's early work is the dark undercurrents running through American life. Fischl has discussed how the postwar American suburb represented a utopian ideal of harmony, equality, and prosperity. Spurred by the GI Bill, cheap land, and urban decay, people flocked to suburbs after the Second World War. These planned residential neighborhoods were to be the place where nature was tamed and domesticated and residents came together in a supportive community. But while all seemed well on the surface, the suburbs were also sites of racial and class exclusion, prefeminist suppression of women, and a stultifying social conformity that masked pathologies of depression, alcoholism, sexual frustration, and invisible violence. In his breakthrough paintings, Fischl explored a world informed by his own experiences as a child of the suburbs, living with an alcoholic mother whose disease was tearing his family apart. Often, in paintings such as *Bad Boy* (1981), *Barbeque* (1982), and *Squirt* (1982), the protagonist is a young boy whose inappropriate behaviors seem to be a cover for deeper insecurities and unacknowledged sexual and antisocial impulses (PLATES 15, 26, 27).

Conflicts between appearance and reality seem baked into the American psyche. This goes back to the earliest days of Western colonization, when settlers hailed the New World as a place of boundless opportunity, replete with the promise of redemption and reinvention. Oblivious to the harsh realities of climate and the presence of an existing Indigenous population, the new arrivals characterized their adopted home as the new Eden, a place of natural abundance and infinite promise where they could break free of the weight of history. In 1630 Governor John Winthrop memorably exhorted members of the soon to be settled Massachusetts Bay Colony to become a shining "city upon a hill," an aspirational metaphor that became the basis for the persistent idea of American exceptionalism. The American Revolution only reinforced this idea: that America was special, a font of individual liberty and social democracy destined to lead the world into the modern age.

Of course, America's lofty ideals have continually clashed with darker realities. The frontier myth of rugged individualism has often devolved into an antisocial selfishness, the notion of individual liberty can be wielded as a cudgel against policies that might make life better for society at large, and proclamations of equality are made hollow by ever starker economic divides. Slavery, Native American genocide, and imperialism exist alongside ideals of freedom, justice, and fairness. The postwar period into which Fischl was born was shaped by the triumph over fascism but was also marked by nuclear fears, civil and racial strife, and Cold War paranoia.

In Fischl's work, these tensions are embedded into open-ended narratives that suggest the ways in which individuals and social units (like the family and the community) have dealt with the contradictions inherent in American life. He continually returns to themes like isolation, anomie, and disconnection through scenarios that emphasize the psychic costs of empty materialism and mechanical pleasure-seeking in a world devoid of spiritual grounding and larger purpose. But Fischl's portrayals are softened by an implicit humanism. He reflects that his initial impulse was to demonize the kinds of people he felt had deformed his childhood, but as he painted them, he discovered that his anger melted into a kind of sympathy. "I had to get inside them, to accept their flawed characters, to understand the tragic aspect of life."[5]

From early work inspired by the sexual and social confusions of his own suburban upbringing, Fischl moved on to other kinds of narratives. Yearly retreats to Saint-Tropez yielded paintings that present jumbles of naked or near-naked pleasure seekers on the beach engaged in what often appear to be forced rituals of relaxation (PLATE 36). Travels to India and Rome allowed him to reflect on modes of spirituality that contrasted markedly with his own indifferent Protestant upbringing. In 1999, Fischl was challenged by one of his art dealers to make a painting that addressed his relationship to Edward Hopper, the twentieth-century chronicler of American loneliness to whom Fischl has often been compared. The result was The Philosopher's Chair, a painting depicting a clothed, bemused older man and a half-dressed younger woman wrestling with her slip (SEE P. 4). Their disconnect in what should be a moment of intimacy is accentuated by the setting—a room dominated by an unmade bed and an upholstered chair covered in a red botanical pattern. This turned out to be the first in a series of paintings titled The Bed, the Chair. . ., in which the chair emerges as a central character as individuals and couples enact various private acts and rituals within this same room (PLATES 18, 19). With works like these, Fischl moved on from the adolescent anxieties that informed his early paintings to explore the complexities of adult relationships.

Fischl was finishing this series when the planes hit the Twin Towers of the World Trade Center on September 11, 2001. From his studio in Sag Harbor, New York, he watched the buildings collapse on TV. In his memoir he writes, "September 11 was a defining event in our history, a national trauma. . . . It left us feeling terrified, helpless, and alone, and the effect that this has had on our country could not have been more insidious."[6] His immediate reaction was to complete the Bed series with a painting of a woman attempting ineffectually to hide underneath the chair, an expression, he remarks, of our often-inappropriate responses to moments of great trauma (FIG. 20).

In the wake of 9/11, Fischl watched the nation lurch from a moment of solidarity to a retreat into tribalism that demonized outsiders of all stripes. As he observed (and shared in) the general post-9/11 sense of confusion and vulnerability, he conceived of a project that he hoped might help salve some of the nation's wounds. He had noticed how, because of the specific nature of the tragedy, the physical nature of the attack's toll quickly disappeared. "After 9/11, there were no bodies, so it was difficult for people to understand the devastation," he recalls. "Instead, the discussion quickly turned toward architecture, and questions like: Do we preserve the footprint? How do we commemorate it as is sacred ground?"[7] As a figurative artist, this seemed wrong to him. He decided to memorialize the tragedy with a sculpture and to reference the only images of bodies the public saw—those of people who had made the terrible choice to fling themselves out the window rather than burn or be crushed alive. At the time, these images had almost immediately vanished from the media, though their imprint lurked in America's collective memory.

The result was Tumbling Woman, a sculpture of a generalized female nude caught as she falls shoulder-first to the ground with her legs stretched in the air (FIG. 21). Fischl notes that he wanted the figure to operate in a metaphorical way. "It was not just about falling," he says. "America had lost its center in that moment, and all was like tumbling sagebrush." The sculpture "was a body in motion, off balance. I had her put out her arm as if for the audience to reach out and grab her hand."[8] Fischl envisioned the work as an emblem of solidarity and communal mourning, and his dealer arranged for it to be installed in the concourse of Rockefeller Center for the first anniversary of the attacks.

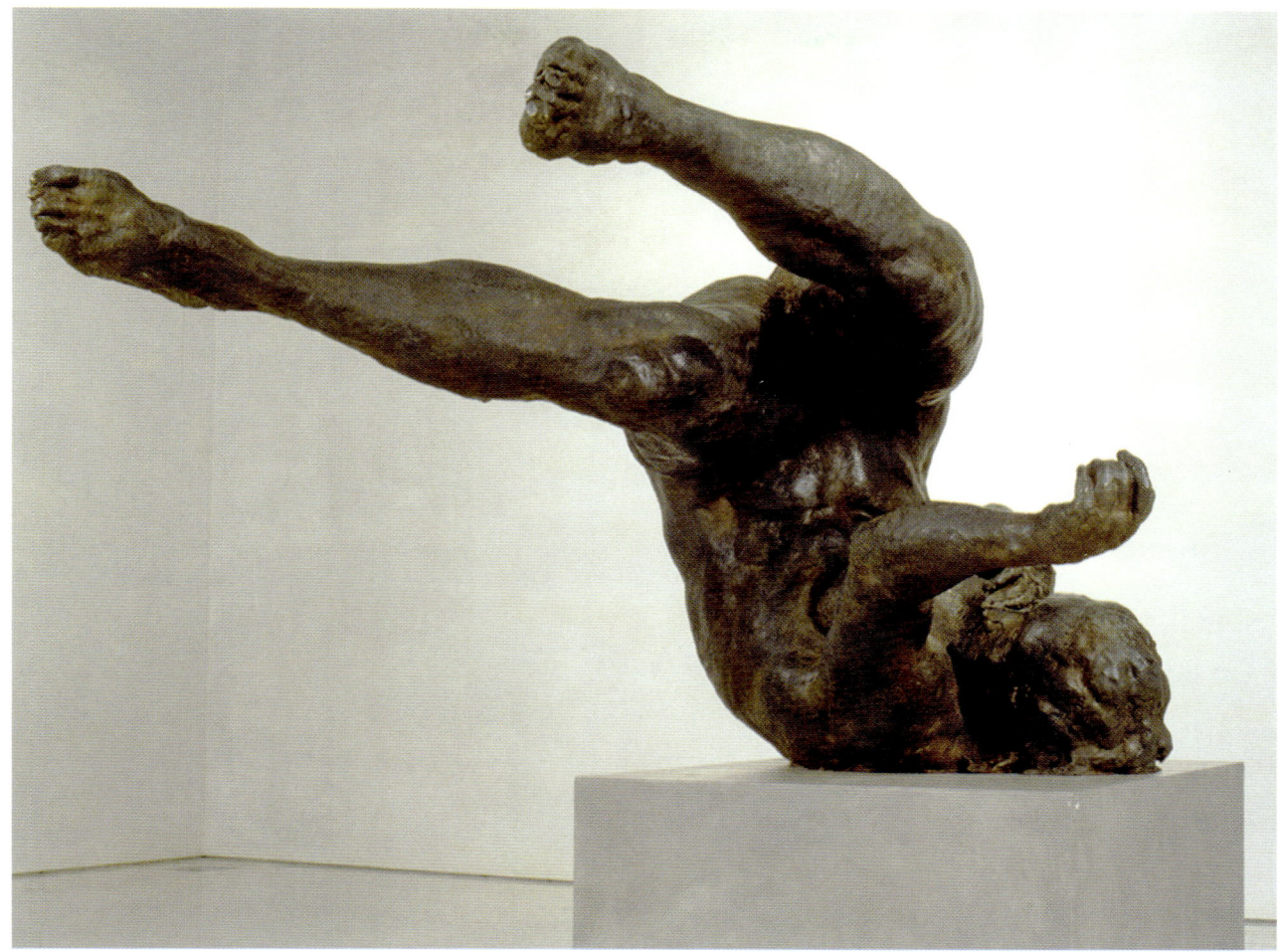

FIG. 21. **Eric Fischl,** *Tumbling Woman,* **2002.** Bronze. 37 × 74 × 50 in. (94.98 × 188 × 127 cm).

Contrary to his expectations, there was an immediate outcry. The work was denounced as exploitive and insensitive, and it was quickly removed from public view. Fischl was taken aback by the response. Looking back at this incident, he muses that memories of the falling bodies were probably still too fresh for viewers to accept this image in the way he intended. And he speculates that the negative response was tied up with the American cultural inability to deal straightforwardly with death. But rather than abandon the idea, he took it back to the studio and continued to work with it in various forms. Fischl connects this motif to his belief that, modernism's iconoclasm notwithstanding, the human body is the best carrier of our deepest feelings of love, fear, anger, and hope. He asks, "If the representation of the body can no longer be an expression of the soul, what is the point of representing it?" He answers himself, "The further art got away from the traditions of telling and retelling our dramas,

reinvigorating our understanding of what it means to be human, what it means to us to be alive, the more it relinquished its central primacy in the culture."[9] Now two decades on, his faith in *Tumbling Woman* appears vindicated. The original sculpture and her various offspring have achieved widespread acceptance as they appear in museum exhibitions and important private and museum collections.

Meanwhile, Fischl continued to mine the themes that he had been exploring in the late 1990s. And he added new subjects—investigating the myths and ceremonies of masculinity in a series of works depicting bullfights, for instance, or the commercialization of art in representations of the vacuous rituals of the contemporary art fair. But post-9/11, his depictions

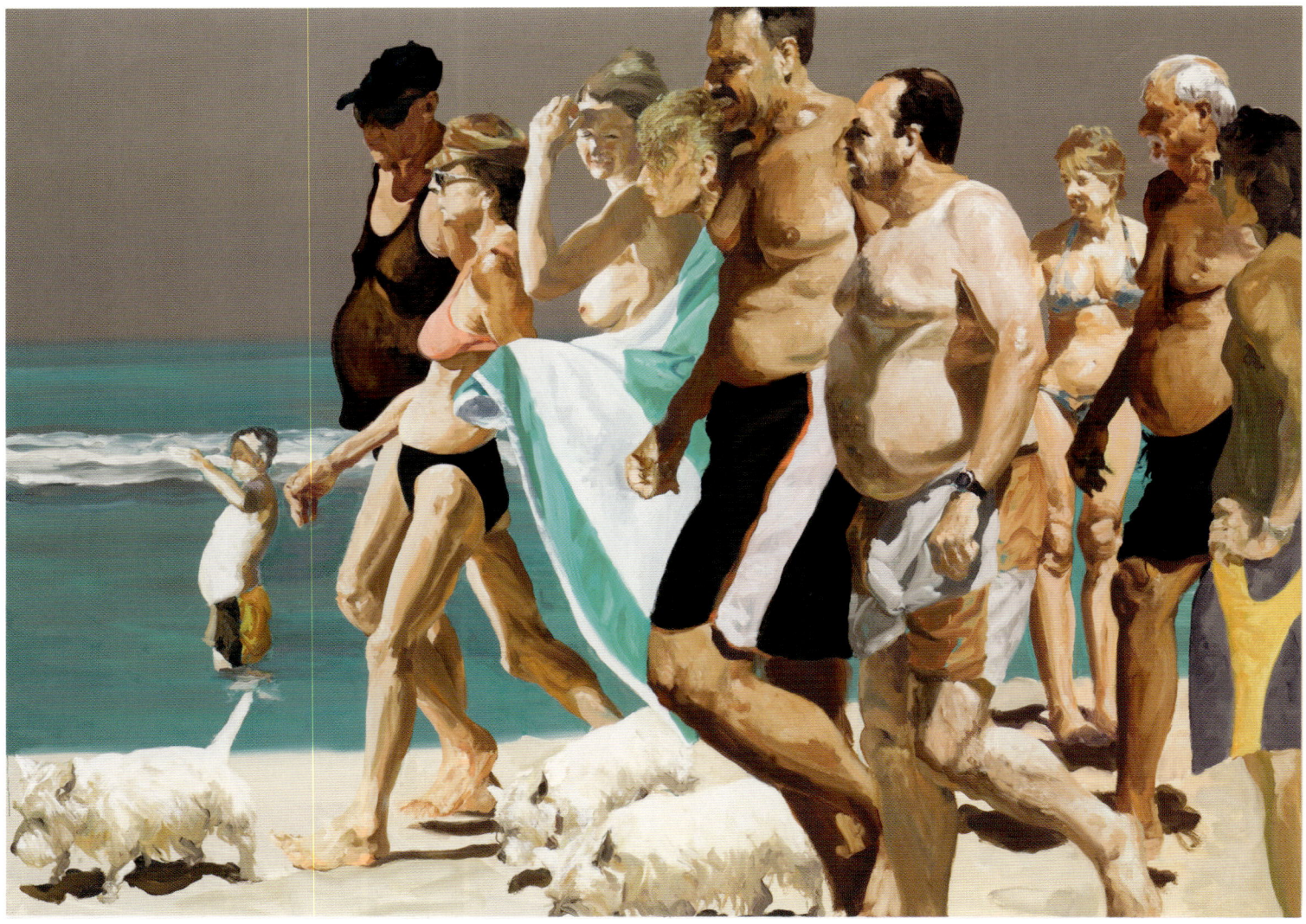

FIG. 22. **Eric Fischl**, *Scenes From Late Paradise: The Parade*, 2006. Oil on linen. 76 × 108 in. (193 × 274.3 cm). Hall Art Foundation.

of relationship dysfunction and psychic isolation seem tinged with an ever more powerful sense of desolation. The series *Scenes From Late Paradise* (2006–2007), for instance, is a return to the beach theme, but the progression of the works deliberately undermines the idyllic promise of its title. The initial paintings present a collection of people arranged in various poses, standing, walking, or reclining, on the sand. But as the series progresses, something happens. Their random movements are replaced by a purposeful-looking march in the same direction (FIG. 22). And then in the last painting, a single character, an overweight man in a green-striped bathing suit, walks off toward the edge of the canvas in the other direction. Around him, the sunny day has turned dark, and ominous clouds threaten a major storm (PLATE 8).

The sky in this painting is very similar to the one that envelopes the woman and child in *Late America 2*. The impending storms in both of these works are especially striking because Fischl's beach scenes usually take place under sunlight so bright and blinding that one can almost feel the heat. The turbulence of these backdrops recalls the seascapes of that other great American realist, Winslow Homer, for whom the sea presented a stage for battles of man against nature. A 2022 exhibition of Homer's ocean paintings at the Metropolitan Museum of Art argued for a social reading as well, suggesting that they were informed by the racial strife and social turmoil that followed the Civil War.[10]

In a similar way, the dark sky in these paintings by Fischl presents a visual metaphor for the chaos and uncertainty that enveloped America as the shock of 9/11 reverberated through society. Fischl believes that one can draw a line from that seismic event to the aftershocks of rage, impotence, and arrogant braggadocio that now characterize our deeply divided country. *Late America 2* belongs to a series of paintings that Fischl created during the COVID-19 pandemic. Titled *Meditations on Melancholia*, the series contains several works in which isolated individuals or pairs act out against the same blue-black sky.

The series title refers to Lars von Trier's 2011 surrealist science fiction film *Melancholia*. The film's apocalyptic narrative is about an incoming comet threatening to destroy our planet. In the days leading up to this collision, we follow the lives of a privileged, dysfunctional family in their idyllic country estate. The hypnotic beauty of the house and gardens provides a sharp contrast to the family's efforts to deny and then hide from the impending disaster. In the end, there is no place to go. The father kills himself, and his wife, young son, and sister-in-law attempt to form a magic circle of protection. In the last scene, they hold hands as the two planetary bodies collide.

In a 2020 interview, Fischl explained the connection of his two *Late America* works to this film: "Though I wasn't thinking about it at the time I painted my earlier work. . . . In *Late America* you can see the cowardly and irresponsible father-figure unwilling and unable to help the child, and in *Late America 2* the mother trying, probably in vain, to protect her child from the complete darkness that is about to envelop them."[11] The obliviousness of the father who ignores his flag-wrapped son in Fischl's 2016 *Late America* is at once a picture of personal insensitivity and a larger allegory of the nation's inability to come to grips with its own demons, paving the way for the shock of the 2016 election. Earlier the same year, Fischl painted a work that presents an even more explicit representation of the social obliviousness of American society. *Rift/Raft* is a diptych that sets well-dressed (and erotically undressed) participants luxuriating at an art fair against a chaotic scene of refugees scrambling ashore from their precarious boat (PLATE 38). This work revisits a theme Fischl explored in his 1983 painting *A Visit To / A Visit From / The Island,* which contrasts a family enjoying a seaside vacation with a group of Haitian refugees arriving on the Florida coast (FIG. 23). Both works underscore the stark divide between privilege and privation, but the art fair setting of the later work gives the contrast a much more biting and satirical edge.

Fischl's Trump- and COVID-era works exude an aura of apocalypse. More recently, he has mined the strangeness of the post-pandemic era. In 2022 he presented a series of works titled *Towards the End of an Astonishing Beauty: An Elegy to Sag Harbor, and Thus America.* The setting for these works is the annual Halloween parade in the beach town of Sag Harbor, where Fischl makes his home. However, the reassuring nostalgia promised by a small-town celebration is undermined by an unsettling weirdness. *You Don't Need a Weatherman . . .* presents a couple of glum fortune tellers who have set up shop on the street against a backdrop of waving American flags and a Blue Lives Matter banner (PLATE 40). They seem to have no takers, and the title, taken from a Bob Dylan song, suggests that the future may be something better left unexplored. These and other works in this series point to cracks in the nation's attempt to return to normalcy in the wake of COVID. Something fundamental has changed, Fischl seems to be saying. Instead of bringing people together, the experience of a worldwide pandemic simply deepened the divisions already tearing the country apart.

Where does this leave someone who still clings to America's professed ideals? Strikingly, despite the ever-darkening tenor of Fischl's paintings, he refuses to relinquish hope for a reconciliation of American ideals with reality. In 2006, he conceived a project he hoped would help heal the rift between art and a traumatized public. It was called *America: Now and Here* and was to be a roving art fair in which his many

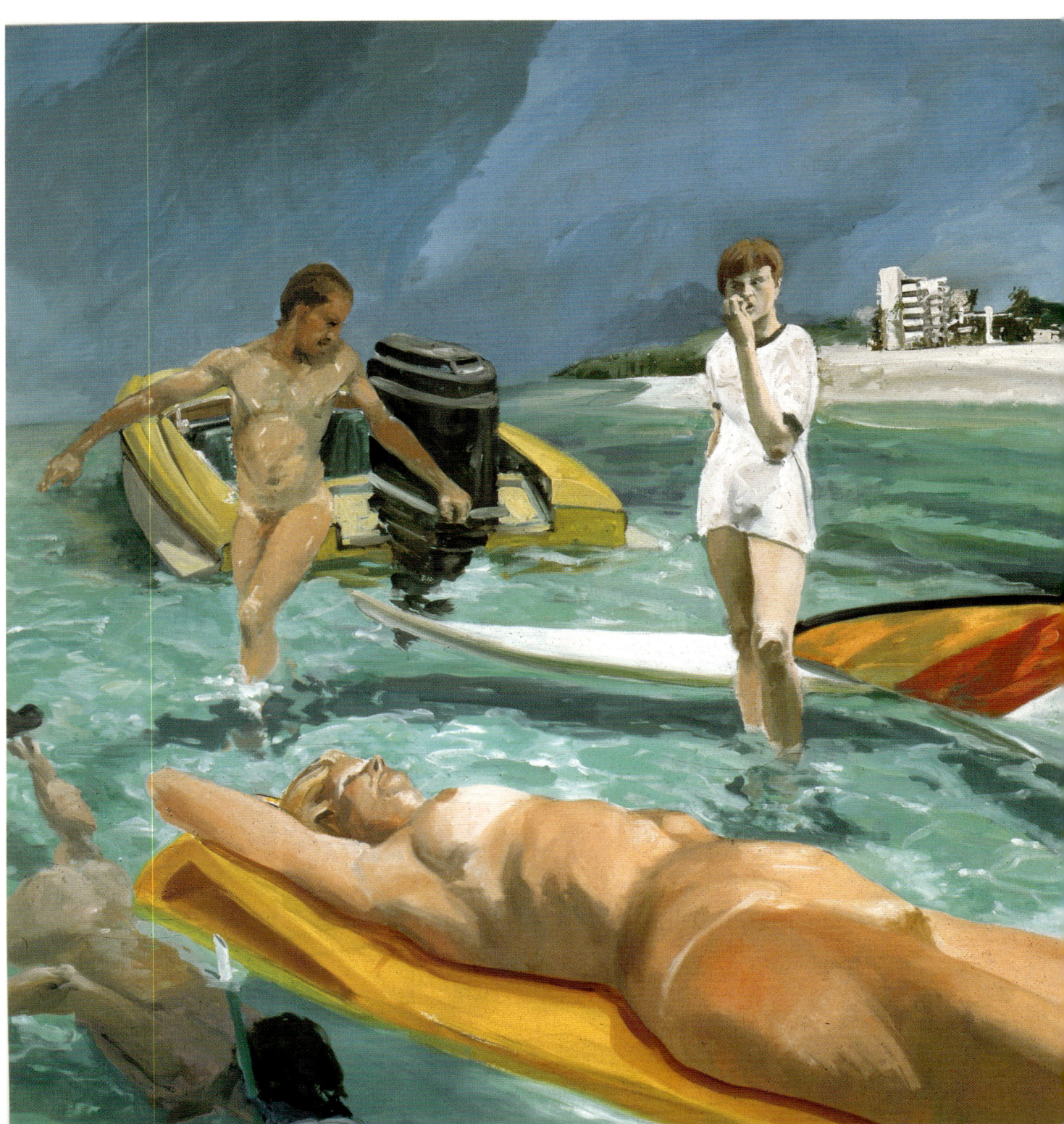

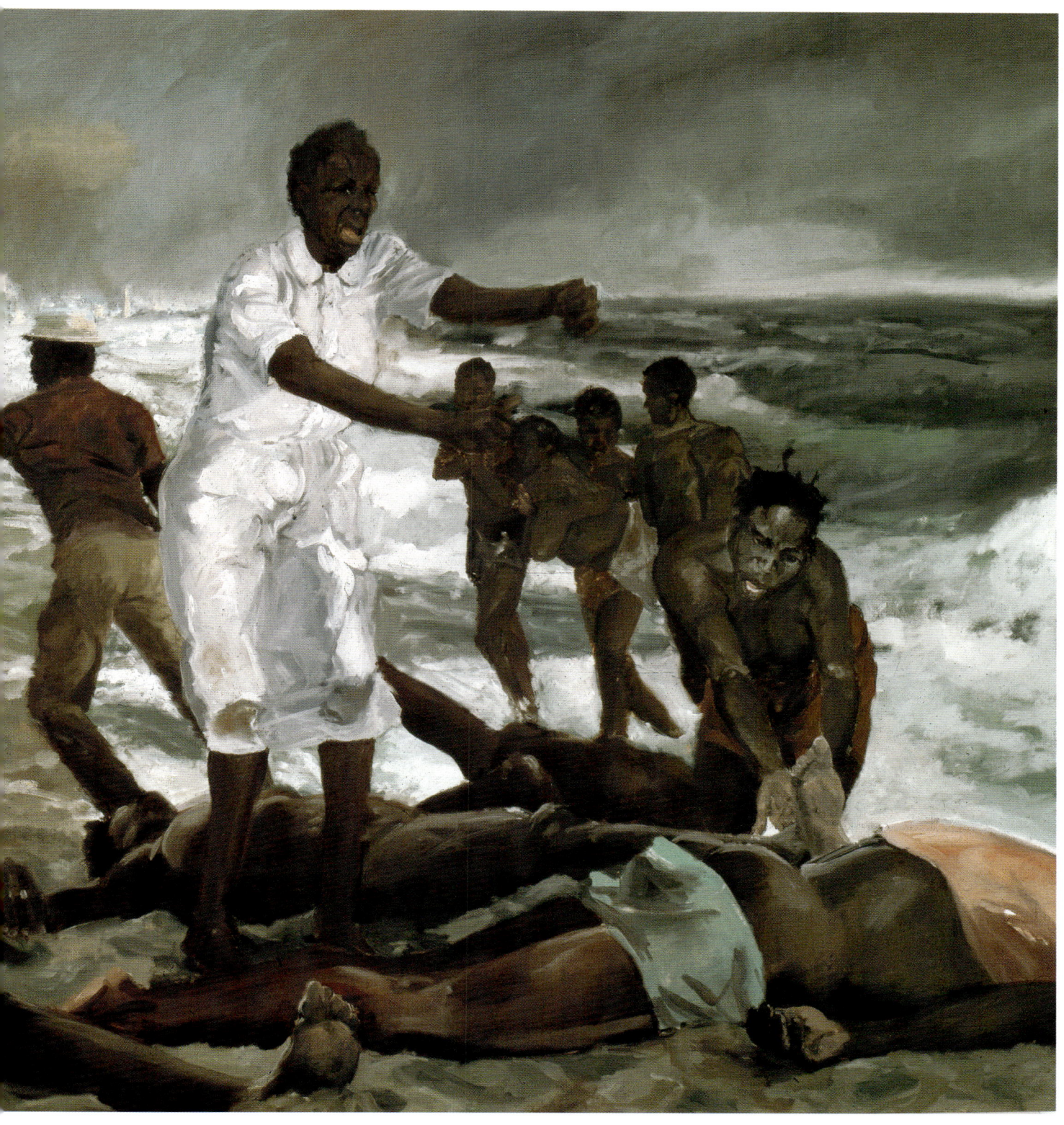

FIG. 23. **Eric Fischl,** *A Visit to / A Visit From / The Island,* **1983.** Oil on canvas, two panels. 84 × 168 in. (213.4 × 426.7 cm). Whitney Museum of American Art, New York, purchase with funds from the Louis and Bessie Adler Foundation, Inc., Seymour M. Klein, President. 83.17a-b.

artist and writer friends would create works that would travel around the country in trucks outfitted like mobile museums. The theme, as the title suggests, was America itself, however the artists chose to interpret it. The reactions from his proposed participants were wildly enthusiastic and funders seemed responsive. All seemed to be moving forward until the 2008 financial crisis gripped the country, and the potential funding dried up. In his memoir Fischl describes his reaction: "I felt sad. *America: Now and Here* was an opportunity to have a conversation, to begin to overcome resistance and partisanship, to get people to stop yelling and screaming at each other, to identify and focus on the source of their anxiety, to demonstrate that they are not alone in their concerns. That's how art works in the culture. It gives us a common language."[12]

Despite the recent pile up of crises—among them 9/11, Trumpism, and COVID—Fischl speaks wistfully of lost possibilities. "Sometimes I feel like America is a family gone rogue," he says. His mixed feelings are encapsulated in a 2023 self-portrait that seems to sum up his sense of his place in the world (PLATE 1). Fischl sits slightly slumped and facing us from a bench in his studio. The foreground is a clutter of paint supplies, palettes, brushes, and rolls of paper towels. Behind him are nude studies in various stages of completion and most prominently, next to him on the bench, a

version of *Tumbling Woman*. Fischl's face is half in shadow as he meets our gaze, and his hands are bandaged. This work was originally painted for an exhibition at The Church in Sag Harbor, a former Methodist chapel that Fischl and his wife, artist April Gornik, have reconfigured as an art space. The exhibition's theme was boxing, understood here as a metaphor for the artist's struggle to follow his muse in the face of emotional, artistic, and social challenges. One reference point for his painting is Paul Simon's song *The Boxer,* which celebrates the persistence of an aging and faltering fighter. The painting's title opens up another interpretation: It is called *Broken Hallelujah*, taken from a phrase in Leonard Cohen's elegiac hymn "Hallelujah." Cohen's song offers an equivocal benediction, weaving together the biblical stories of David and Samson to suggest the pain and sense of loss that comes from love. It ends, "And love is not a victory march/It's a cold and it's a broken Hallelujah."[13]

One suspects the phrase resonates for Fischl, not only as a description of his struggles but also as a way to understand his complicated feelings toward the idea of America. As the song suggests, the lover may be betrayed by the object of his devotion, it may change almost beyond recognition, but the lover cannot abandon it. Fischl's America is such a love object, and he refuses to let it go. ■

## Notes

1   Eric Fischl and Michael Stone, *Bad Boy: My Life On and Off the Canvas* (Crown, 2012), p. 315.

2   Phoebe Hoban, "Eric Fischl's Late America," *Riot Material,* June 21, 2017, https://www.riotmaterial.com/eric-fischls-late-america/.

3   Fischl, interview with the author, June 4, 2024.

4   Fischl and Stone, *Bad Boy*, 159.

5   Fischl, interview with the author, June 4, 2024.

6   Fischl and Stone, *Bad Boy*, 314.

7   Fischl, interview with the author, June 4, 2024.

8   Fischl, interview with the author, June 4, 2024.

9   Fischl and Stone, *Bad Boy*, 320.

10  *Winslow Homer: Crosscurrents,* exhibition at the Metropolitan Museum of Art, New York, April 11–July 31, 2022.

11  Karen Rosenberg, "Dancing Into the Apocalypse: Eric Fischl on His New Paintings About America in the Age of Covid," Artful Jaunts (website), November 18, 2020, https://www.artful-jaunts.com/magazine/eric-fischl-on-his-new-paintings-about-america-in-the-age-of-covid.

12  Fischl and Stone, *Bad Boy*, 336.

13  Leonard Cohen, "Hallelujah," produced by John Lissauer, track 11 on Leonard Cohen, *More Best Of*, Columbia, 1997.

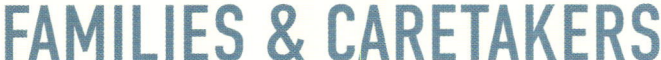
FAMILIES & CARETAKERS

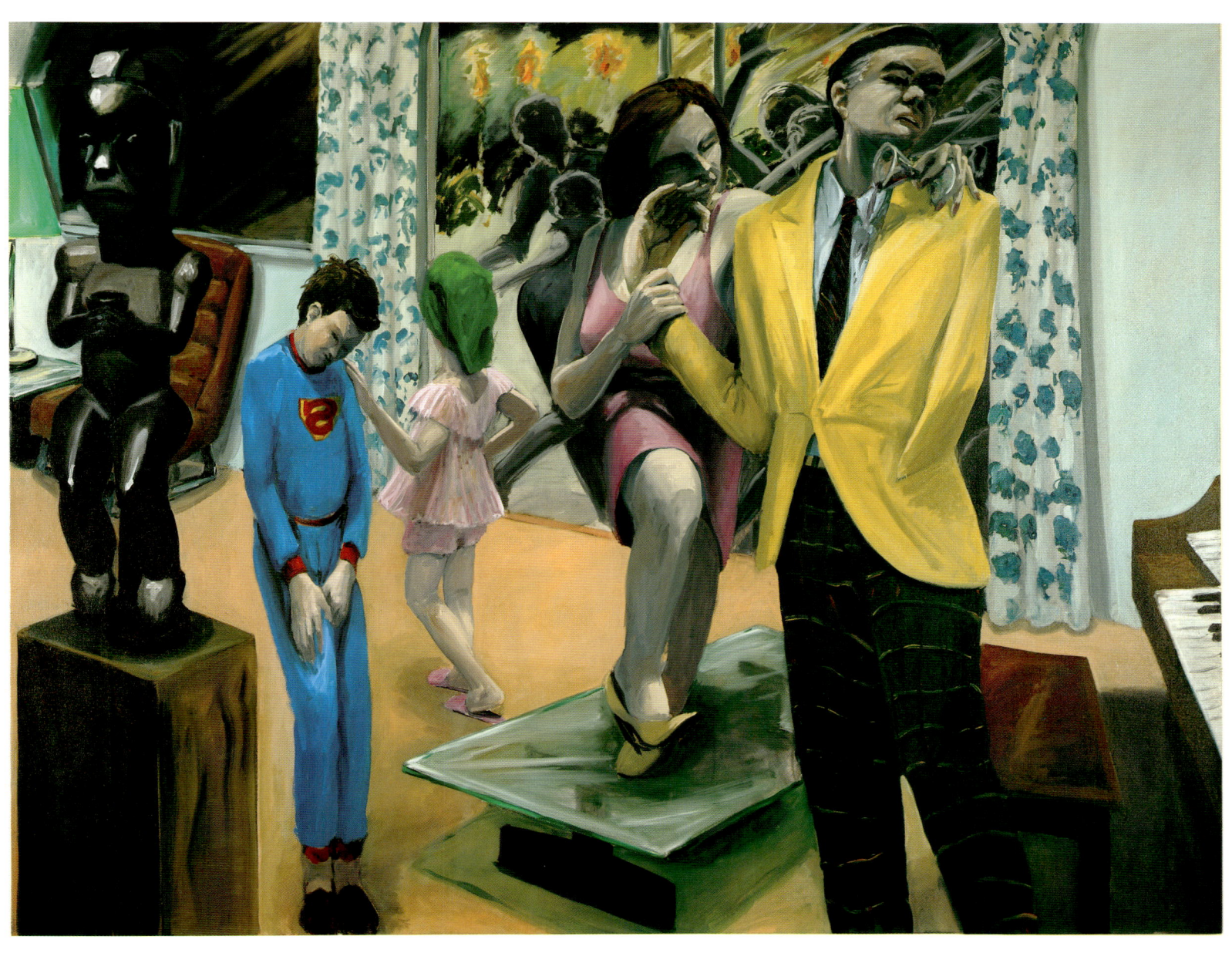

PLATE 24. *Time for Bed*, 1980

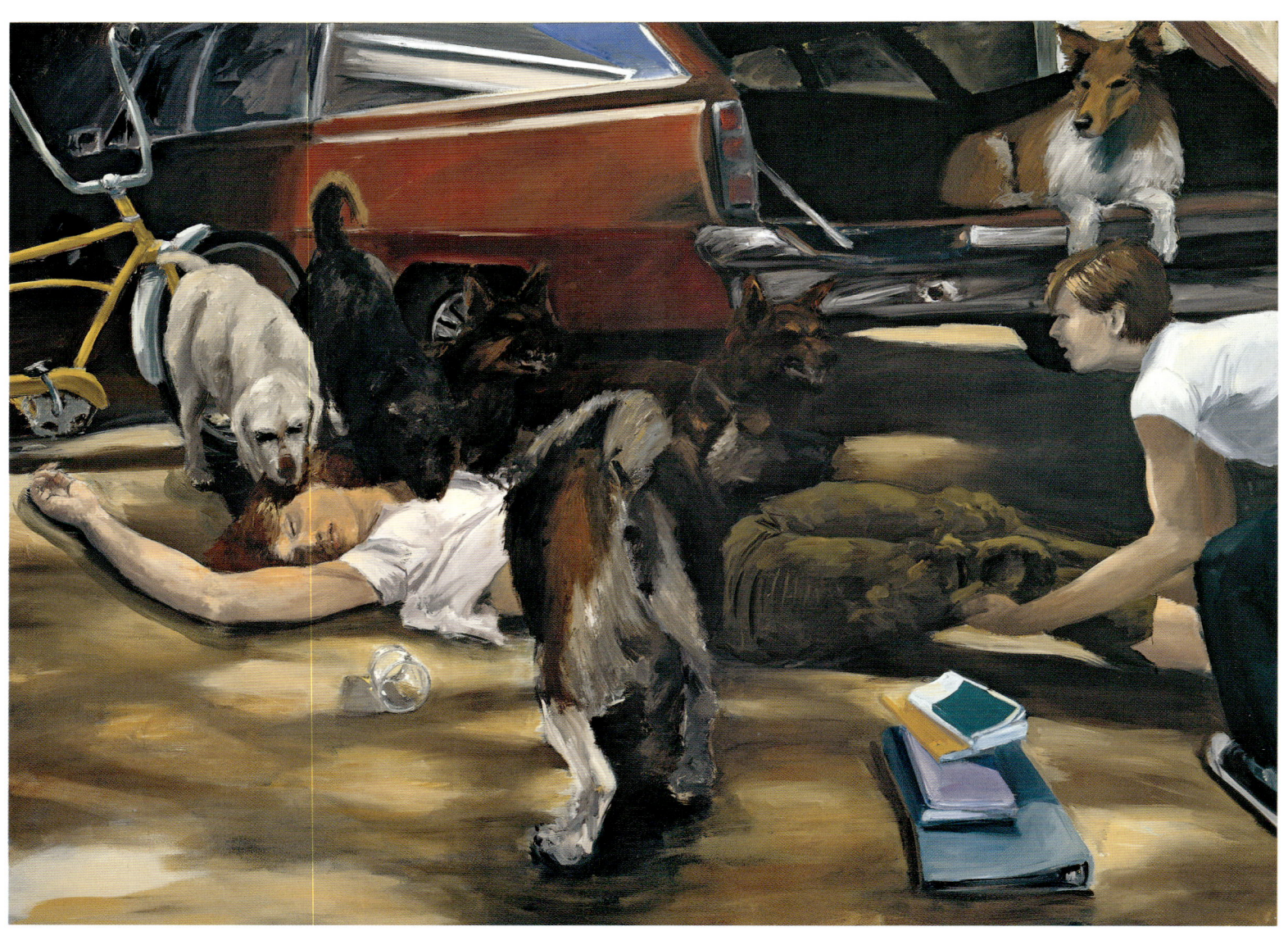

PLATE 25. *A Woman Possessed*, 1981

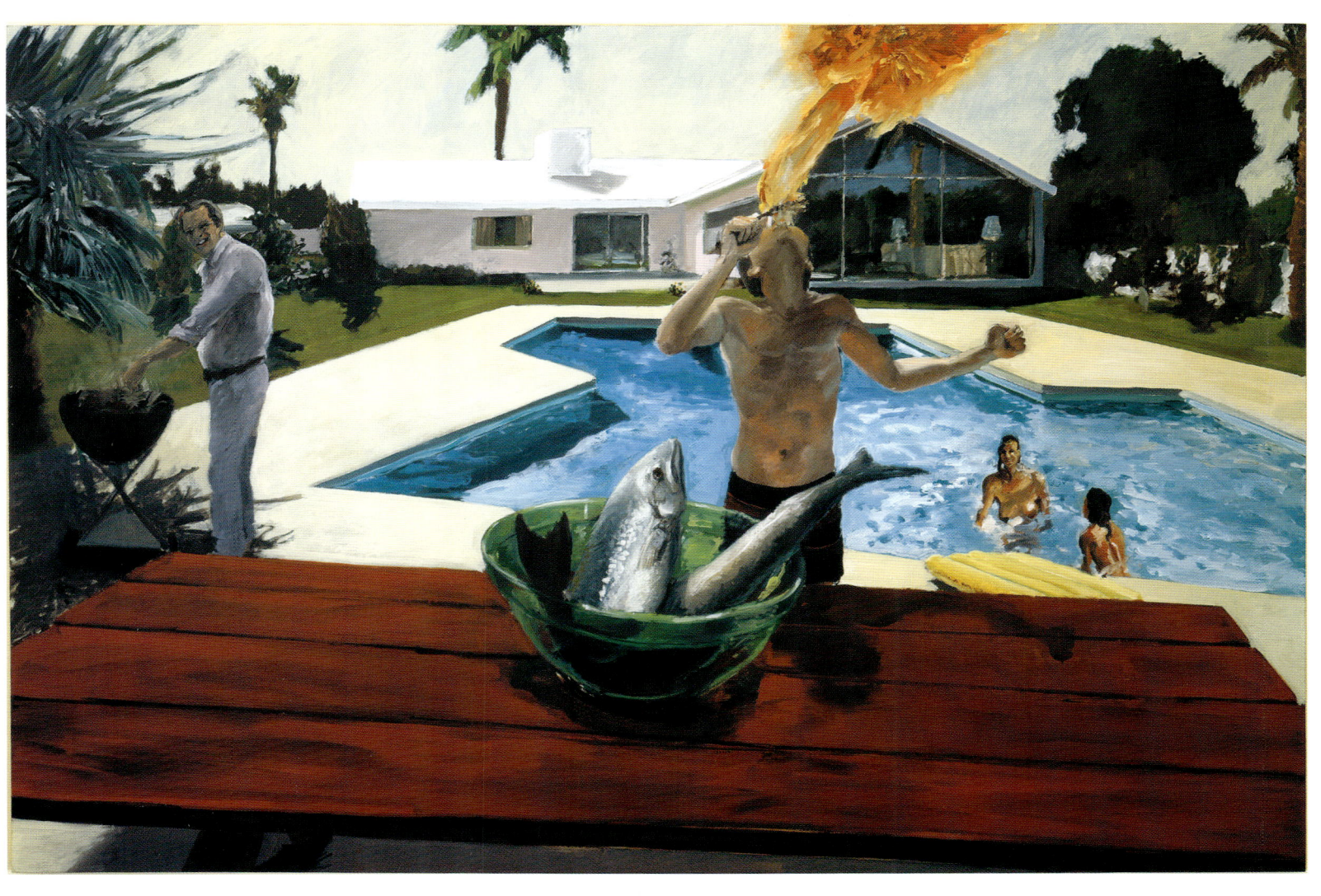

PLATE 26. *Barbeque*, 1982

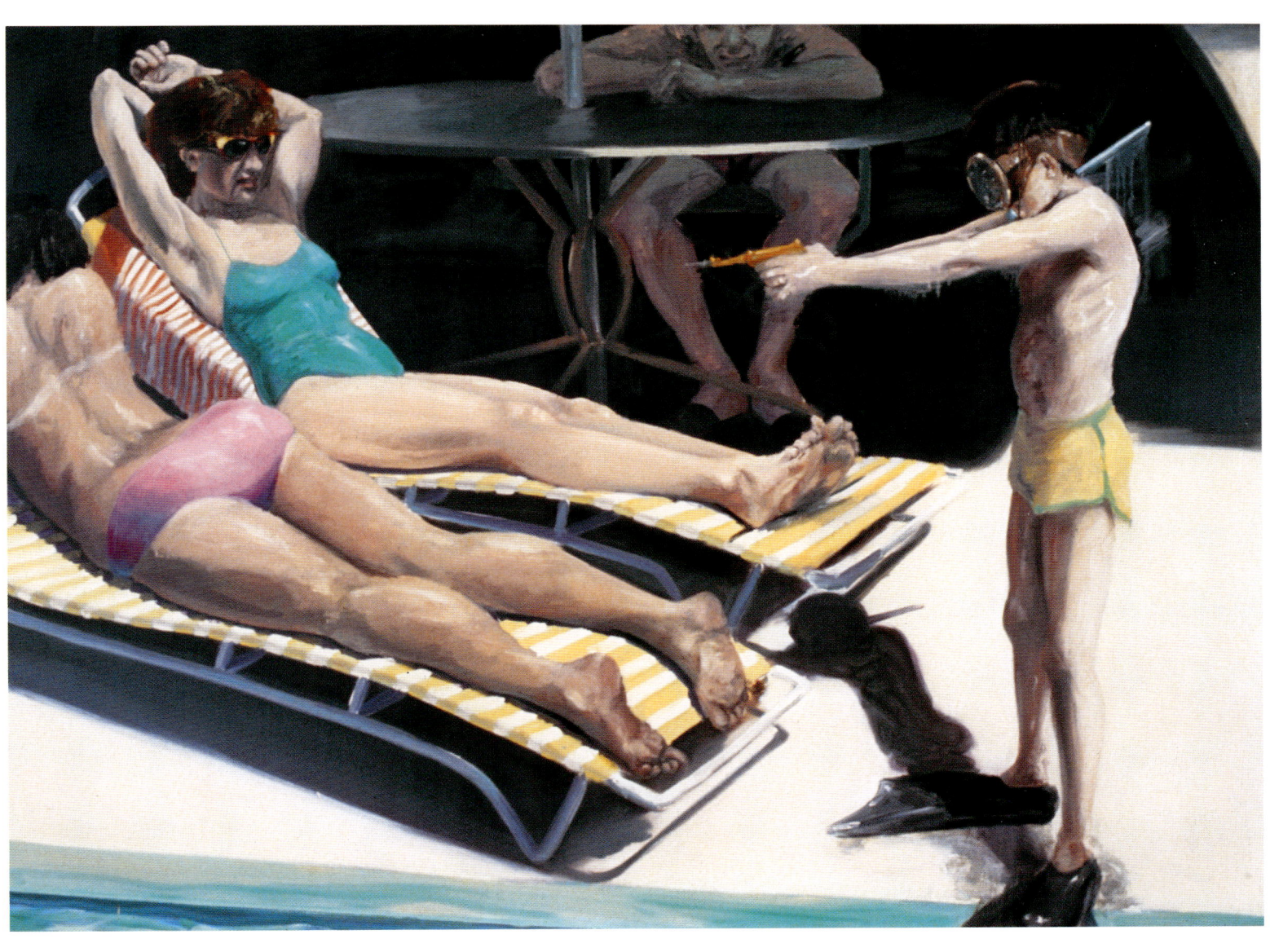

PLATE 27. *Squirt*, 1982

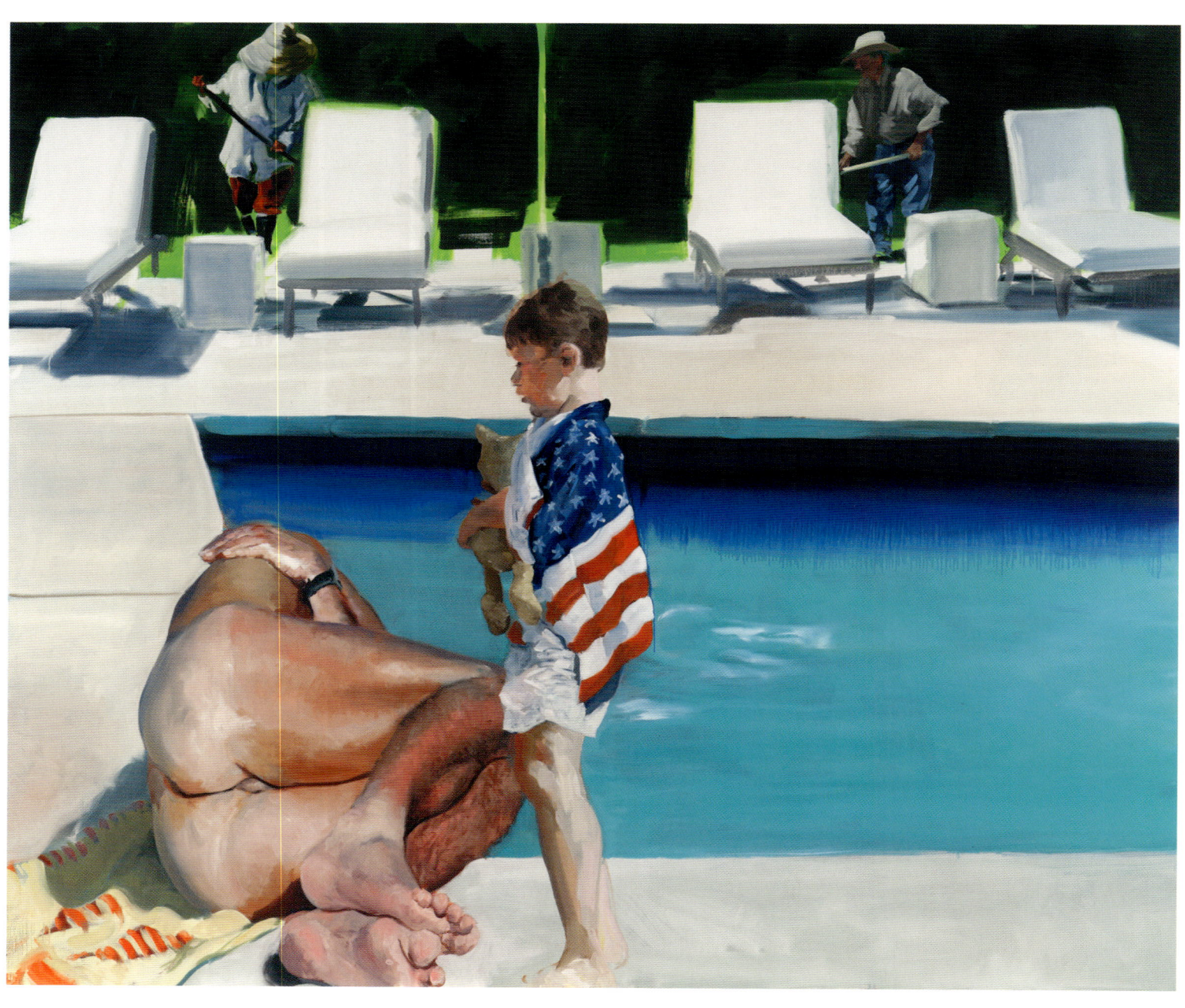

PLATE 28. *Late America*, 2016

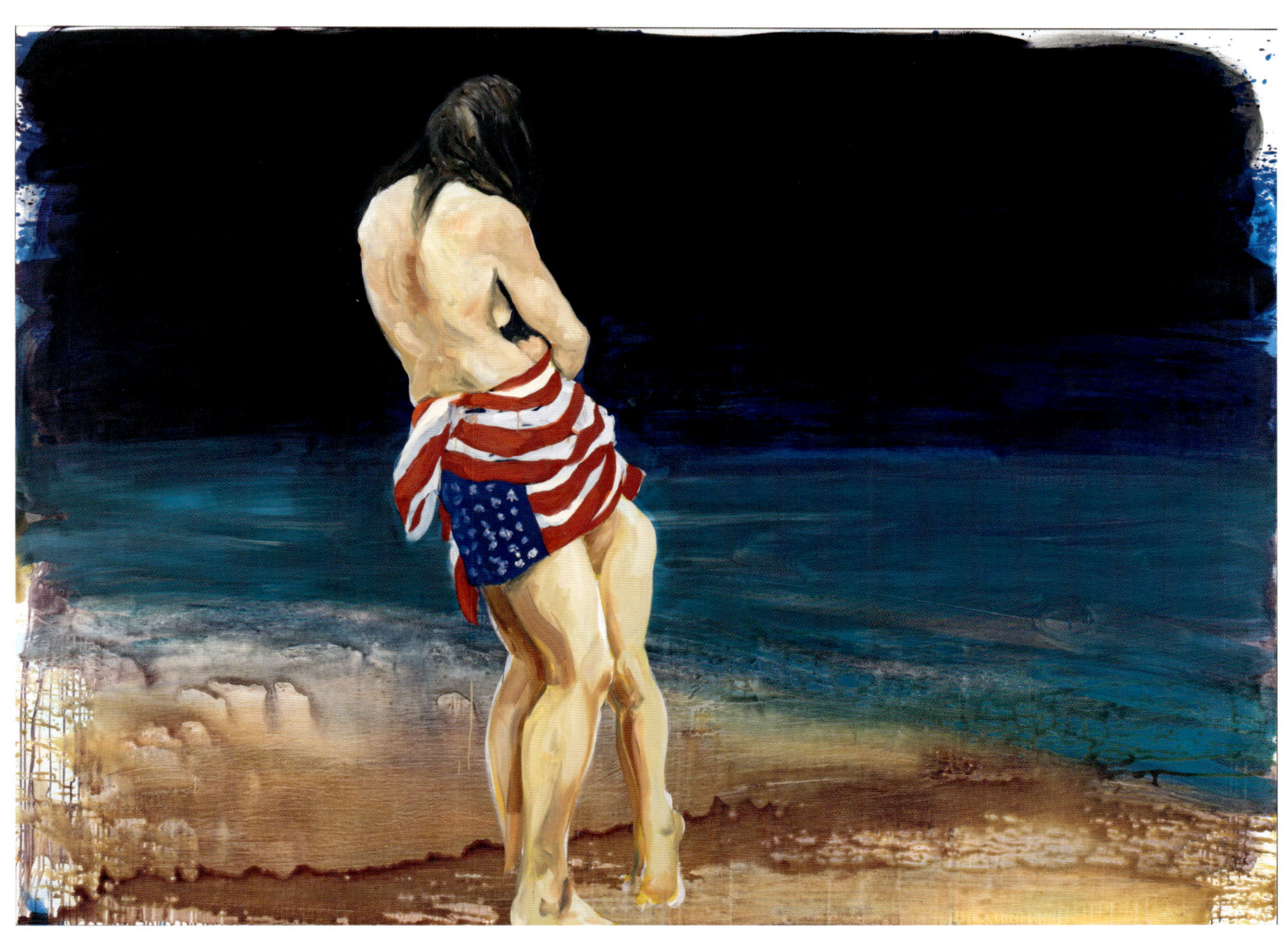

PLATE 29. *Late America 2*, 2020

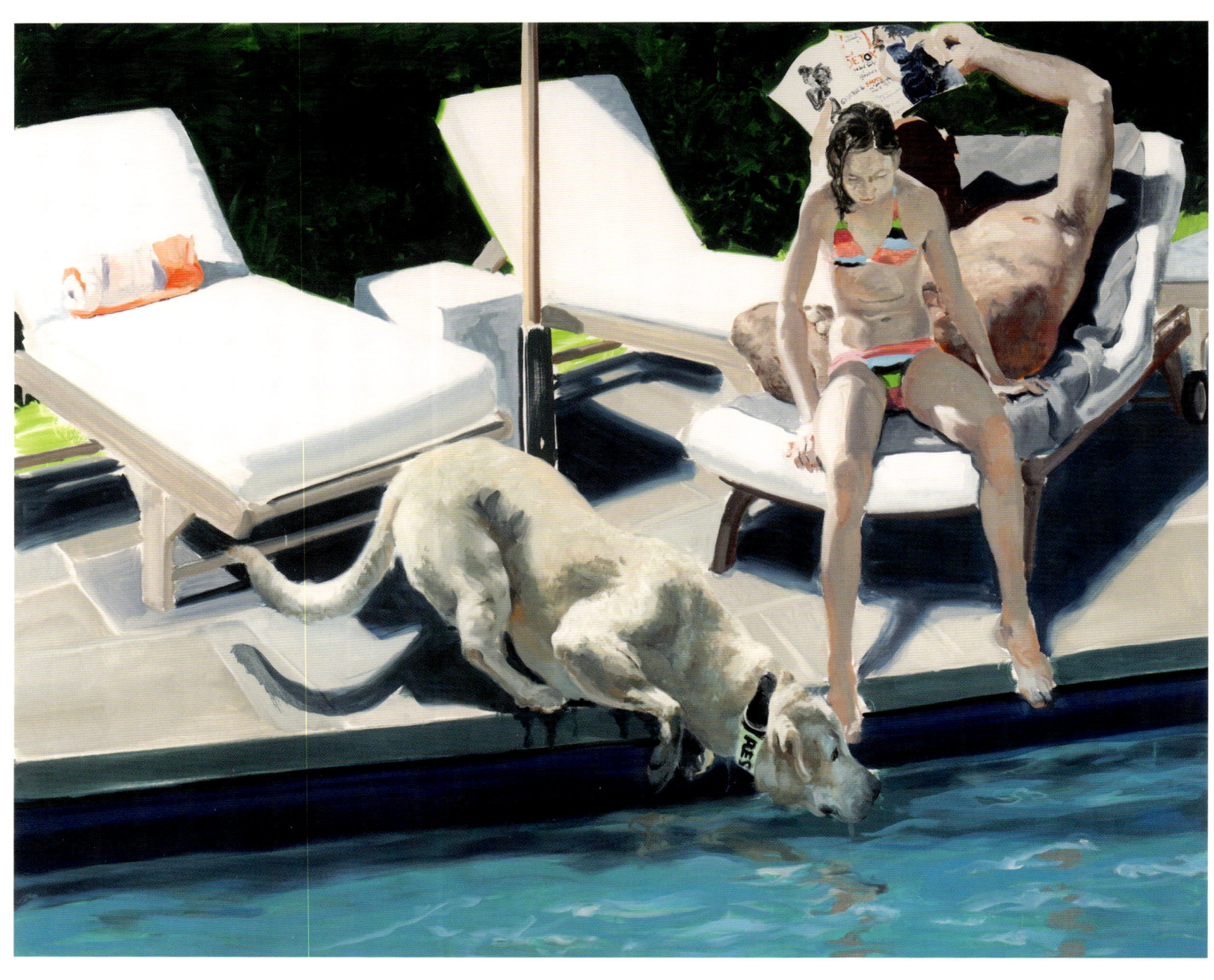

PLATE 30. *Daddy's Girl Age 11*, 2017

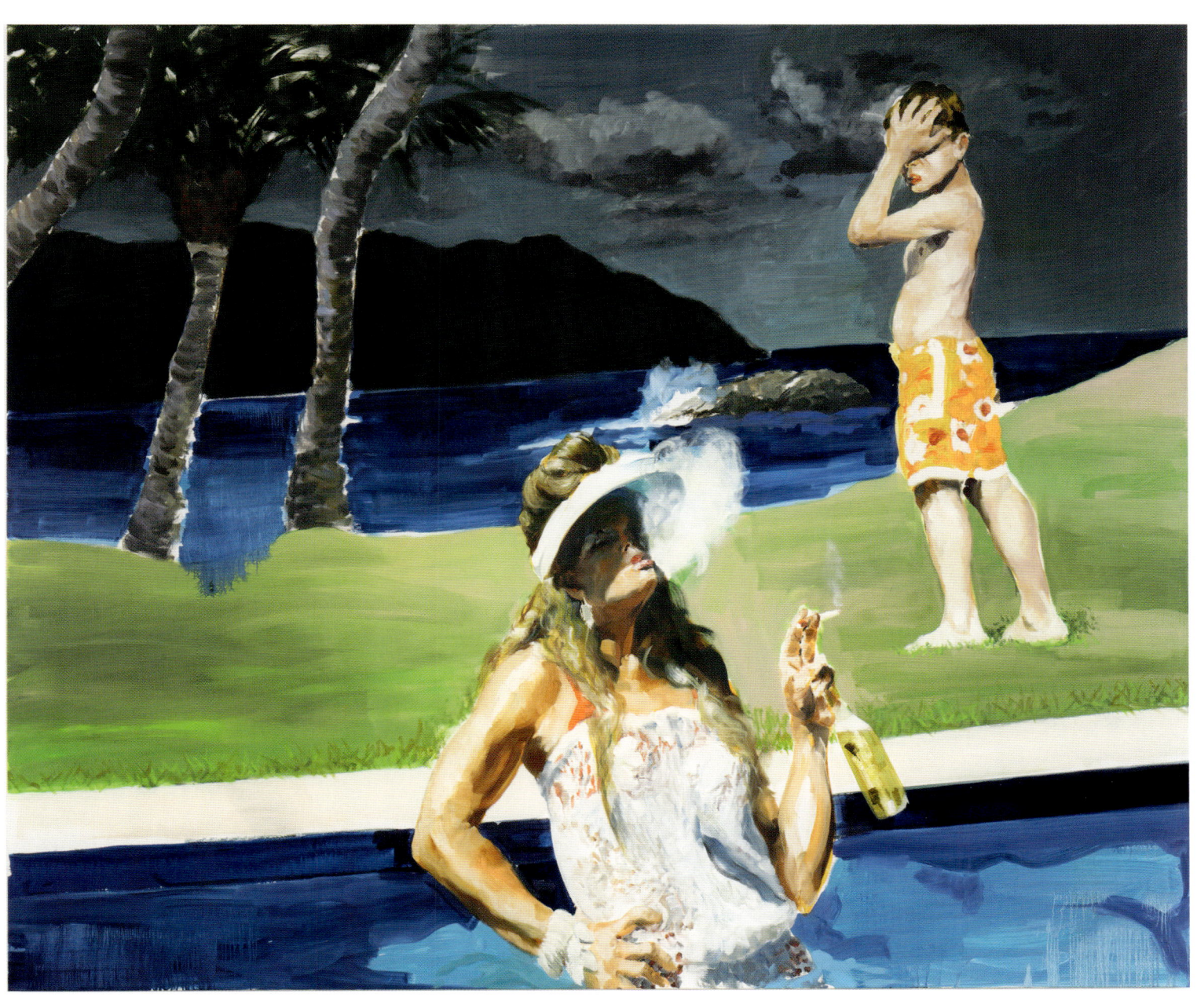

PLATE 31. *Island of the Cyclops: The Early Years*, 2018

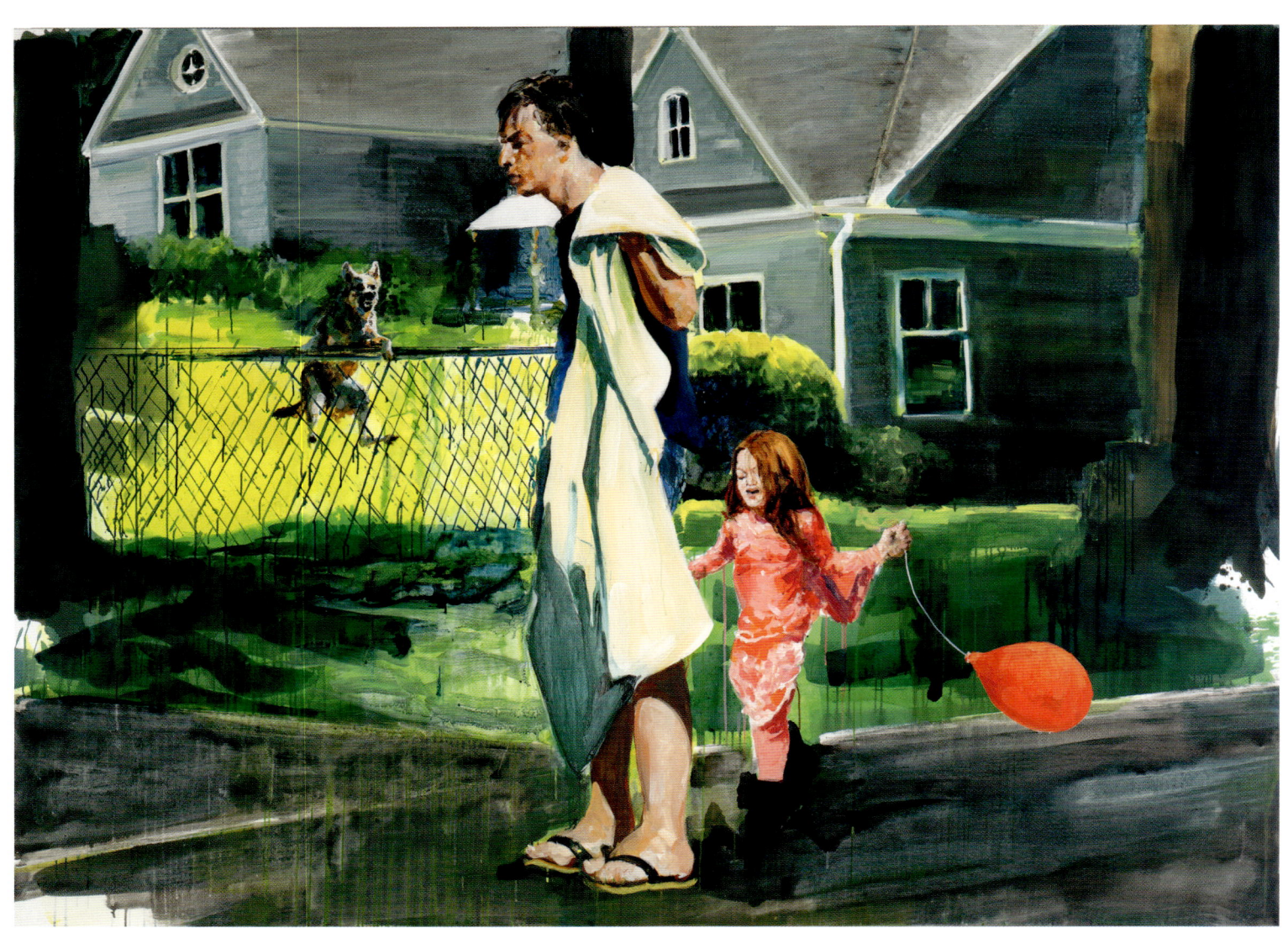

PLATE 32. *My Old Neighborhood: Red Balloon*, 2021

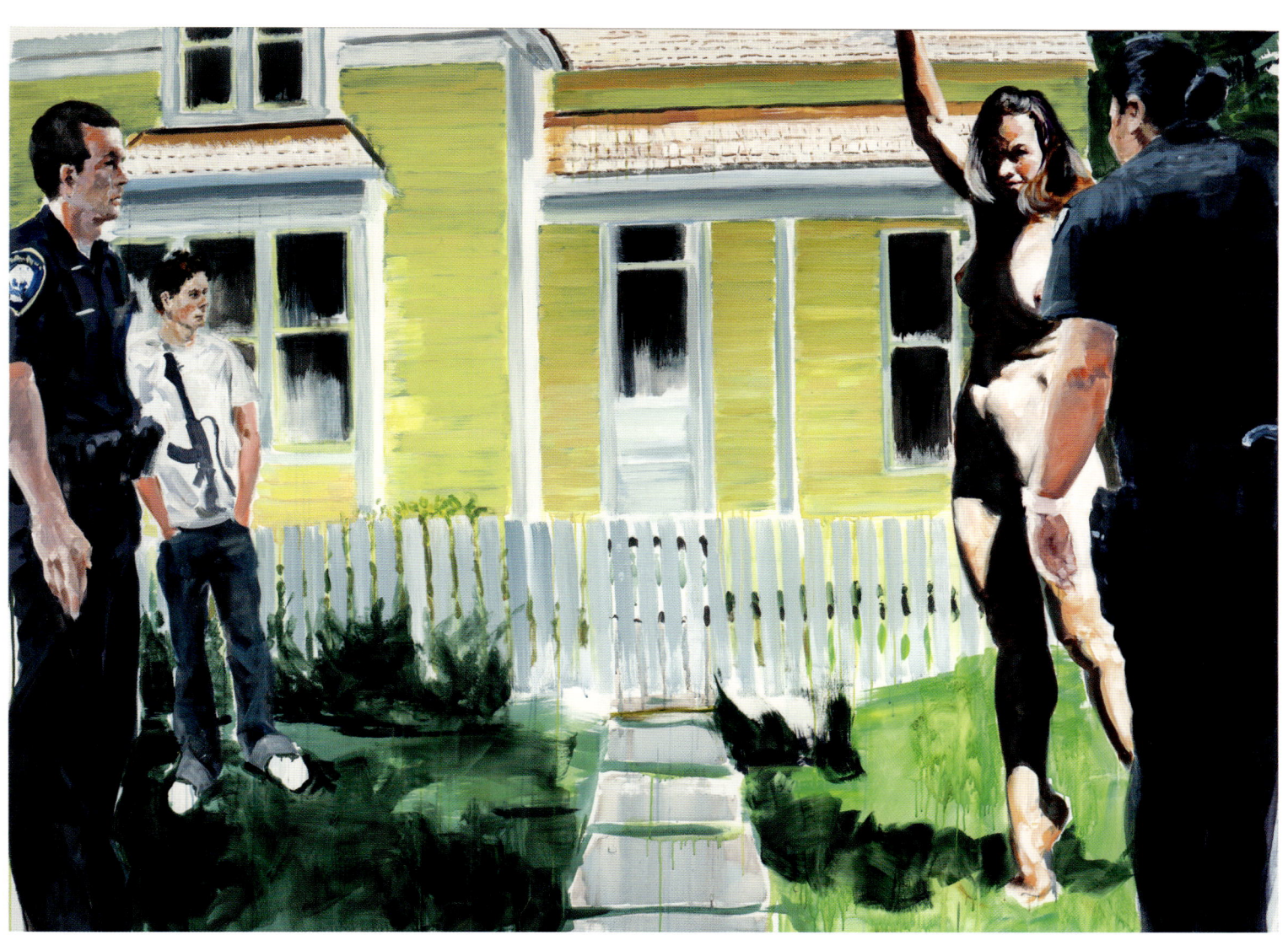

PLATE 33. *My Old Neighborhood: Private Property,* 2021

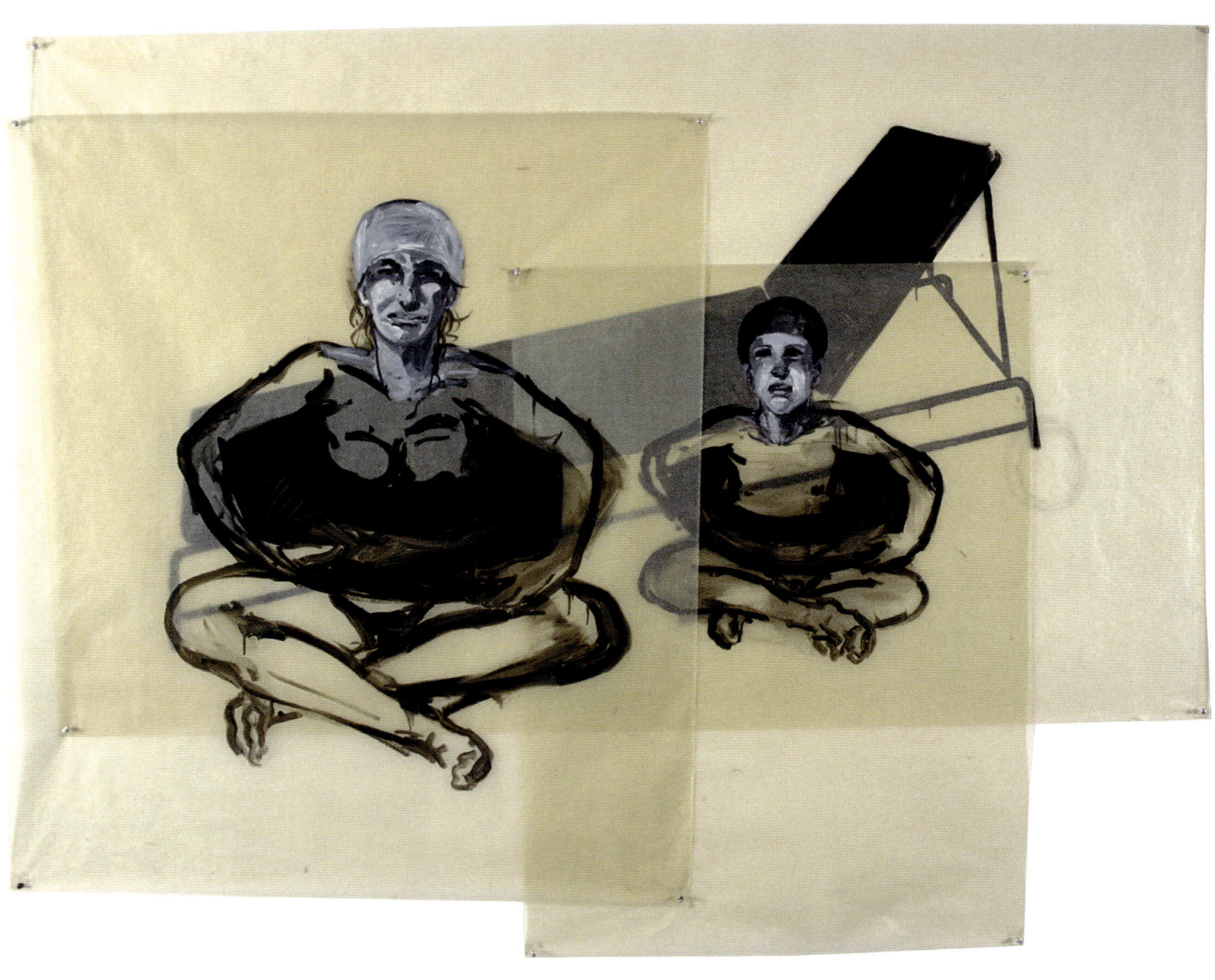

PLATE 34. *Life Saver/ Life Preserver,* 1979

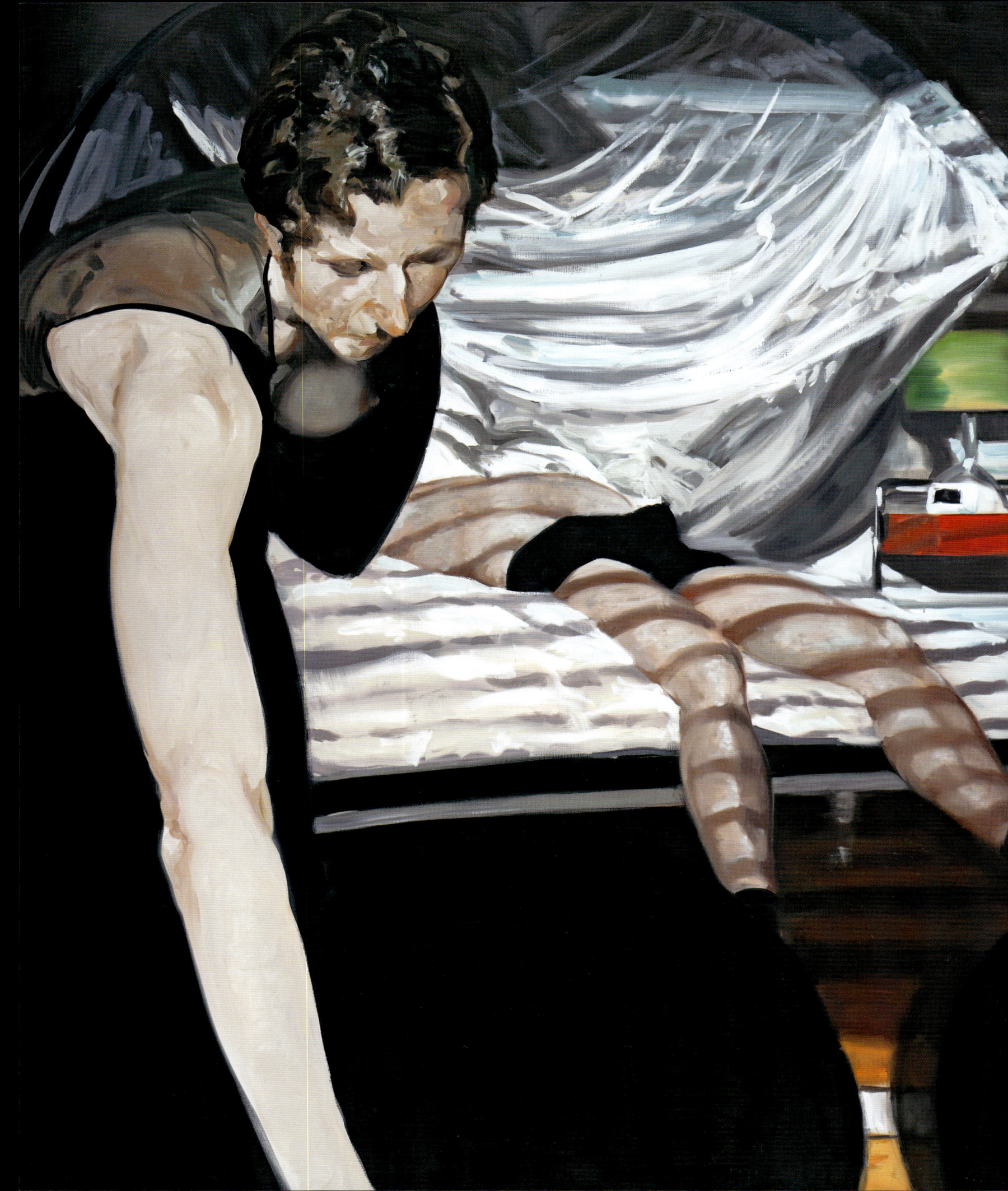

# TO SING THE BODY ELECTRIC
## ELEANOR NAIRNE

. . . Pleasure
as a means,
and then a
means again
with no ends
in sight. I am
absolutely in opposition
to all kinds of
goals. I have
no desire to know
where this, anything
is getting me.

EILEEN MYLES, "PEANUT BUTTER," 1991[1]

I find it hard to resist the carnal quality of Eric Fischl's painting. Each work is a reminder that the act of painting is itself erotic. Objects in the studio have a practical function of course, but that barely conceals their sensual pleasures: the rabbit glue to size some cotton duck or linen canvas, the smears of oil on a palette, the fistful of brushes soaking in a tin of turpentine, the collection of soiled paint rags. There is an intimate mystery to what has happened between an artist and their canvas, pinned to a wall or propped on an easel where it can meet their gaze. (And so the seedy wonder of Jackson Pollock dripping paint directly over his work on the floor.)

This is not news to painters. In her 2013 lecture "On Color," Amy Sillman marveled at an art historian who

didn't know that identical tubes of cadmium red and cobalt violet could be felt apart by their differing weights—he had never *held* color, only *beheld* it.[2] Alison Katz has written recently about the hedonism of paint's application, recalling a blog she once read on Gustave Courbet and the motif of hair-touching in his paintings, which was interpreted as a reflection of the method of brush painting. "That is, hair equals paintbrush, everyday touch indexing visionary touch. I find the argument compelling, kinky, smart. I am back to being a young girl in sleepaway camp, when we would brush hair for hours on end (each other's, our own). A feeling close to perfection. What else were we doing then if not practising painting?"[3]

Born in New York in 1948, Fischl grew up in suburban Long Island and later Phoenix. He experimented with modes of abstraction, the earliest of which he told art

Detail of PLATE 20

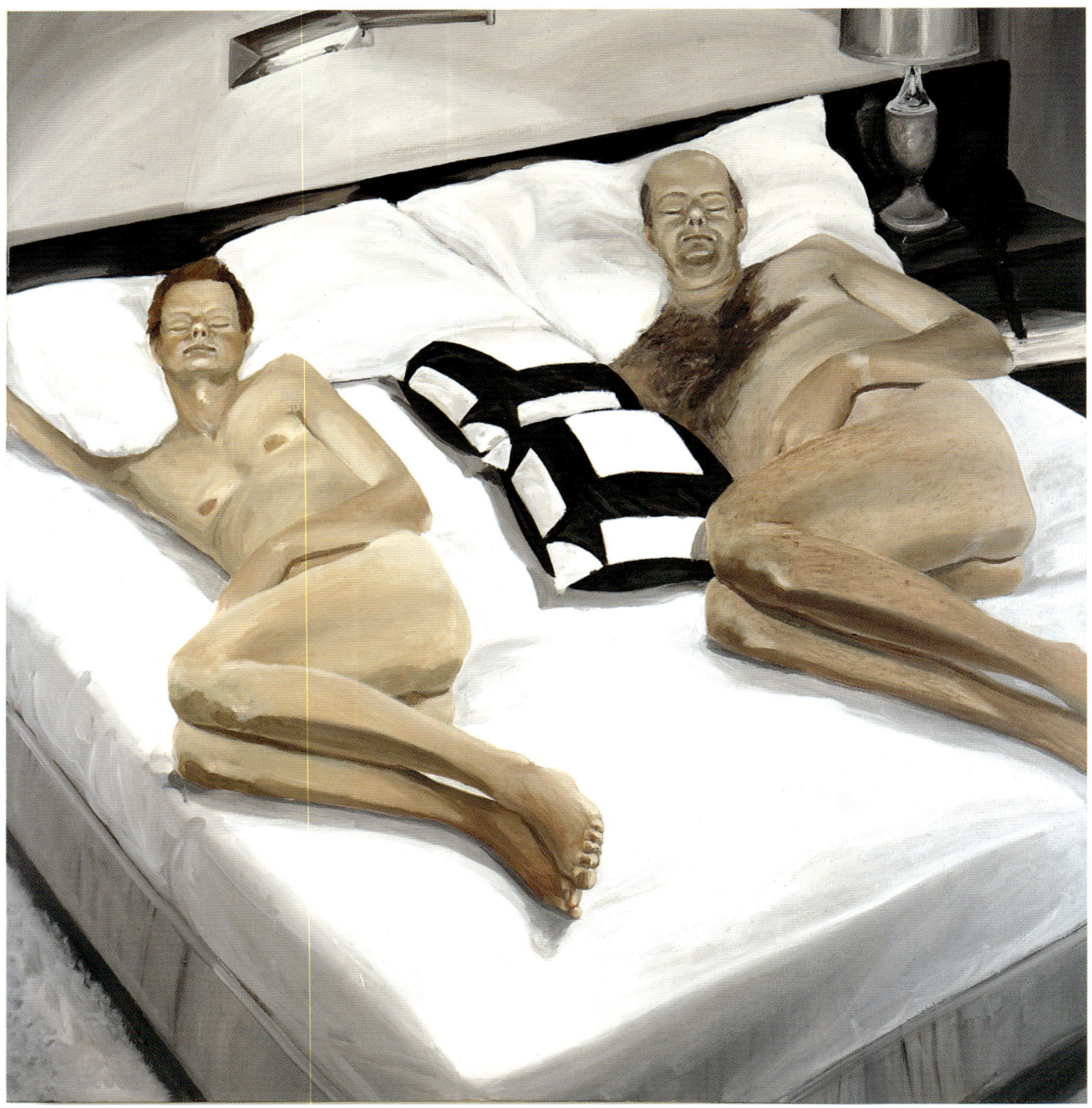

FIG. 24. **Eric Fischl**, *Father and Son Sleeping*, **1980.** Oil on canvas. 72 × 72 in. (182.9 × 182.9 cm). Collection unknown.

critic Peter Schjeldahl "looked like salad going down a drain," before settling into figuration.[4] He came back to Manhattan in 1978 and allowed the libidinal quality of his painting to spill directly into his scene. By 1980 he was showing with Edward Thorp Gallery and receiving significant critical attention.[5] He had his first mention in *The New York Times* when Vivien Raynor reviewed a group exhibition about realism— the so-called phoenix of art styles—at the Robeson Gallery of Rutgers University, Newark, that summer.

"His large canvas of a naked father and son sleeping in the same bed," Raynor wrote, "is startling in its pathos and intensity. The figures, flesh-colored in an otherwise black and white surrounding, are separated, as if they were a courting couple in Colonial New England, by two cushions" (FIG. 24).[6]

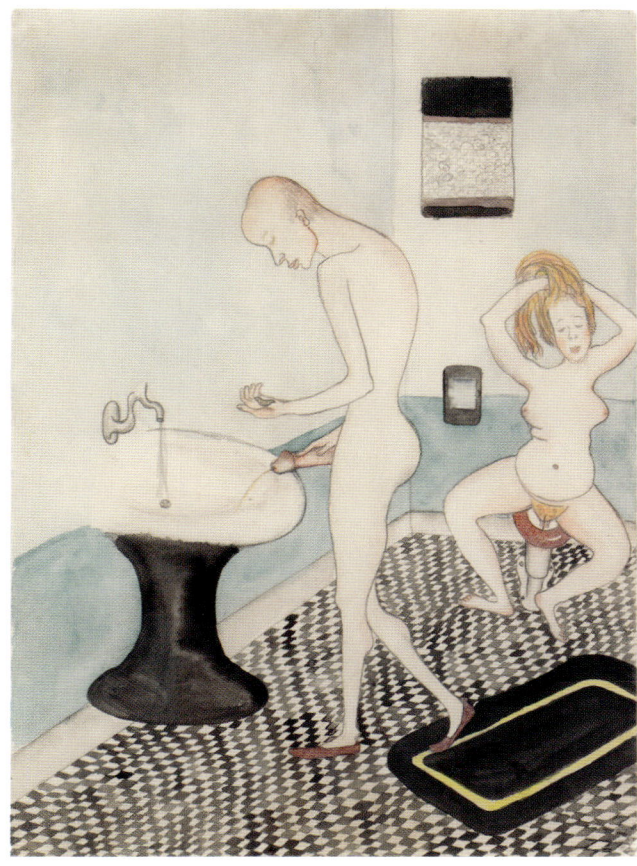

FIG. 25. **Alice Neel** (American, 1900–1984), **Untitled (Alice Neel and John Rothschild in the Bathroom), 1935.** Watercolor and graphite on paper. 11⅞ × 8⅞ in. (30.2 × 22.5 cm). Collection of Nancy Magoon. © The Estate of Alice Neel. Courtesy The Estate of Alice Neel and David Zwirner.

The painting was based on a text by Paul Bowles, a fellow Long Islander who had a notoriously bad relationship with his father, a frustrated violinist-cum-dentist. The short story isn't specified but must be "Pages from Cold Point," first published in 1949 and deemed too scandalous to be included in his British collection *A Little Stone* in 1950. The story is told in the menacing first-person voice of Norton, a university professor who considers his career to have been "an utter farce," and so retires to a remote island with his son, Racky. He becomes "envious of the lithe body, the smooth skin, the animal energy and grace" of his son and resentful of his escapades with others his age, and then one night he goes to bed with him.[7]

The horror of the story is amplified by the cold simplicity of Bowles's language: "I shall never know

whether or not he was really asleep all that time. Of course he couldn't have been, and yet he lay so still. Warm and firm, but still as death."[8] Fischl called his painting *Father and Son Sleeping*—as if to underline the question of whether that is really all that has occurred in the image. The canvas is perfectly square (seventy-two by seventy-two inches, just taller than the average American male), but the composition is all diagonals, the double bed viewed on an angle from above, and the two bodies mirroring one another with their knees drawn up, each with their left hand resting on their middle. Their eyes may be closed and their faces serene, but everything else is askew.

A detail in the painting: the father has a white mark on his wrist from where his watch has been. What better way to emphasize the uneasy nakedness of this parent than with a reminder of the accessories of everyday life that have been set aside. There is something unseemly but also unashamedly funny about this tan line, a motif that Fischl would continue to delight in as a perfect image for human vanity. This grubby underside of American life doesn't often find its way into painting, but it's where Fischl makes a home. There's the suggestion of depraved want, sure, but also the simpler fact of flesh that's white and clammy from lack of exposure to the sun. The painter Alice Neel, the most senior figure in the Robeson Gallery show, was aiming for a similar effect, I think, when she depicted her sometimes lover John Rothschild pissing into the sink with nothing but a pair of red slippers on (FIG. 25).

The sexual act became a more explicit topic in *Inside Out* (1982), a painting selected for the Whitney Biennial in 1983 (FIG. 26). The left-hand panel of the triptych features a couple recording themselves having sex, the man fixated on his own image being relayed on the television screen at the foot of the bed. The TV is arguably the most potent of American fetishes; as Don DeLillo puts it in his novel *White Noise* (1985): "waves and radiation. I've come to understand the medium is a primal force in the American home. Sealed off, timeless, self-contained, self-referring. It's

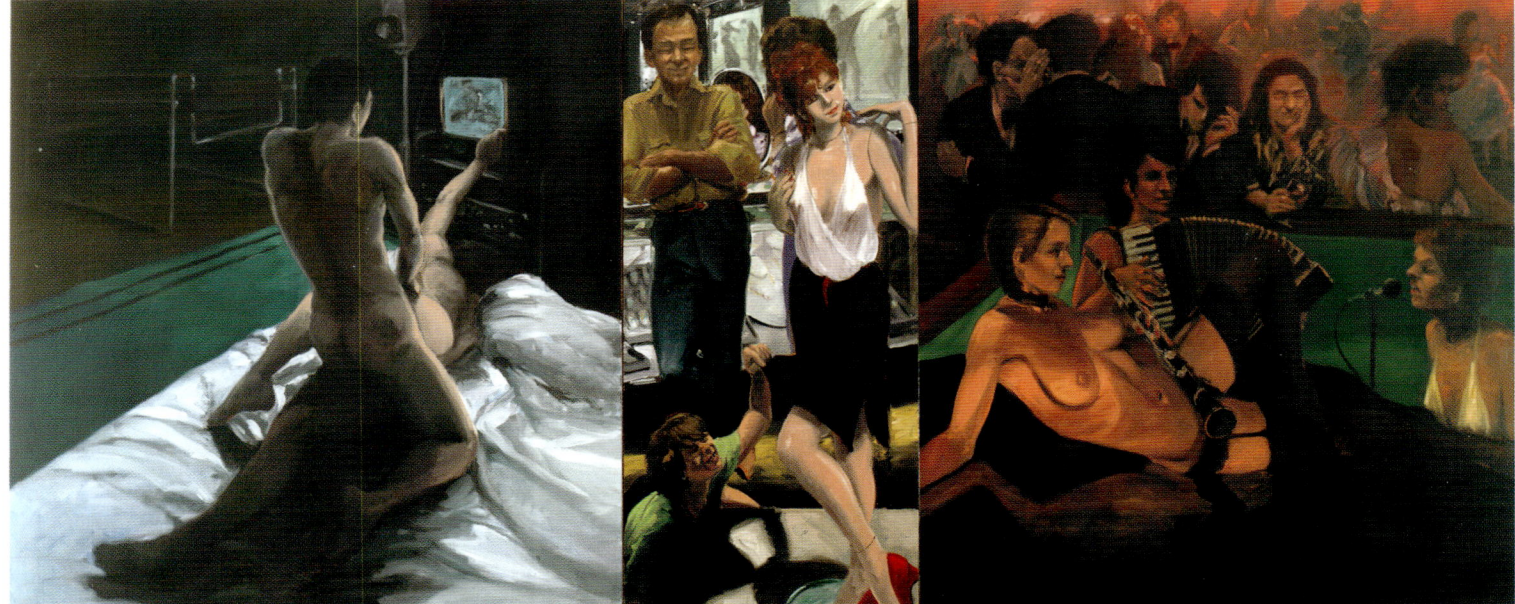

FIG. 26. **Eric Fischl**, *Inside Out*, **1982.** Oil on canvas, three panels. 72 × 178 in. (182.9 × 452.1 cm). Collection unknown.

like a myth being born right there in the living room."[9] Fischl plays on the religious connotations of the three-panel format to worship at the altar of everyday lust and our attempts at its ignition. Never one to remove himself from the fray, for the following Biennial, in 1985, Fischl exhibited *Portrait of the Artist as an Old Man* (1984), in which he envisions his own rock 'n' roll demise: Naked save for sunglasses, a lilac short-sleeved shirt, and black slippers, he turns his back on a Van Gogh wheat field, his right hand covering his crotch with a newspaper while the other slips beneath it (PLATE 11; see FIG. 19).[10]

This kind of sexually fraught humor is applied by Fischl to bodies pretty much regardless of their gender, but the depiction of alluring women in states of undress was bound to be a catcall for certain kinds of critics, especially amid the feminist politics of the 1980s. You can hear the tone of derision slipping into Grace Glueck's review of *Social Studies* at Barbara Gladstone Gallery in June 1985: "Eric Fischl subur-ban-baits as usual in 'Birth of Love,' a fleshy, sullenly lighted poolside scene in which a youth lays explor-ative hands on a leering woman."[11] And in the tele-vision series *State of the Art*, the curator Joan Borsa laments the ways in which "many of Fischl's paintings simply restate the attitude towards women that is so prevalent in the commercial patriarchal culture he

denounces." She continues, "In this way, Fischl's work succumbs to the culture it attempts to expose."[12]

The operative words here are *denounce* and *expose*. But are those really Fischl's aims? What if the works are simply bearing witness to sexuality and its discon-tents? Take *Sleepwalker* from 1979: a naked teenager stands in a shallow paddling pool on a suburban lawn, his knees softly bent, his head lowered as he mastur-bates into his fists (FIG. 27). The boy is at an angle, so we see nothing racy beyond his clenched bum, and there is something almost protective about the way the rim of the pool encircles him. In an interview in 1986 with Douglas C. McGill, Fischl recalled wanting to make "a shocking picture" but also one that was benign towards its hero: "I felt sympathetic to this boy, acting out his independence and giving himself pleasure. It seemed very positive. . . . The point at which a child discovers himself sexually is one of the most profound events of his life."[13]

And yet where do we see that moment pictured? Were you to search the internet for "an art history of mas-turbation," as I just have, you will find embarrassingly

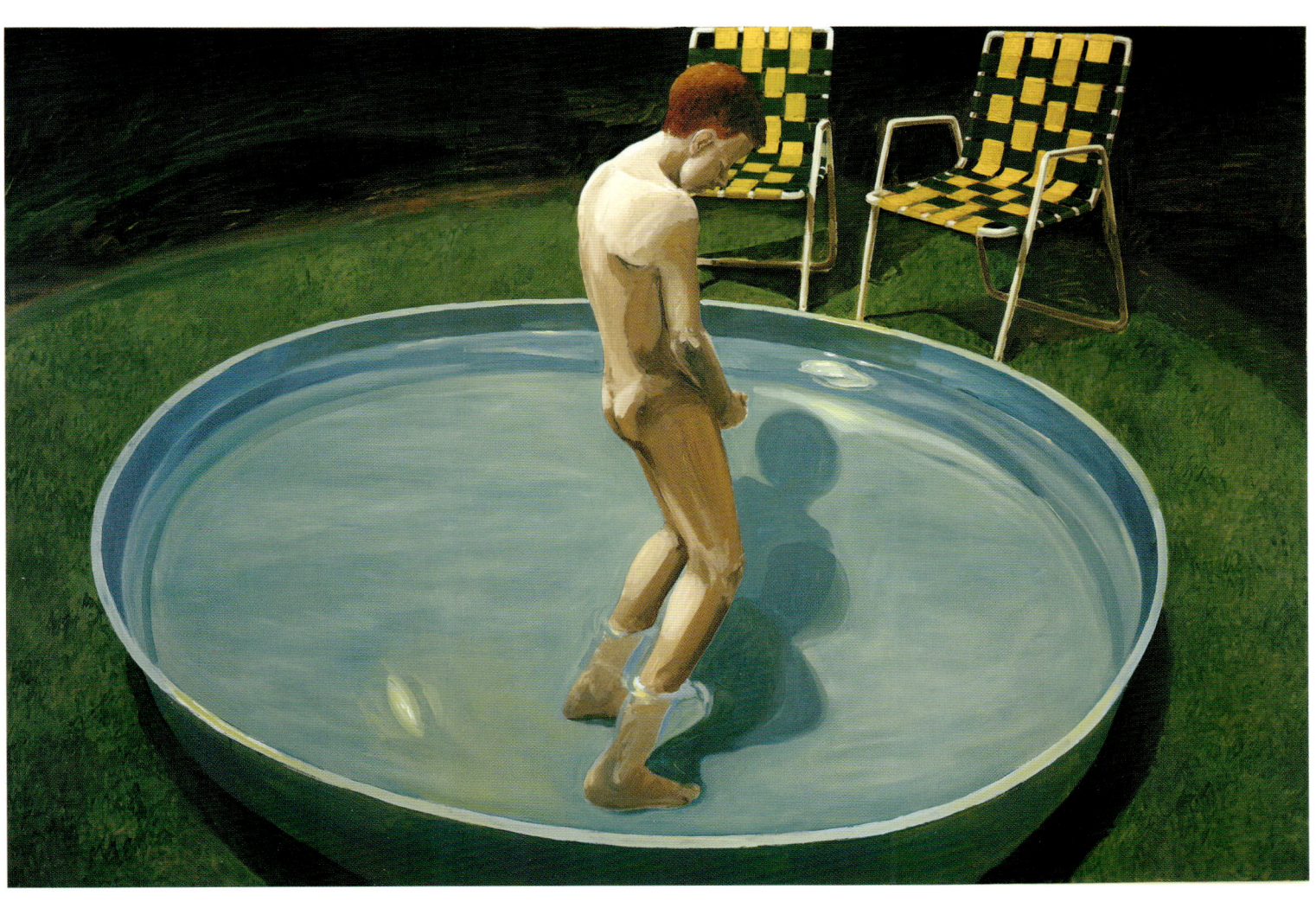

FIG. 27. **Eric Fischl**, *Sleepwalker*, **1979.** Oil on canvas. 69 x 105 in. (175.3 x 266.7 cm). Private Collection.

little (on topic). There are certainly cinematic scenes of one kind or another, from Hedy Lamarr in *Ecstasy* (1933) to Naomi Watts in *Mulholland Drive* (2001). But in the art world there is a striking gap between the Greco-Romans and Vito Acconci's *Seedbed* (1972) —a performance piece unironically described by the Metropolitan Museum of Art's website as "seminal," in which he lay beneath a wooden ramp at the Sonnabend Gallery in SoHo, voicing his fantasies as he masturbated to the sound of visitors walking above: "you're on my left. . . . I'm pressing my eyes into your hair."[14]

Of course, there is a certain charm to pubescent self-discovery which is not quite true of some of Fischl's paintings that wade into Oedipal waters and darker realms of sexual longing and frustration. *Daddy's Girl* (1984) presents a naked father and young daughter lying on a lounge chair by a white modernist house, with nothing but sunshine and a glass of iced tea for company (FIG. 28). The insinuations of the title are uncomfortable, but are they really there in the image? We are made conscious of our own unease, which was one source of inspiration for the work after Fischl spent a summer in Saint-Tropez and found himself stunned by the languor of naked French families on the beach (PLATE 36). As Robert Enright has remarked, "there are times looking at his work when you feel you are less a viewer than a private investigator, wondering about the motivations and the actions of the characters in the paintings. What you end up activating is something like a forensic gaze."[15]

There is an equally powerful temptation to look for traces of Fischl's own life, only more so since the release of his autobiography, *Bad Boy*, in 2012.[16] The title must have been irresistible: snatched from his notorious 1981 painting in which a naked woman lies with her legs folded up while a young boy stares, transfixed, with a hand slipped behind his back into her purse (PLATE 15). A childhood marred by his mother's alcoholism and its inevitable emotional chaos left Fischl with no shortage of familial material to work from, but the episodes that he paints have such a

strong flavor of film noir that it's clear there is nothing literal about them. Nor are these transcriptions of psychoanalytic concepts, tempting as that reading might be. The truth for Fischl is more ambient; drawn from the dissonance felt between the glint of public suburban life and the ache of it inside.

*Daddy's Girl* was one of the first occasions on which he had used his own photography as source material for his painting. With that shift in technique came the added charge of voyeurism and a connection to the circulation of explicit imagery in domestic and professional spaces. Photography offered something else too: a sheer mass of detail. When a work is drawn directly from life, the mind tends naturally to simplify what it sees in order to make it renderable. Our memories are even more fallible in terms of omitting critical information about color, light, and texture which seem irrelevant to the emotional heft of the incident. As Fischl puts it, photography can "capture life in such thin slices that everybody is off balance and everybody is in motion."[17]

This effect is in full force in the Krefeld paintings (2002–2006; FIG. 29; PLATES 20, 21). And now there is another element to the drama: Fischl has hired actors. The project began as a conversation with the Kunstmuseum Krefeld in Germany, which has turned two former homes designed in 1928 by Mies van der Rohe into contemporary art spaces. Fischl furnished the rooms back into domestic environments and worked with two actors to play out a series of unscripted scenes that he photographed and filmed over two days. The results are compelling and devastating; a *pas de deux* in which our protagonists are intimately alienated. Amid the light and elegance of a modernist utopia, in the living room, the sunroom, the dining room, the bathroom, and the bedroom, they reach for but elude one another. One moral of the story: no Barcelona chair can secure your happiness.

Crucially, there is nothing condemnatory here or indeed elsewhere. Fischl's distinctly warm palette and

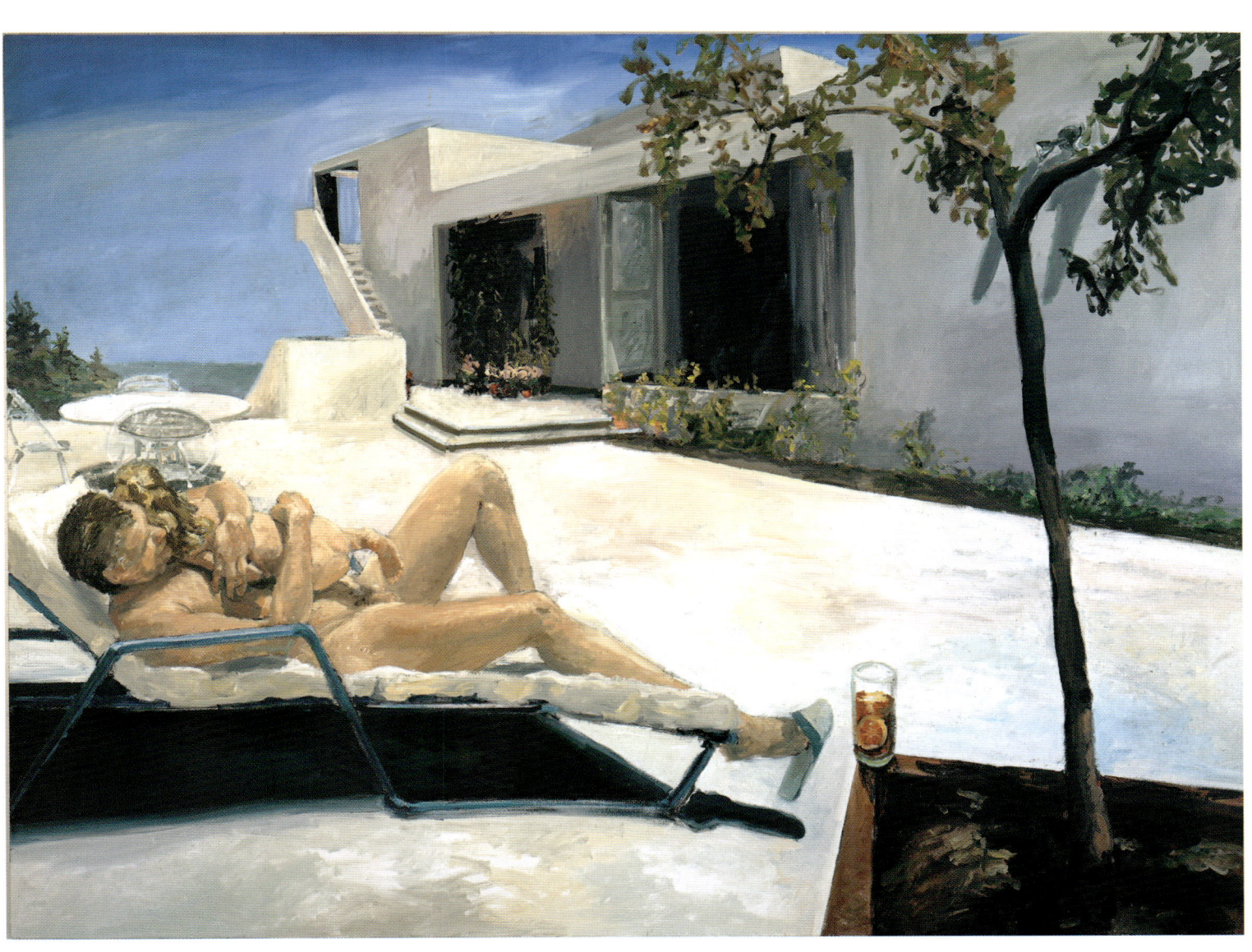

FIG. 28. **Eric Fischl**, *Daddy's Girl*, **1984.** Oil on canvas. 78 × 108 in. (198.1 × 274.3 cm). Udo and Anette Brandhorst Collection.

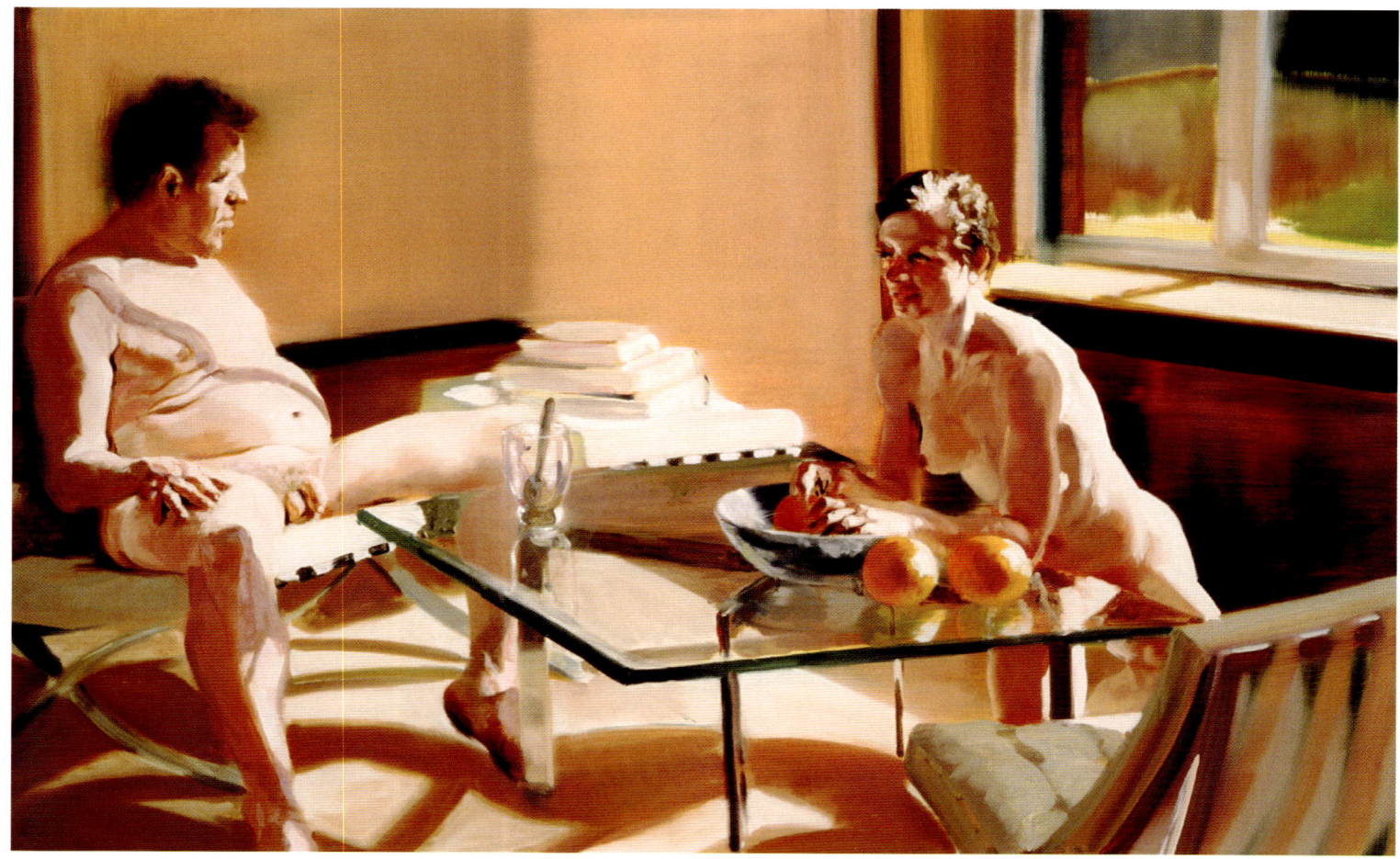

FIG. 29. **Eric Fischl**, *Krefeld Project; Sunroom, Scene #3*, **2002**. Oil on linen. 40½ × 65 in. (102.9 × 165.1 cm). Collection of Michael A. Young and Family.

increasingly sumptuous handling of paint reflects the depth of compassion with which his pictures have been made. However awkward the narrative unfolding, Fischl is fundamentally kind to his subjects. These are the anxieties and desires, regrettable and otherwise, of ourselves and our neighbors. As he put it simply to Schjeldahl: "I like that my work makes certain kinds of emotions seem ok to have."[18] There may be humor in his portrayal but never bitterness. Like Walt Whitman, Fischl is a painter driven by "the curious sympathy one feels when feeling with the hand the naked meat of the body." And so even in the most poignantly tense of sexual encounters, his paintings hum with something like Whitman's hymn to physicality, "I Sing the Body Electric":

*To be surrounded by beautiful, curious, breathing,*
*        laughing flesh is enough,*
*To pass among them or touch any one, or rest my arm*
*        ever so lightly round his or her neck for a moment,*
*        what is this then?*
*I do not ask any more delight, I swim in it as in a sea.*

*There is something in staying close to men and women*
*        and looking on them, and in the contact and odor*
*        of them, that pleases the soul well,*
*All things please the soul, but these please the soul well.*[19]

## Notes

1   Eileen Myles, "Peanut Butter," in *I Must Be Living Twice: New and Selected Poems* (HarperCollins, 2015). © 2015 by Eileen Myles. Courtesy of HarperCollins Publishers.

2   Amy Sillman, "On Color," originally a lecture delivered at Harvard in 2013, republished in Isabelle Graw and Ewa Lajer-Burcharth, eds., *Painting beyond Itself: The Medium in the Post-medium Condition* (Sternberg, 2016), p. 103.

3   Allison Katz, "Artery," in *Artery*, ed. Sam Thorne and Martin Clark (MIT Press; Nottingham Contemporary; Camden Art Centre, 2021), published in conjunction with a traveling exhibition of the same title, 2021–22, p. 24.

4   Peter Schjeldahl, "Bad Boy of Brilliance," *Vanity Fair*, May 1984, https://archive.vanityfair.com/article/1984/5/bad-boy-of-brilliance.

5   "Realism is the phoenix of art styles. Whenever it seems to have disappeared, it springs forth from the ashes, alive and thriving." David L. Shirey, "Art Sampler," *New York Times*, September 27, 1981.

6   Vivien Raynor, "Realism at the Robeson Gallery," *New York Times*, August 9, 1981.

7   Paul Bowles, *Pages from Cold Point and Other Stories 1910–1999* (Peter Owen, 1968), p. 87.

8   Bowles, *Pages from Cold Point,* 98.

9   Don DeLillo, *White Noise* (Picador, 1986), p. 51.

10  For further discussion of this self-portrait, see Kathryn Brown in this volume.

11  Grace Glueck, "Art: At the Whitney, Michael Heitzer Work," *New York Times*, June 28, 1985.

12  *State of the Art: Ideas & Images in the 1980s*, episode 4, "Sexuality," an Illuminations production for Channel 4 (Britain) television, https://www.illuminationsmedia.co.uk/product/state-of-the-art/.

13  Douglas C. McGill, "Probing Society's Taboos—On Canvas," *New York Times*, March 2, 1986.

14  Vito Acconci, *Seedbed*, 1972. A gelatine silver print from the performance is in the collection of the Metropolitan Museum of Art, New York, 1993.116, https://www.metmuseum.org/art/collection/search/266876. One of the few other examples of onanistic works of art is Georg Baselitz's brilliantly titled *Die große Nacht im Eimer* (*The Big Night Down the Drain*) from 1962–63.

15  Robert Enright, "Desiring Ambiguity," in *Eric Fischl, 1970–2000* (Monacelli Press, 2000), p. 66.

16  Eric Fischl and Michael Stone, *Bad Boy: My Life On and Off the Canvas* (Crown, 2012).

17  Eric Fischl interview with Steve Miller, *Musée* 15 (2016), https://museemagazine.com/features/2023/4/13/from-our-archives-eric-fischl.

18  Schjeldahl, "Bad Boy."

19  Fischl would be just the man to paint "eye-fringes," "hind-shoulders," and "lung-sponges," terms that Whitman coined in the poem. Walt Whitman, "I Sing the Body Electric," 1855, https://www.poetryfoundation.org/poems/45472/i-sing-the-body-electric.

CROWDS & PARADES

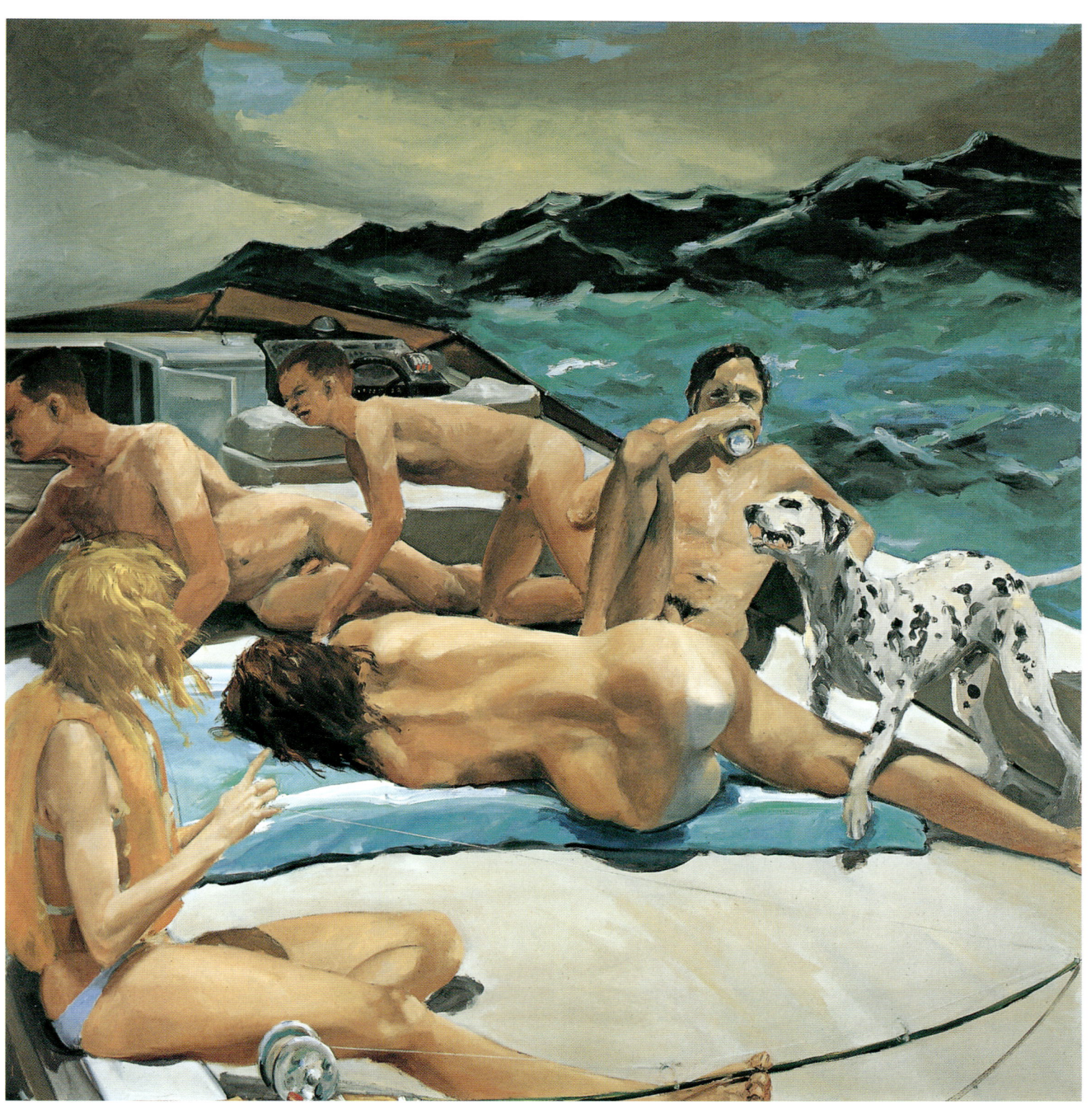

PLATE 35. *The Old Man's Boat and the Old Man's Dog*, 1982

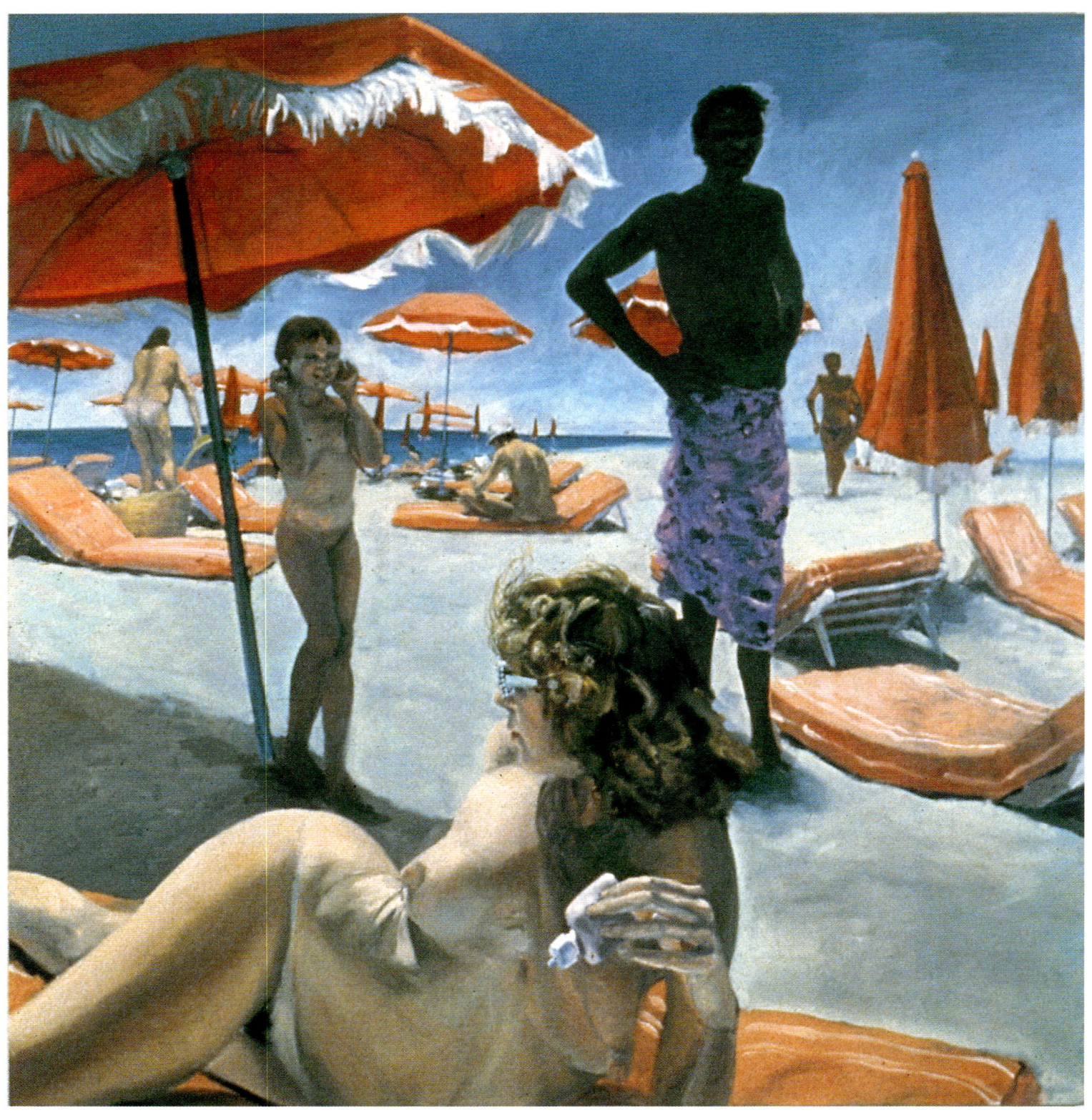

PLATE 36. *St. Tropez*, 1982

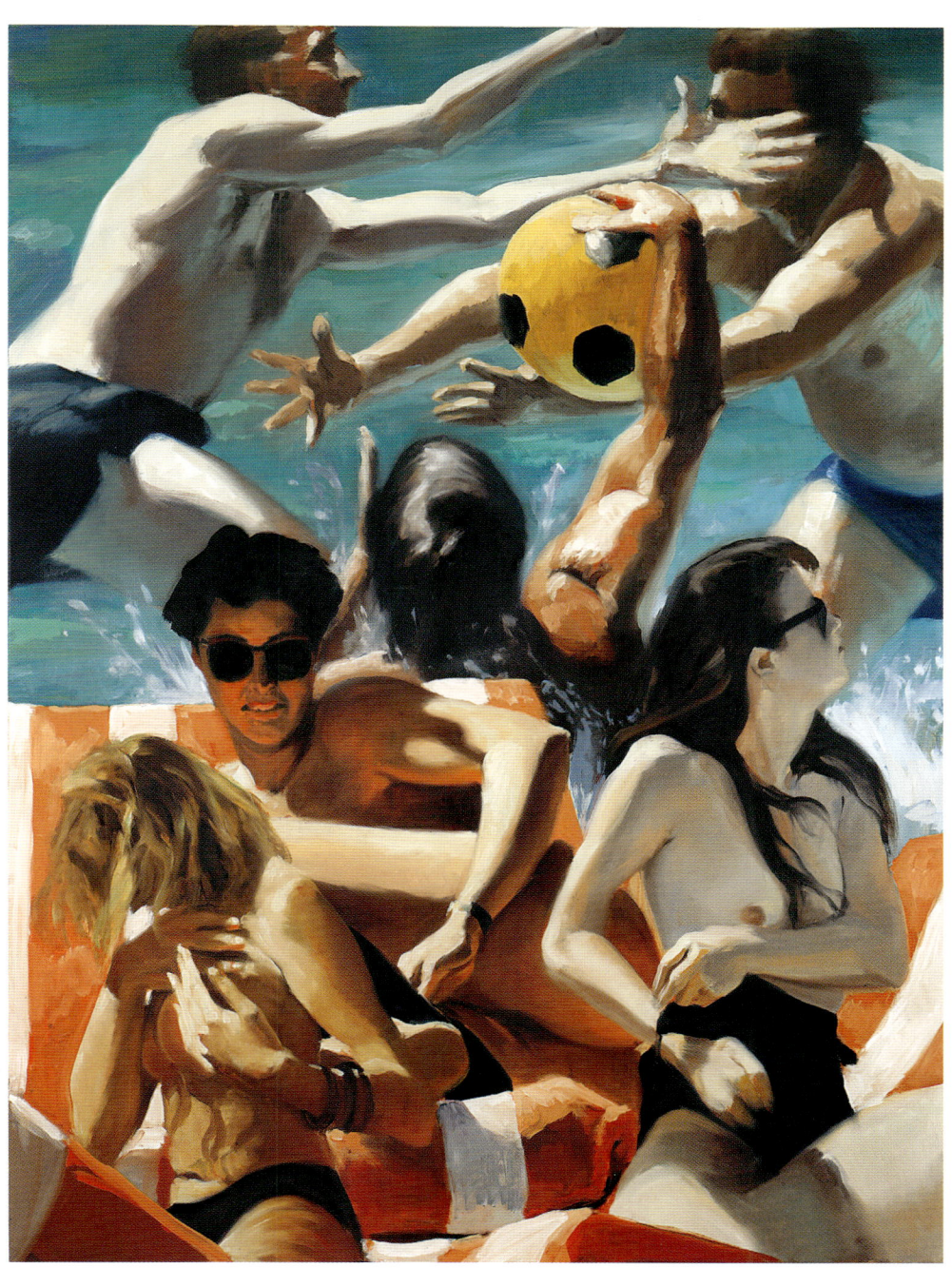

PLATE 37. *The Call of the Ball*, 1993

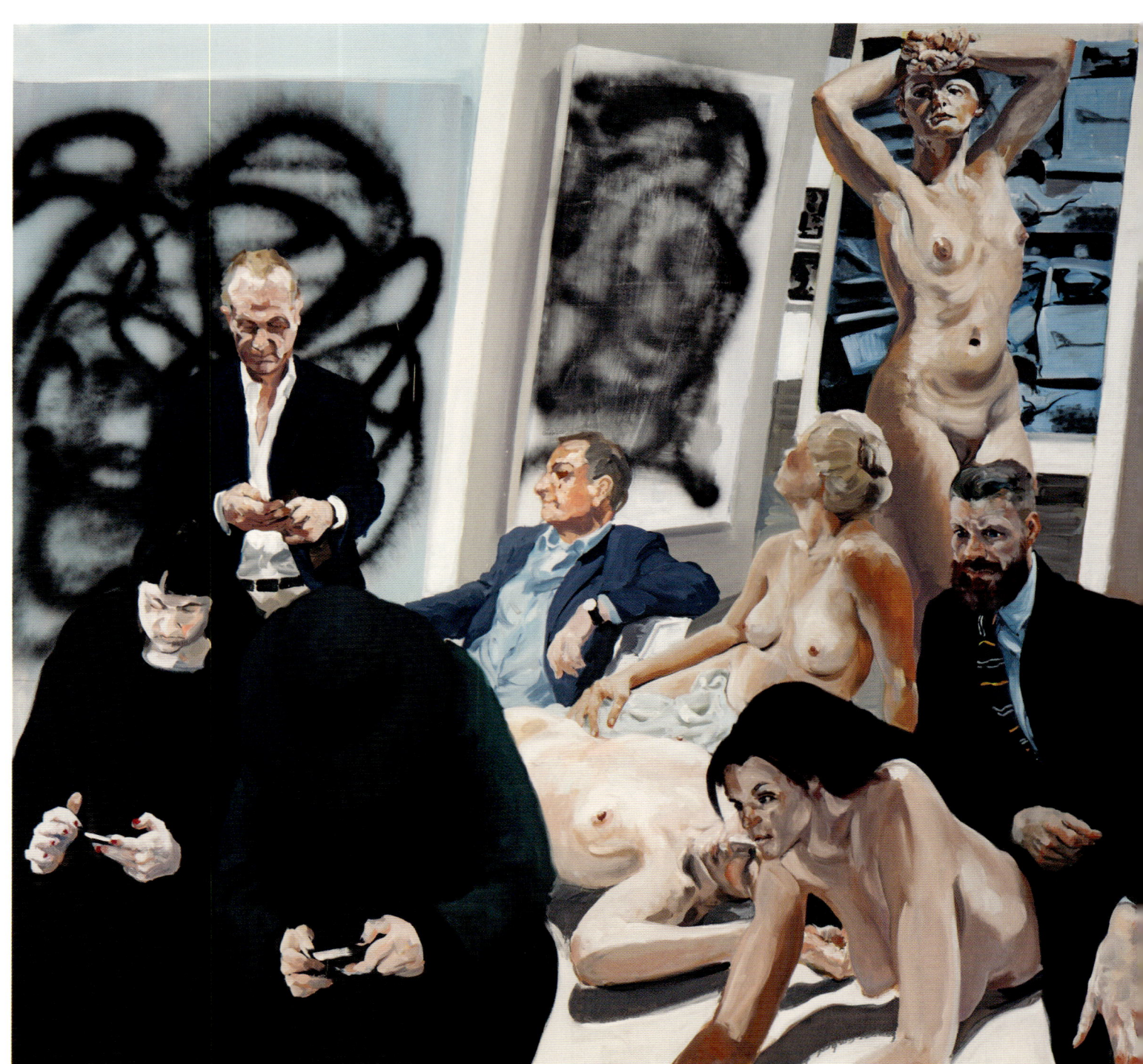

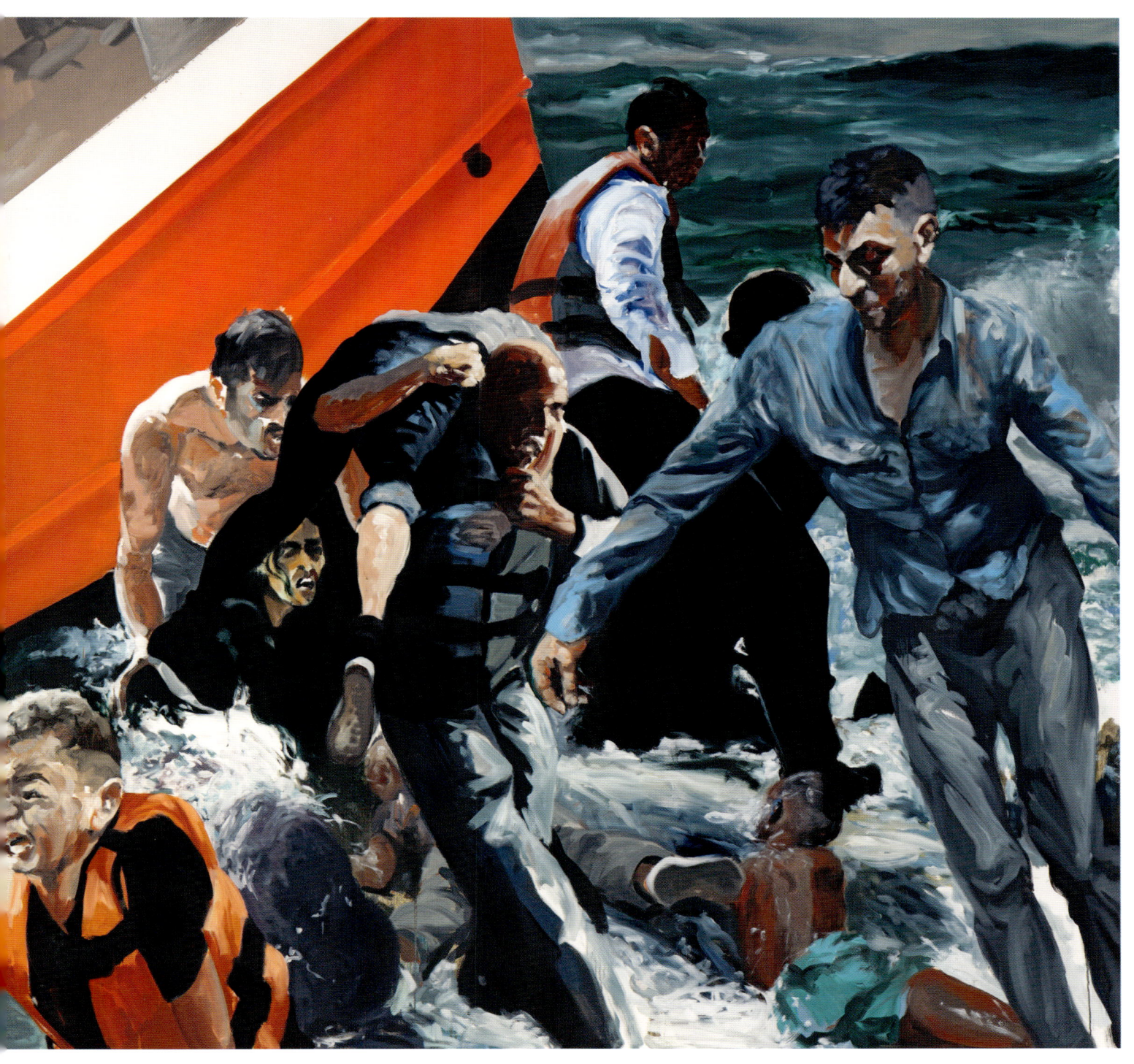

PLATE 38. *Rift/Raft*, 2016

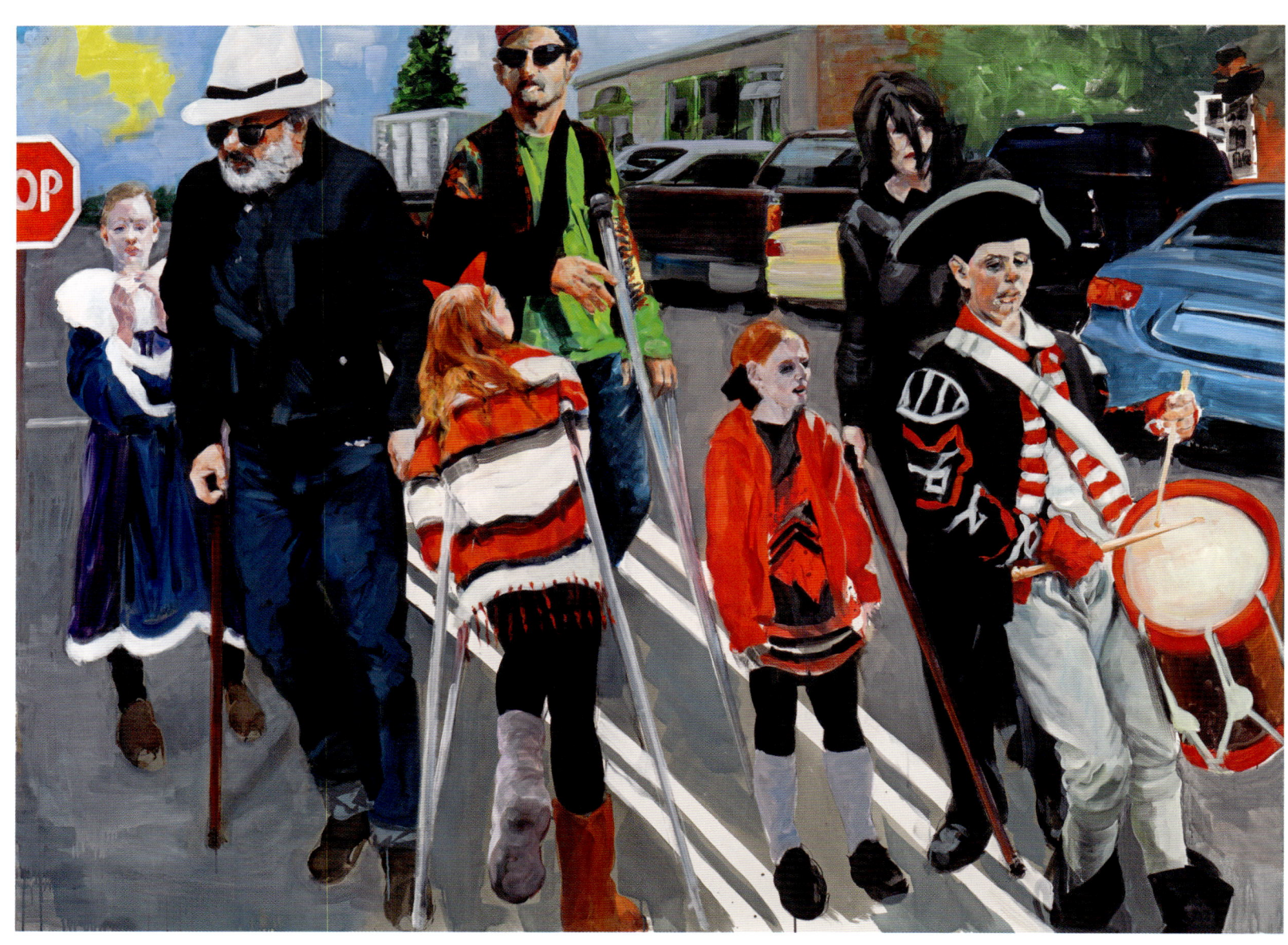

PLATE 39. *The Parade Returns*, 2022

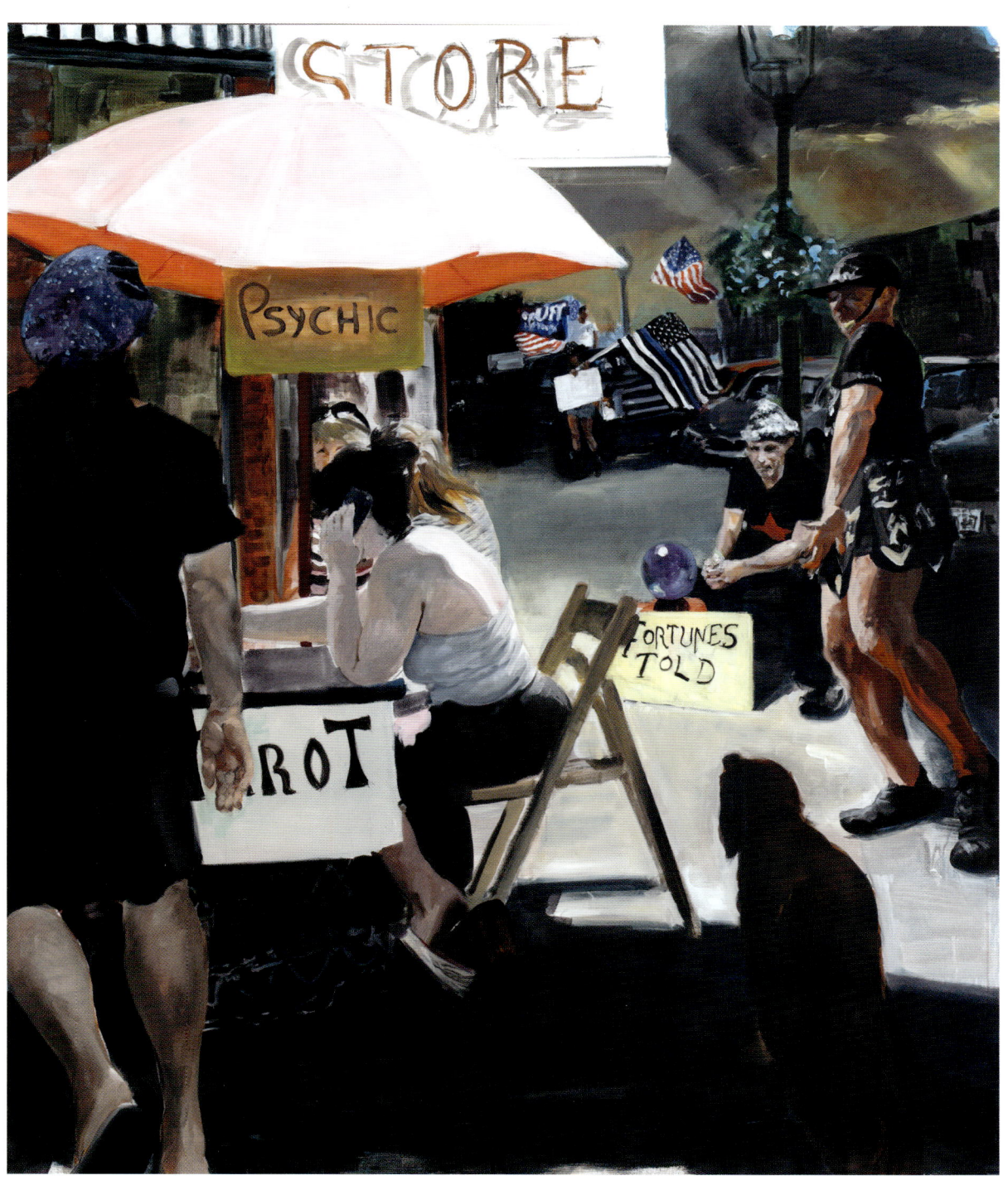

PLATE 40. *You Don't Need a Weatherman...*, 2022

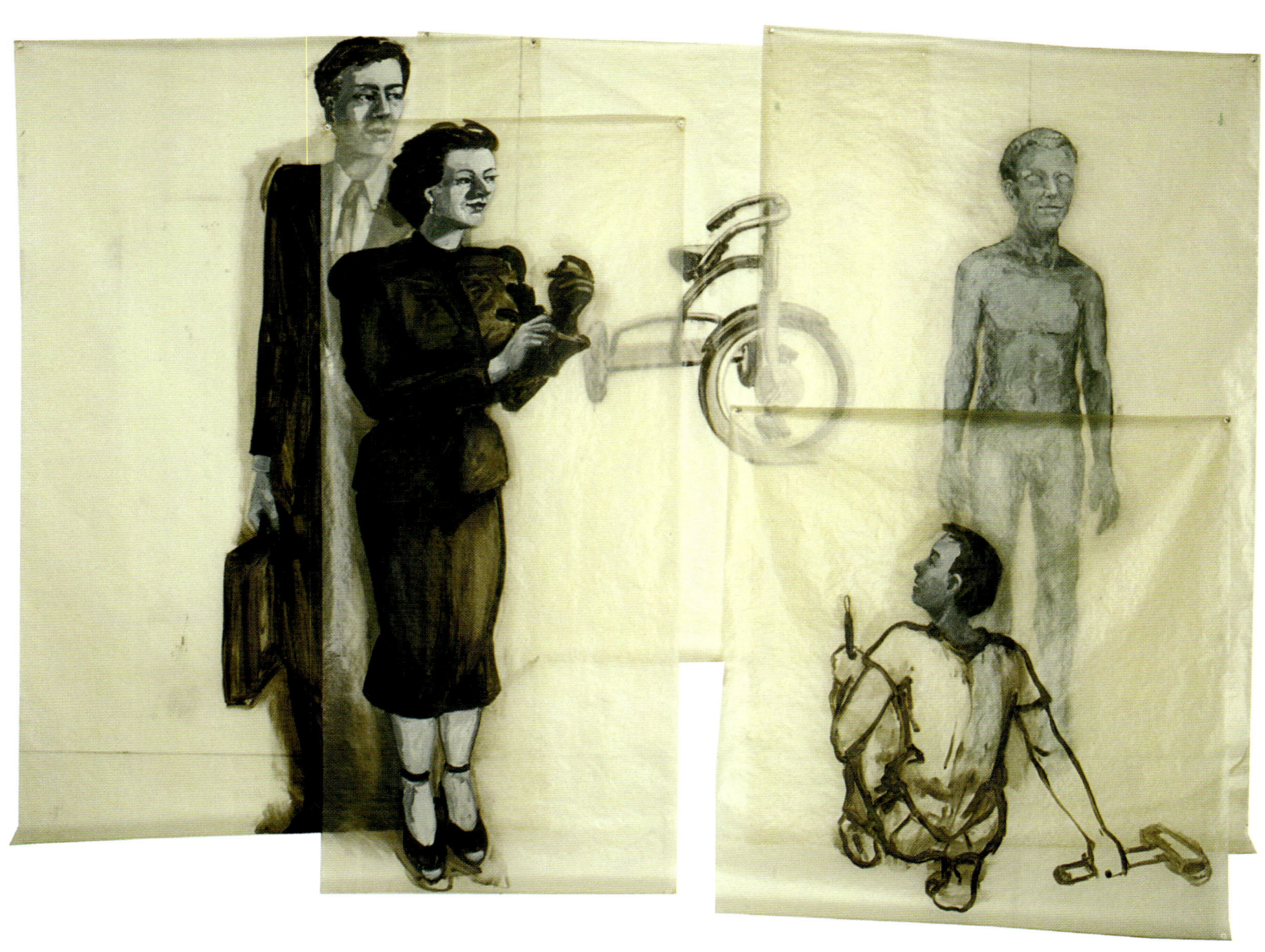

PLATE 41. *The Critics*, 1979

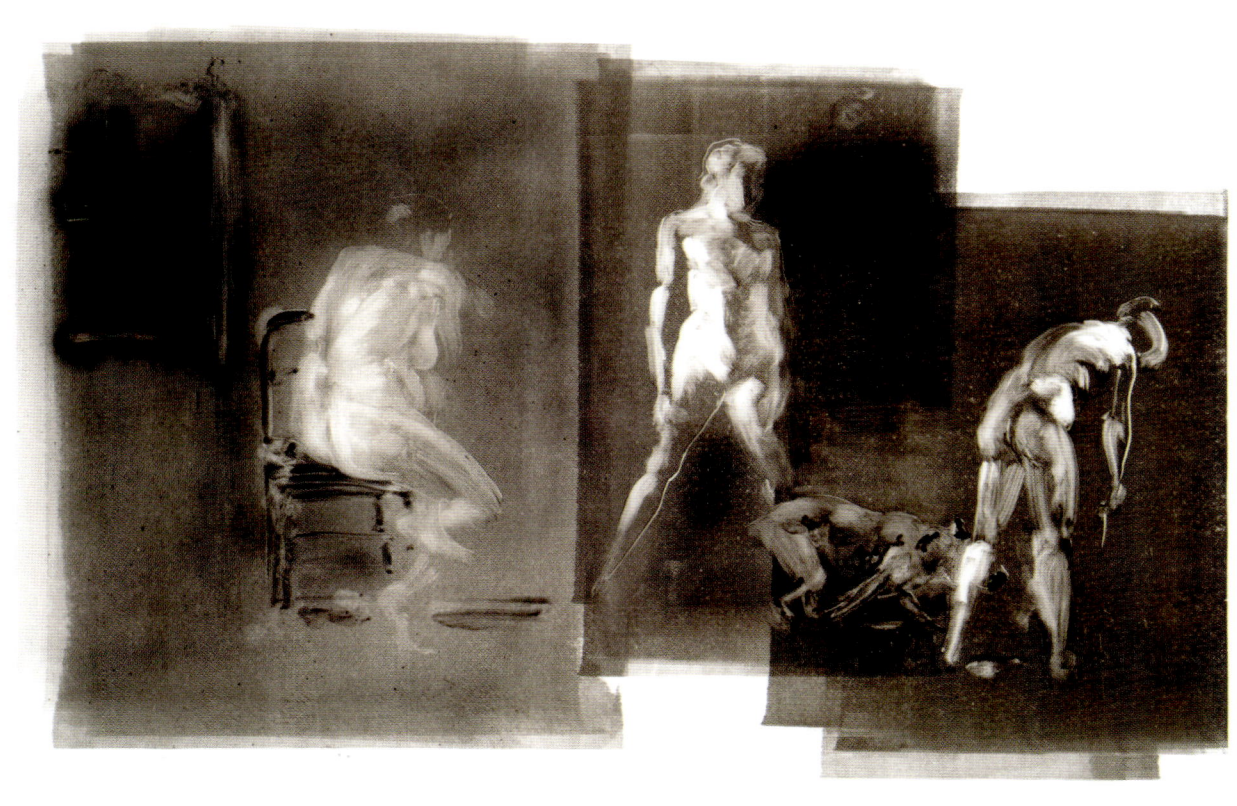

PLATE 42. *Scenes and Sequences: Fable,* 1986

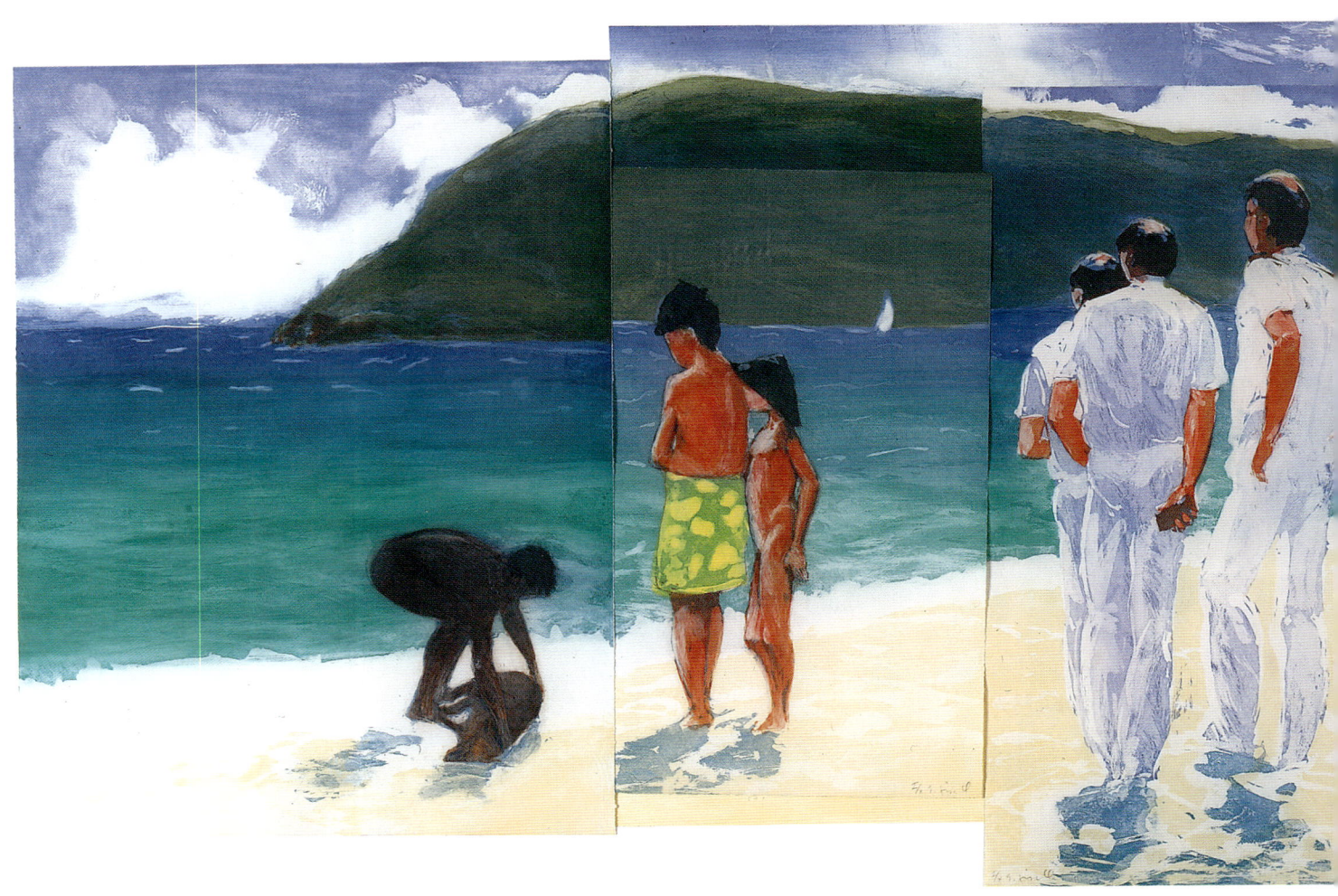

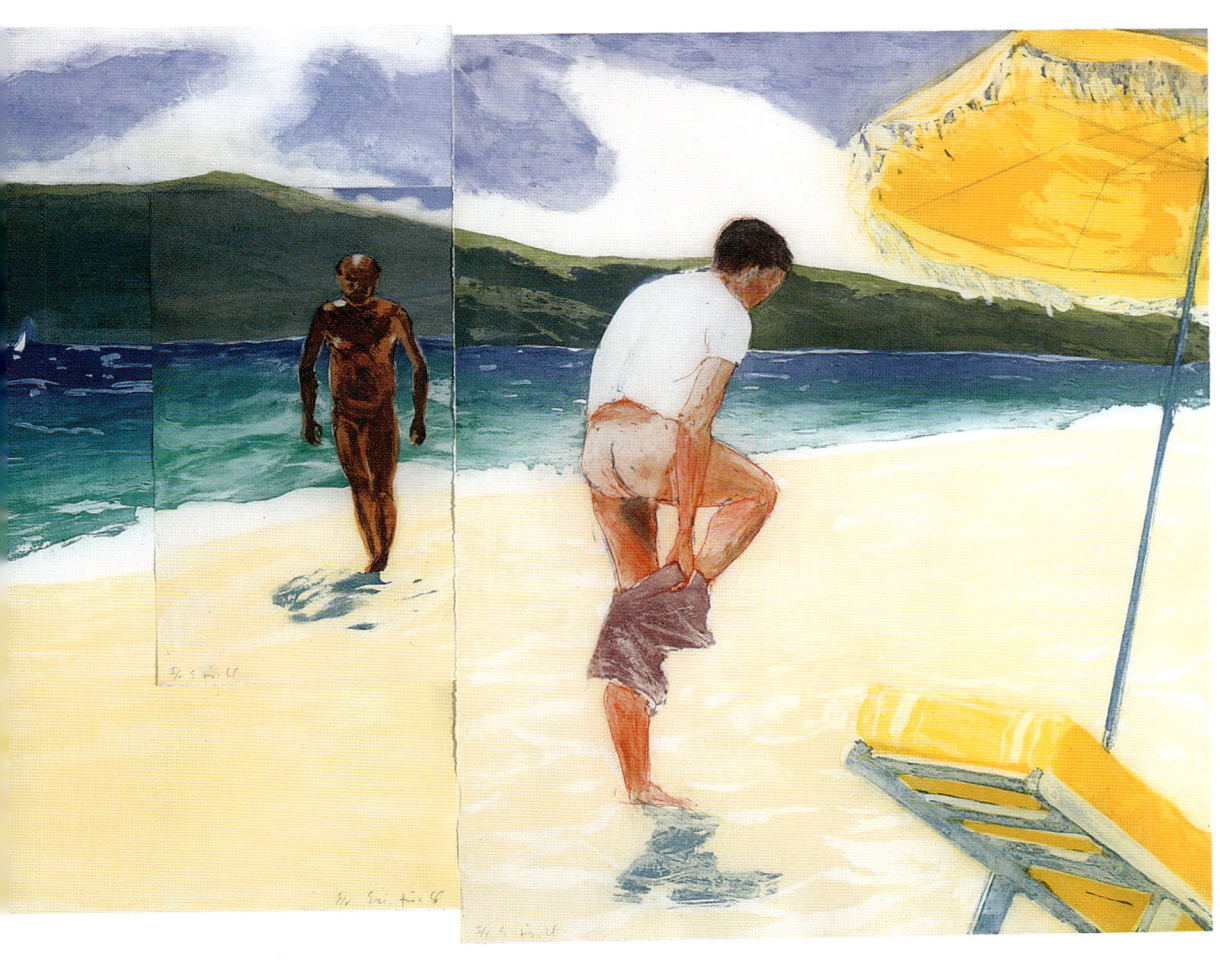

PLATE 43. *Year of the Drowned Dog*, 1983

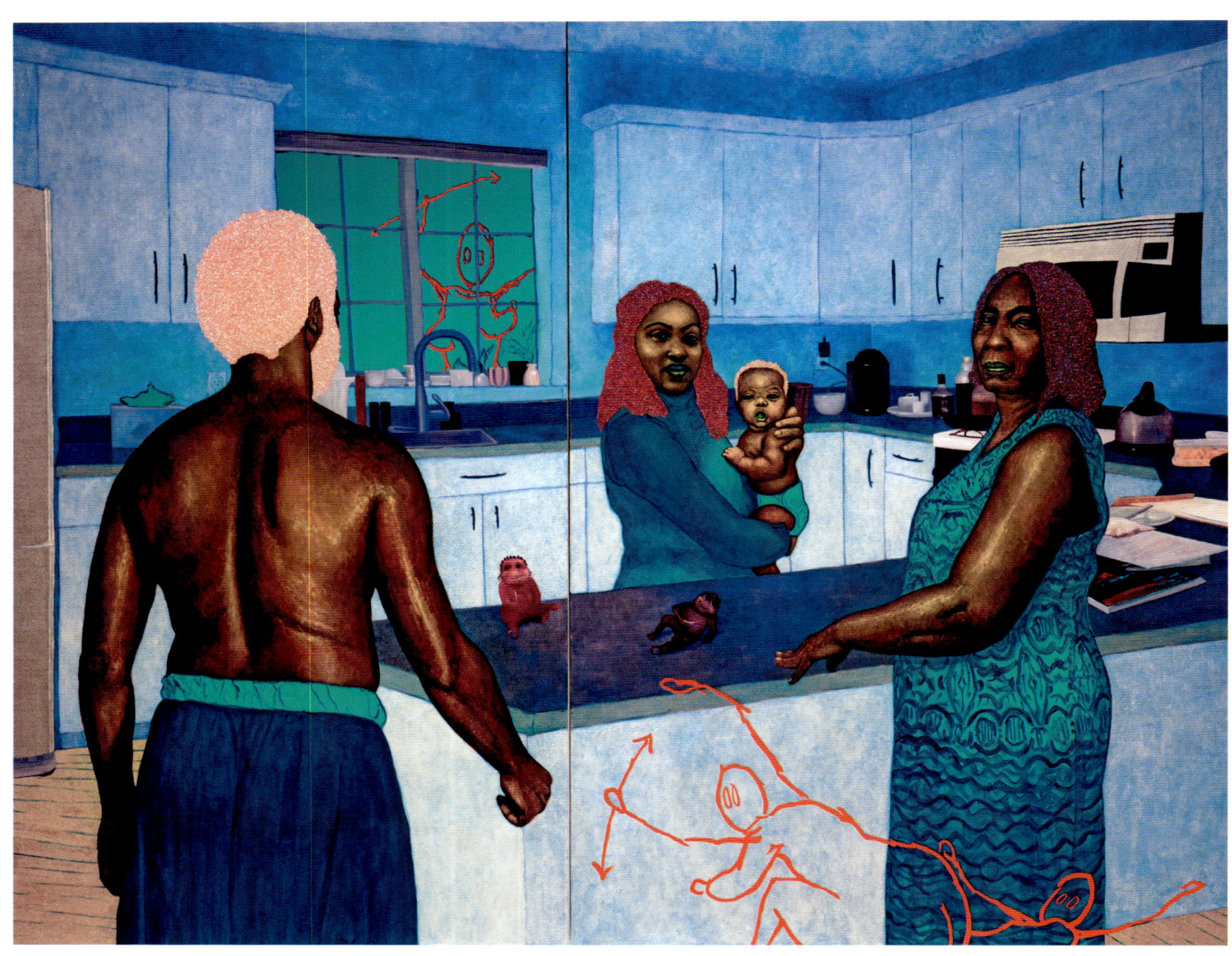

FIG. 30. **Arcmanoro Niles** (American, b. 1989), *Does a Broken Home Become a Broken Family*, **2019.** Oil, acrylic, and glitter on canvas. 77 × 92 in. (195.6 × 233.7 cm). Collection of Phoenix Art Museum, Purchased with funds provided by the Dawn and David Lenhardt Emerging Artist Acquisition Fund (2019.7.A-B).

# PAINT WHAT YOU KNOW?
## A CONVERSATION BETWEEN ERIC FISCHL AND ARCMANORO NILES

**ARCMANORO NILES.** I remember the first time we met, about ten years ago at PAFA [Pennsylvania Academy of the Fine Arts], during your exhibition *Dive Deep: Eric Fischl and the Process of Painting*. A teacher introduced us, and we talked for about five to ten minutes. The next day at your talk, you spoke about how you started painting, about being from the suburbs where all these things were happening that you couldn't really see on the surface. That really interested me.

What was the decision like for you to paint from your life? When I was in school, I was painting about my life but covering it up, saying "this is a story about Zeus" or "this is a Caravaggio copy." Even now, it's hard for me to fully commit and say, "this is about me."

**ERIC FISCHL.** I had a similarly long process to come to this realization. When I started, I did everything I could to disguise any personal references in terms of specificity of who these people are and what the situation is. When I first started doing narrative work with oil on glassine overlays, I always tried to keep all the furniture like isometric silhouettes of a chair or sofa or table so that it didn't have any economic or lifestyle references. So it didn't have any specific associations. It took me a long time to put in a chair which was more literal and specific to what you find in a middle-class suburban home. Then all of a sudden the people in my paintings became more real and more familiar to me.

**NILES.** What was the thing that made you finally be like, okay, I'm going to start showing more of me in my paintings?

**FISCHL.** The simple answer is that the more the questions around what art is, what it could be or should be, became simpler to answer the closer I got to the truth of my life, because the truth couldn't be taken away. At the time, choosing to be a painter was a negative and choosing to be a figurative painter was a double negative in terms of what the art world was looking for. So I thought, just get it irreducible, get it down to where, whether you like it or not, it's real. And that's the best I can do.

**NILES.** I agree with all of that. And for me it was seeing contemporary artists do it.

In high school, I watched this documentary on Caravaggio, and it started off by saying that his religious paintings were based on his life, people in Rome, and sort of seedy back alleys. The church wanted religious commissions, so Caravaggio just put his life into those stories.

**FISCHL.** He even painted himself into *The Martyrdom of Saint Matthew* (FIG. 31).

**NILES.** Yeah, he's in the back. The idea of the artist always leaving a piece of their life in the painting and being honest about it. Hearing you talk about it at PAFA slowly gave me the courage to say, "OK, this is about me."

Painting has always been a way for me to connect with people. In my daily life, I'm kind of shy, and it's a way for me to share that I went through this and someone else probably did too.

**FISCHL.** For painters, we communicate with a visual language. It's the way we organize information, experience the world through shapes, colors, relationships of form that have both visual and emotional significance. I am a painter not because I wanted to be an artist, but it's how I see and organize everything in a clearer and more meaningful way. The next thing is, how do I get better at it? And what is better? How do you both find your themes and find a language that best describes those themes? You keep trying to expand your language to see if you can get clearer, because clarity of expression is what we're after, right? It's through that clarity that you touch people.

**NILES.** Clarity is a good word because as time goes by, my images get reduced, become clearer. I remember when I was a student, I would throw a bunch of stuff in a painting just to see if I could do it.

**FISCHL.** It's a good thing for students to do because they don't know what they're capable of or what is going to stick. It's something that you also carry on throughout your career: every now and then throwing a lot of shit at a painting. Can it take you to some other place because the place that you've been in for a while is used up?

Robert Motherwell said that he started every painting with a series of mistakes, and the process for him was correcting the mistakes.[1] And I like that. I like it more than I like his paintings. You get into a problem-solving situation very quickly in painting. Even when I do my Photoshop collages to build the image, I basically have to intuitively find a reason why making a painting would be better than leaving it as a photo collage.

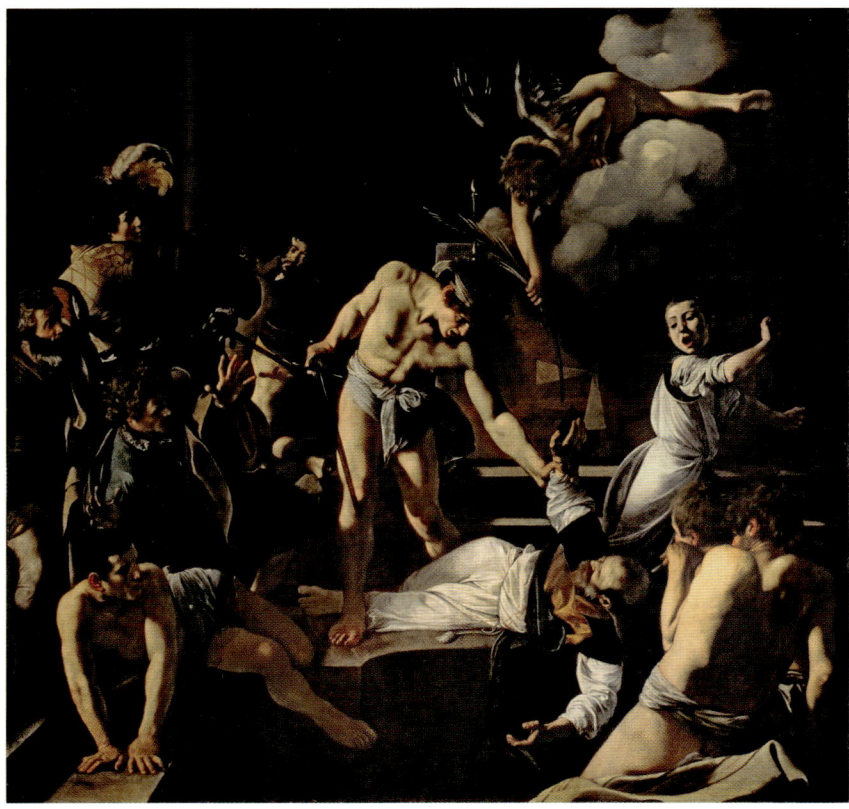

FIG. 31. **Caravaggio (Michelangelo Merisi da)** (Italian, 1571–1610), *The Martyrdom of St. Matthew*, **1599–1600.** Oil on canvas. 129 × 137 in. (328 × 348 cm). Contarelli Chapel, S. Luigi dei Francesi, Rome, Italy.

That starts with letting a painting do what photos can't, coming in with what I can do with my hand that I can't do with a computer keyboard or a mouse.

**NILES.** Mistake is another good word, because it always feels like I'm correcting whatever I just put down—correcting, correcting, correcting. By the time I start each new painting, it almost feels like I forget how to do it. Do you sit down sometimes and think, "I don't even remember how to do this"?

**FISCHL.** I don't want to remember, especially after I switched to painting in acrylic during the pandemic. It gave me the opportunity to correct the mistakes immediately. I didn't have to wait for it to dry or scrape it off; I could gesso it out or paint on top of it. But freedom also brought trying different approaches each time, and I found that I've got to control it more.

The Abstract Expressionists started each painting not knowing what it was going to be: finding their way into it, fighting with it, scraping it off, and putting it back on. But it would still end up looking like a de Kooning painting or a Pollock or a Frankenthaler. At a certain point, you have a language, and you're trying to make that language stay vibrant every time you make a painting. Exciting to you first and then to the audience.

**NILES.** Maybe I also don't really want to know. Every time I sit down to paint, I must be tricking myself.

I've heard you mention Edgar Degas as an influence, and I was wondering what your relationship is to his paintings.

**FISCHL.** I hugely admire his work, particularly the later work with the influence of photography. Degas understood photography as a way of liberating painting by introducing whole new compositional possibilities. You couldn't get at it through the language or history of painting. Photographers accidentally click something, or a hand is in the frame, and because they're looking for a pure image, it is a mistake. Degas understood that you can have things entering and leaving the rectangle that are controlling compositional focus, but they're incidental. Instead of painting a portrait of a woman where she's at the center, the vase of flowers next to her was at the center. It was brilliant. And his sort of deep voyeuristic sense, especially with the dancers. He would create a scene in which you were seeing the whole moment, but you also were seeing through the crooked arm of this dancer to this other dancer who's tying her shoe. That becomes the real focus of the painting. Those kinds of inventions I find incredibly profound in terms of visual language.

He was very much a sort of emotional and psychological painter, so there was always that edge in his work. There was beauty and in some cases utter banality, but it was still fraught with significance. It was different from Édouard Manet, who I also admire and who was painting at the same time. He emptied out that kind of content from painting. For Manet, it was all

just beautifully, simply painted images but emptied of any real meaning other than how he painted it. I struggle with trying to figure out what is that relationship between those two things: painting taking the meaningfulness out of it, or painting maintaining meaningfulness but keeping up with the issues of the contemporary moment.

That's our job moving forward. We've inherited a long history of painting that has successfully tried everything. How are we keeping painting alive? What is it that we can bring into this moment?

**NILES.** Although the artist Eugène Delacroix didn't influence me much, in his journal there's a passage where he talks about everything should be painted like it's on a gray day. The shadows and lights should just be mere accidents. Basically, he was talking about how the real color of the thing is in between the light and the shadow, and that should be the main subject. Then with Caravaggio, it is chiaroscuro, so the light is really bright, and then you have a lot of shadow. I've always thought: What if you combine both of those? Have all the color, but still have heavy lights and shadows? I've just been thinking about that for a while, and that's kind of how I came up with whatever it is I do.

**FISCHL.** Well, the Walters [Art] Museum in Baltimore has some great historical paintings, Baroque paintings, and I was standing with a friend in front of a Bernardo Strozzi painting. It is heavy in terms of what you're talking about, color and dark and light. I said to him, "the problem with modernism is it took all the shadows away and when you take the shadows away, you take a part of your creative mind away too." There's a lot in the darkness where our mind is very active, and it can imagine the unseen.

Starting with Impressionism, it moved painting into an obsession with light itself rather than light, shadow, and that conflict. Then art carried on with flatness, which became part of the language of modernism. Where are the possibilities for shadows to occur?

Shadows destroy flatness and create space. Within the contemporary moment, maybe pulling the shadows back into painting is a wide-open door, because there's definitely limitations to an only light-filled kind of experience.

**NILES.** Time to bring the darkness back.

We've touched on how painting is an art form that is heavily bound in tradition, especially figurative painting. At times in my life, this has felt like a burden, something I couldn't get away from. In 2011, I made this painting at PAFA of me as Atlas (FIG. 32). I'm painting at a palette and hunched over. At other times, [the history of painting] has felt like a gift. The older I get, it feels like something that's guiding me, showing me different paths that I can take. Less of a weight. It reminds me of your painting, *The Sheer Weight of History* (1982; PLATE 3). It's like my painting with this little kid hunched under a sculpture. What were you thinking about?

**FISCHL.** I was thinking about two things. One is the weight of art and cultural history. The painting that you're referring to was inspired by a room in the Uffizi Museum in Florence where you see painting after painting with great thematic narratives, incredible stylistic changes. [Art history] carries a weight for a young artist trying to figure out how to compete with it, how to use it, how to . . .

**NILES.** . . . get away from it.

**FISCHL.** . . . depart from it. All those things are present. So that's a weight.

The beautiful sculpture in the painting looks at first like a lounging woman. When you walk around it, it turns out to be a hermaphrodite, and you see the male genitals. So it's like, "Whoa, that's a surprise." Then it has these niches on the wall with portrait busts of powerful men. From the perspective of my painting, you see a lounging sexy woman and a wall of male figures staring at her in an almost judgmental

way. The young boy underneath the table is overwhelmed by both the history of art and the questions around manhood.

**NILES.** Do you still feel that weight, or is it a little lighter?

**FISCHL.** I feel the weight of my ambition all the time, and my ambition is to sustain creative vitality in my life and to keep finding ways of connecting meaningfully through my work to the time. I used to think that it would get easier, because you would know so much, experience-wise. I find instead that it gets harder and harder, because the questions don't seem to go away. You think you're answering them, but you're only answering them for that painting or that body of work. The weight changes a bit in terms of what it is that's weighing you down, but the weight itself. . .

**NILES.** I wanted to talk about the gaze in your paintings and how you use it. What does it mean for you?

**FISCHL.** For a figurative painter, there's no way there is no gaze. You make a painting by making judgments and decisions about the formal things and of the person I'm painting. Who is this person I'm painting to me? Is this person the focus of the painting? Is there another person who is the focus? Where am I understanding this moment from? The magic of painting is that you can create images of people that feel real.

In my paintings, the witness could also be a chair, television set, window. So for me, gaze—in terms of creating the work—is about trying to find where the consciousness is, where the witness is in this work.

**NILES.** Is the person in the painting ever witnessing the person outside of it?

**FISCHL.** Sure. If you paint a figure whose gaze does not connect with yours, then you're painting a painting of somebody that's in their own world. They're thinking

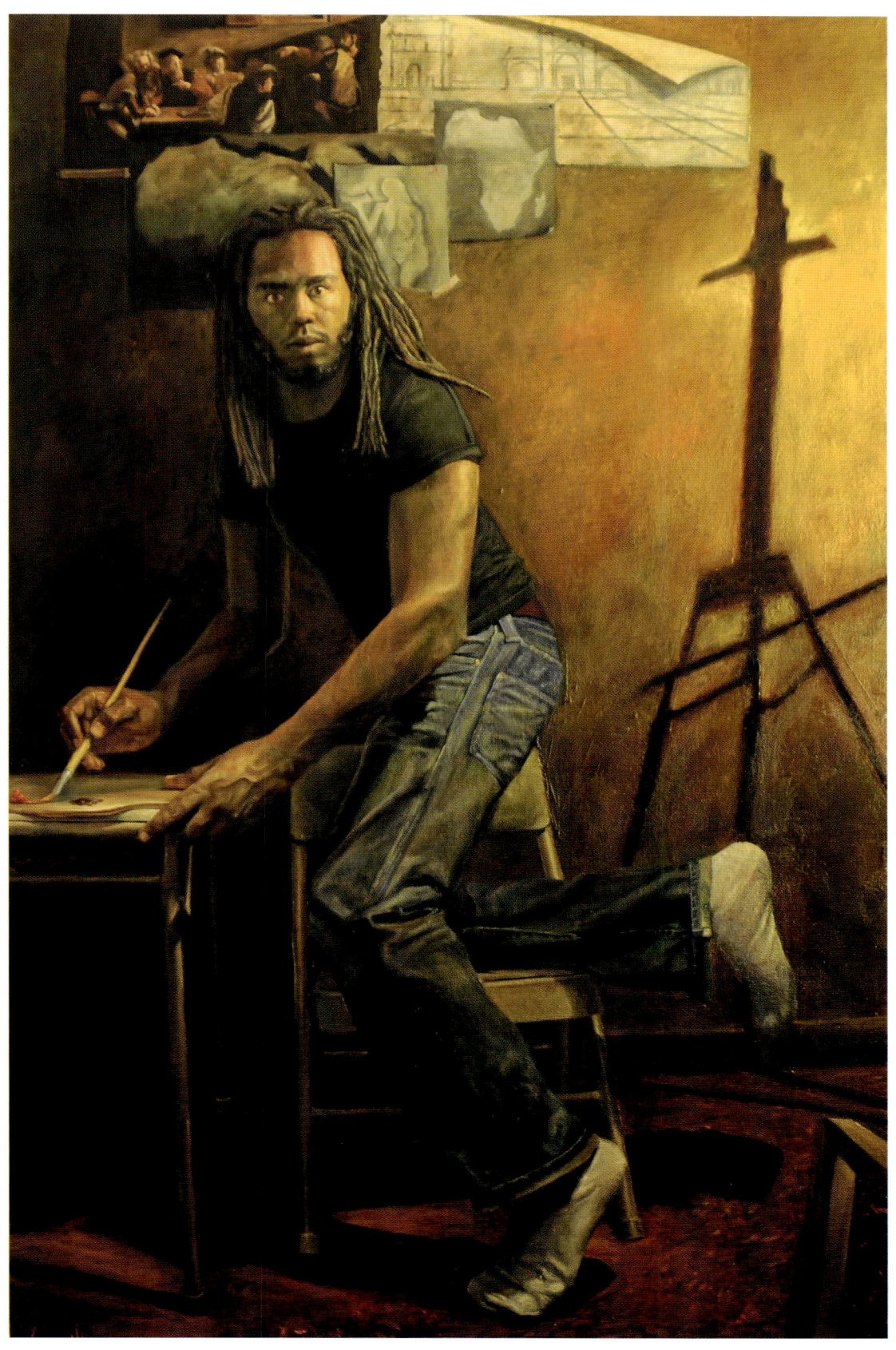

FIG. 32. **Arcmanoro Niles** (American, b. 1989), *The Tribulation of Atlas*, **2011.** Oil on canvas. 72 × 48 in. (182.9 × 121.9 cm). Lehmann Maupin, New York, Seoul, and London.

and feeling something that's got nothing to do with you. If you paint a person who is staring right back at you, you're part of the moment, part of their thinking and feeling. They may be happy you're there, they may be pissed that you're there, they may be confrontational. All those things are there, and that's a whole other dynamic.

Then you paint two people in a painting, and they're interacting with each other, and again, you're separated from it. You're looking into a moment, and they're not aware of you being there. You're watching them behave and having thoughts, judgments, and feelings about what's going on. Then you paint three or more. Now there's this weird triangulation of awareness and obliviousness. These are all dramatic tools for telling stories, for creating moments. I explore all of them.

**NILES.** The person looking at the painting, I want them to feel like they're part of it in some way. Either they're coming in right before the person in the painting notices you, and you're catching something that they're doing, or they're engaging with you.

I think a lot about identity and the roles I am or have been—son, lover, friend—but also roles I've never had but seen from my perspective: mother, father. I say I paint my experiences, which gets misinterpreted as I paint what I know, but that's only partly true. Most of the time, I'm painting what I don't know. The part of the experience that I have questions about, [that] keeps me up at night, and may not ever have any real answers even once I have painted it.

There're a few things in there, but I guess the first thing is perspective. If I do paint a mom, it's through a son's eyes, and this is my idea of what that feels like. That's kind of what you were touching on. I don't know if I ever really separate it, because when I'm painting a woman or specifically a sister or a mother, I'm thinking about me looking at them. I try to put whatever feelings I have into it. I feel like the viewer is seeing it through me, and it will bring up

feelings of what they think about when they think about a mother.

**FISCHL.** Yeah. I think there's the "paint what you know," but what you're really doing is you're using what you know to discover what you don't understand.

The process of painting is the process of coming to understand something. Right? We've all had these experiences that are profound in our lives, meaningful. They involve things that are also not only specific to us but are general to everybody. Everybody has a mom. There is a kind of web of relationships between people that are from time immemorial and that are constantly being reinterpreted. Who are we, and what just happened? Then you paint what just happened, and it leads to both an understanding and a continued mystery.

**NILES.** In the *Hotel Stories* series, which you just finished, I noticed there seems to be a looseness and simplified clarity that seems freeing. I imagine it comes with experience, something I think about a lot. I was wondering, does working in watercolor or with monotypes or even the iPad help inform or develop this way of painting? I'm specifically thinking about the painting of the hotel and that back foot of the guy in the red shirt (FIG. 33).

**FISCHL.** I'm creating a visual narrative. I'm telling a story. I'm putting a moment together in which something is both familiar and unfamiliar. I can tell you everything that's in the painting, but I don't know what's going on, just a kind of feeling. It has been painting to painting, starting to get someplace and then trying to get to someplace else. Along the way, comes the question of who and what is the most important thing in this painting. Does it require the most detail, the most finish? What does it take to indicate the rug? Am I describing it in detail, or is it a swash of color that's on a plane so you accept it as a rug? All those questions are happening in the moment as I make the piece. I'm setting up a hierarchy of language trying to say "pay a lot of attention to

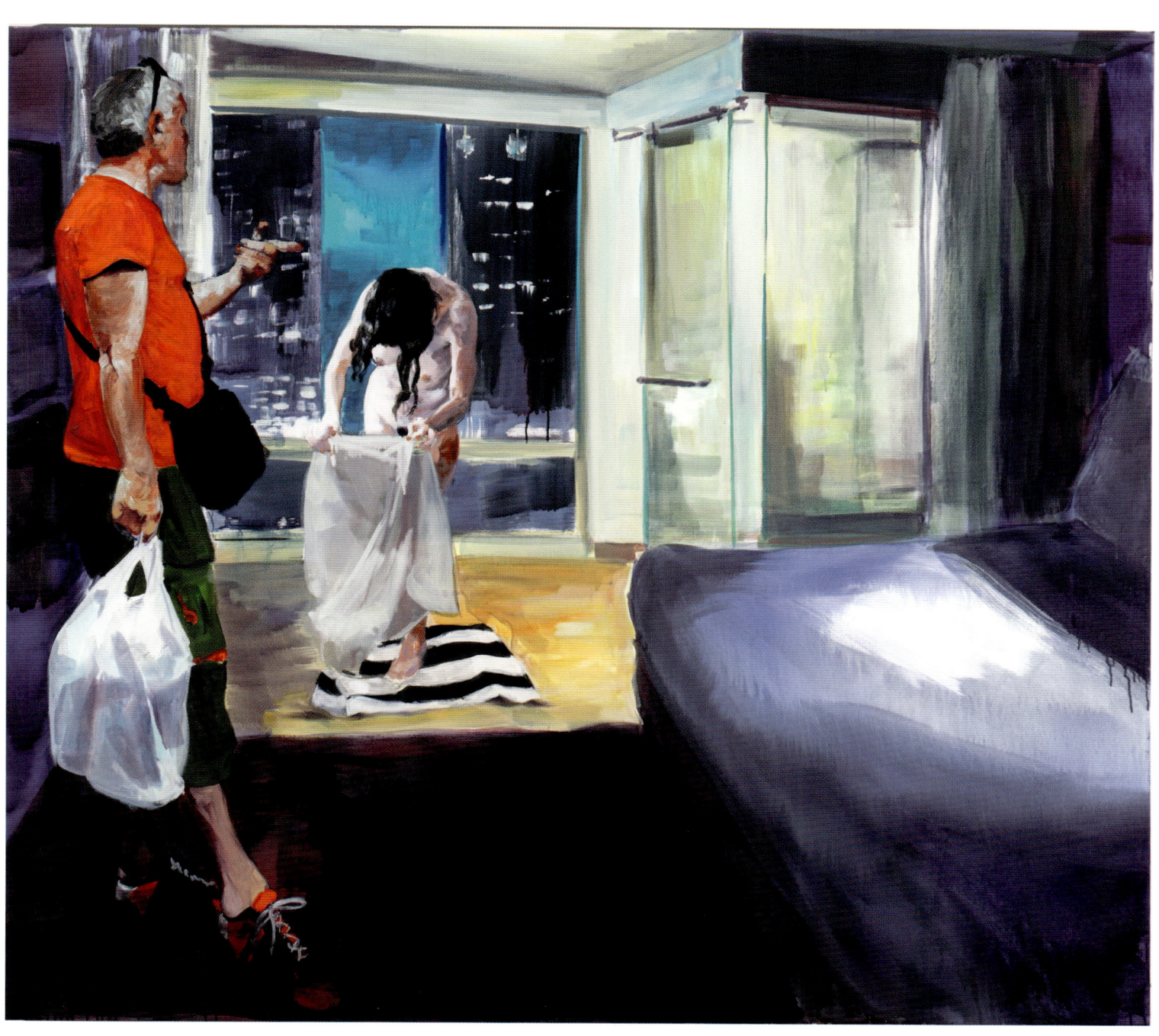

FIG. 33. **Eric Fischl,** *Snapshot of a Marriage,* **2023.** Acrylic on linen.
62 × 72 in. (157.5 × 182.9 cm). Private Collection.

this" or "don't spend a lot of time on this." Just know that it's there.

**NILES.** When you use photographs and collages, is it pretty much set when you get to the painting, or does it change quite a bit?

**FISCHL.** It changes dramatically. The collage is just a way of starting something. I treat the collages the way other artists sketch. I intentionally don't have canvases that are the same size as the collage, so the first thing I do is adjust it to fit. I don't grid. I'm not interested in that kind of precision of placement or specificity of detail. When I get to the canvas, I change compositional stuff in a way that maintains the significance of the moment.

Sometimes as I am approaching the canvas I'm nervous, so I sketch out the figures or the things that would be the most important. And then sort of paint around it. Other times I just start smearing on paint that has nothing to do with the color it ultimately will be or the shapes that ultimately will happen. I am doing it to get rid of the white and then go back in and try to block in things that are part of the scene.

That's all by way of saying that, from painting to painting, I approach it differently. Even though the collage is the same in terms of the process of Photoshop, where I start in a painting is different each time. If I find that in the course of painting, I am not as interested in that person, then they must go. If they leave a hole, what goes in that hole? I'll go back to Photoshop and start throwing things at it until I find something, and then put that in.

**NILES.** Listening to your process, I don't know if I'd be able to do that. I can only focus on one thing at a time, I'm thinking about composition first. Then the rest of the painting process is mostly color. At least for now, for some reason, I don't want both at the same time.

**FISCHL.** You can't go back and forth.

**NILES.** Little things can shift, but big things, not yet. I'll let you know in thirty years.

In my still lives and interiors, my objects usually become a bit of a portrait. If I'm painting a bedroom, well, it actually says a lot about the person and is also a portrait of a person. I was wondering, do you think about still lives or empty spaces in these ways? I'm thinking back to your earlier work when you would not be descriptive with the type of furniture. Do you think your objects have a bit of a portrait to them?

**FISCHL.** I don't think of them as portraits. I think of them as having a lot of resonance. It's a certain kind of person that would have that kind of chair type of thing, or this is a room that is too tidy or too confusing.

**NILES.** I use the word portrait loosely. How do you define portrait?

**FISCHL.** A portrait is so much about trying to make a person be there with undercurrents going on, and you feel that there's something that got him to this moment and is moving him past this moment.

There are two small portraits of the same guy by Rembrandt done ten years apart [that] I saw in Dresden. In the first portrait, he's in his thirties, and in the second he's in his forties. They're side by side and clearly the same person, but there's something in the second portrait that fills the gap of those ten years. The younger person looks out to the world with confidence and a sense of self-possession. In the later one, there is wariness and fatigue. It's amazing that you can feel that in a portrait of a person, but it's clearly there.

It's certainly possible to do a portrait of a couch and get feelings out of that couch. This couch is tired of people jumping on it. But the way I use the environment, it either reinforces or it goes against the characters.

**NILES.** What if there's no character? Have you done this?

**FISCHL.** I've only done a couple of paintings that have objects and no figures. I know what you're talking about. I never figured it out enough to expand into an object. There's certainly examples in history where you don't need [figures]. You look at Giorgio Morandi's paintings, and you don't need any people to get experiences of life.

**NILES.** That's how I think about it. I'm wondering if [Rembrandt] had also painted the guy's bedroom ten years apart, would you know more about what happened in those ten years? Would one be more of a portrait than the other? Especially if it's a self-portrait, I wonder what would be more revealing and what would show more of who I am and what I'm going through?

I was also thinking about outdoor[s] versus indoor[s]. Specifically, I find when people are outside, it feels more about everyone versus the individual. It captures more of a certain time and feels less like a real person to me. Do you think about this in terms of where you're placing people? I'm thinking about *Late America* and *Island of Cyclops* where, especially in the latter, you can't even really see their faces (PLATES 28, 31). It feels more about something in the air.

**FISCHL.** Each room in a house has its own psychological and emotional memory. If you choose to put a scene in a bathroom, it is different than if you choose a kitchen or a living room. Each of these places—you could put it in a closet, the basement, in the attic— they all have very different energy, resonance, metaphor and archetypes.

Then you have the front and backyards. The front yard is a presentation space. It is the person from the house greeting the public, greeting the neighbors. . . . Then the backyard is a semiprivate space. You're paying less attention to the public whether you're barbecuing, hanging out, throwing a ball, or swimming. These are all things that I consider.

Then you get to the public spaces, parks or the beach, consider the difference between a bunch of people on a beach versus one person staring out at the vast horizon. What I'm saying is that all of them are available spaces to explore meaning with their own conditions.

**NILES.** I guess when it's inside the house, there's more specificity. It feels like a portrait of a person or a specific family. But when it's out in a public space, it feels more like a portrait of a time or a place or, say, America.

**FISCHL.** You travel across the country, and you see things that are beautiful or strange. I'm looking at this landscape in Iowa, or I'm looking at these mountains. I'm seeing these people in these funny costumes in a parade. And then, can I use it as an environment or a backdrop for my paintings? And then it changes. I am not drawn to doing a large-scale work of a lot of people doing different things that are not connected to some other meaningfulness. ∎

Notes

This interview was recorded on June 11, 2024, at Fischl's studio in Sag Harbor, New York. It has been edited for clarity.

1   Full quote: "I begin painting with a series of mistakes. The painting comes out of the correction of mistakes by feeling. . . . The final picture is the process arrested at the moment when what I was looking for flashes into view." Robert Motherwell (American, 1915–1991), quoted in William C. Seitz, *Abstract Expressionist Painting in America* (Harvard University Press, 1983), p. 94.

# ARTIST CHRONOLOGY
## COMPILED BY DAWN BERG AND HEATHER SEALY LINEBERRY

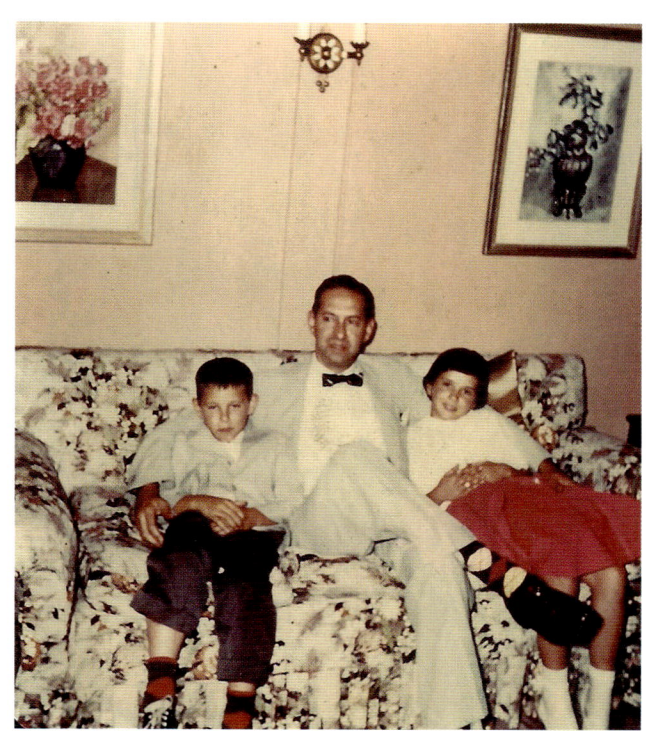

Fischl with his father, Karl, and older sister, Holly, c. 1954.

## 1948–55

Born March 9, 1948, in New York City. Father, Austrian American Karl Fischl, is a salesman for an industrial filmmaker. Mother Janet Fischl stays at home to care for Eric, his older sister, Holly, and younger siblings, Laurie and John. Family moves to Long Island and settles in a suburban commuter town on the north shore.

Like the Fischls, many white, middle-class families decamp to the suburbs in the early 1950s. They subscribe to the American Dream, believing everyone has the prospect of success and the opportunity for upward mobility. By 1955, more than half of Americans have a television, which, along with movies and popular magazines, entertains and reinforces values related to faith, patriotism, consumerism, and conformity to social norms.

At the same time is the rise of the modern civil rights movement. Martin Luther King Jr. and others organize nonviolent protests against racial discrimination throughout the South. On May 17, 1954, Supreme Court decides in *Brown v. Board of Education*, legally ending segregation in US public schools.

## 1956–57

Karl Fischl candidly discusses Janet's alcoholism and depression with the children, cautioning them not to share the information beyond the family. Later Fischl says, "It was this secretive nature of it that planted a seed of shame and deceitfulness that snakes through my childhood like a toxic vine."[1]

His childhood is defined by his mother's alcoholism and related, vicious arguments between his parents. Becomes a caretaker for his mother and siblings, resenting his father for not shielding them from a tumultuous home life. Janet often walks around nude, and on several occasions flees the home, resulting in at least one police encounter.

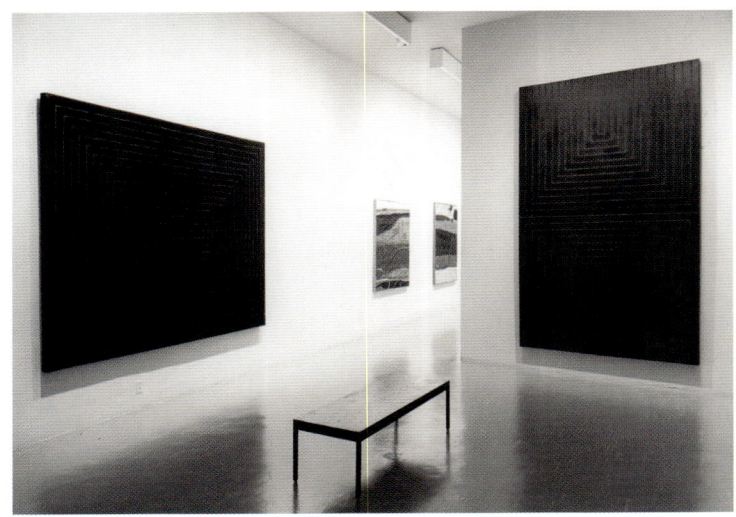

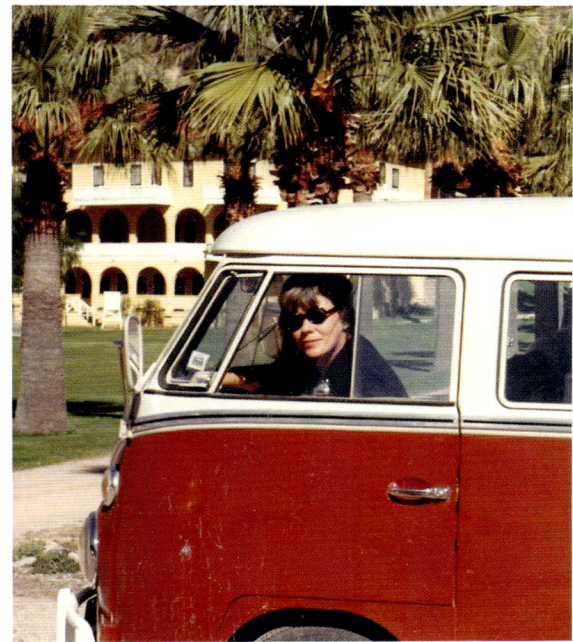

Installation view of *16 Americans* at the Museum of Modern Art, New York, December 16, 1959–February 17, 1960.

Fischl's mother, Janet.

## 1959

Minimalist painter Frank Stella exhibits his *Black Paintings* series at the Museum of Modern Art (MoMA), New York, as part of curator Dorothy C. Miller's *16 Americans* exhibition.

## 1963

At 15, sent with his sister Holly to boarding school at West Nottingham Academy in Maryland. He is an indifferent student but observes and learns to navigate the complex social scene. Has his first romance and gets into trouble hanging out with a crowd of outsiders. Leaves Nottingham for holiday breaks, although prefers boarding school over the chaos at home.

## 1966

Graduates from West Nottingham Academy and attends Waynesburg College, a small, liberal arts institution near Pittsburgh. At his father's advice, enrolls in business courses. Concludes his first year with poor grades and leaves school.

## 1967

Janet struggles with emphysema, and the family moves to Phoenix for the desert climate.

Rather than moving with his family, Fischl travels to San Francisco with friends. Lives communally in Haight-Ashbury, experimenting and exploring the profoundly antiestablishment Summer of Love. It is exhilarating but exhausting. Rejoins his family in Phoenix, which is a tremendous shock after San Francisco and suburban Long Island.

## 1968

Seeking to meet new people, enrolls in the local community college, Phoenix College, and takes a foundational art class. Artist and professor Merrill Mahaffey introduces him to painting. "He stressed alternative processes that demystified and democratized art and took it out of its traditional contexts: the academy, the museum and the gallery."[2] Finds energy and focus in making art. Janet is pleased, Karl is not.

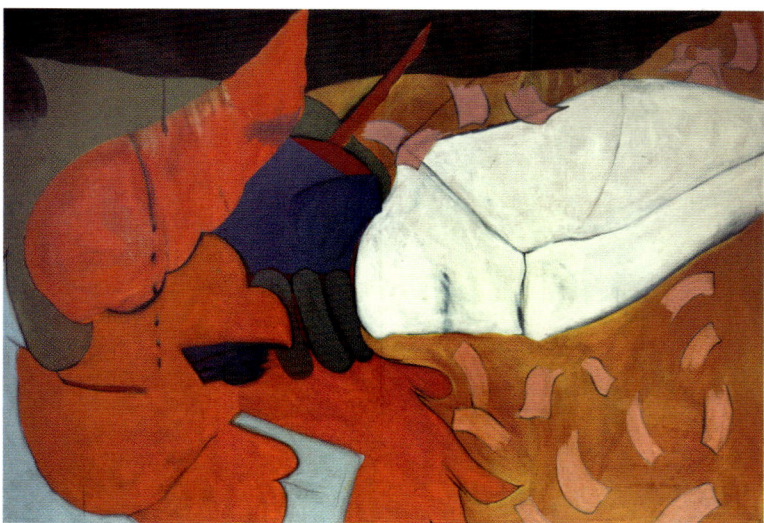

Eric Fischl, *Untitled*, 1969. Oil on canvas. 48 × 72 in. (121.92 × 182.88 cm). Private Collection.

## 1969

Receives notice to report for the Vietnam War draft lottery. Opposed to America's involvement in the war, which began in the 1950s, he was lucky that Phoenix had already satisfied its quota.

Transfers to Arizona State University (ASU) and enrolls in the BFA program. Under the mentorship of instructor and painter Bill Swaim, explores art history, particularly modernism and abstraction. "Bill opened my eyes to his midcentury enthusiasm for the Russian avant-garde, especially [Wassily] Kandinsky. I discovered the formal, intellectual, and spiritual demands of pure abstraction. My world had suddenly gotten bigger."[3] Shares a studio space near ASU's campus with Mahaffey.

Paints a white bed floating in abstract space; beds will play a significant role in his work.

## 1970

Reads in major art publications that painting is dead. The pervasive dialogue in the art world is that painting, particularly figurative painting, is no longer relevant with focus instead on Minimalism, Conceptualism, and a range of new art forms. Later recalls, "I'm a painter, so obviously I believed that the activity had value, but I always believed that your job was to prove it. . . . So every abstract painting was an attempt to prove that it was still alive, and every image painting was an even greater effort to bring back integrity to something that had been degraded."[4]

Encouraged by Swaim to apply to California Institute of the Arts (CalArts) and receives a full scholarship to their inaugural class. Convening a faculty of some of the most forward-thinking voices of the time across visual art, design, film, music, theater, and dance, the progressive institution favors independent work and collegial relationships instead of traditional curricula and professor-student hierarchies. The school's visual art program features innovative artists/professors including Judy Chicago, Allan Kaprow, Nam June Paik, John Baldessari, and Miriam Shapiro. In its first and famously chaotic academic year on an interim campus in Burbank, the school becomes a counterculture center with parties, protests, and social experimentation.

Days before classes start, Janet dies in a car crash after drinking heavily.

Paints large, abstract paintings under the mentorship of Allan Hacklin and Paul Brach, the CalArts painting faculty. Later describes his work, which is praised by Hacklin, as "canvases primed with flat, primary colors—where I floated squiggly tubular shapes."[5]

Shares a studio with student and painter David Salle. Disagree on issues related to their respective practices but become close friends.

## 1971–72

Invited by a classmate to help paint murals in a Los Angeles bar. Fischl paints a figurative scene of a naked couple. The man, to his surprise and chagrin, bore a resemblance to President Richard Nixon. Remembers it as "the most fun I'd had painting in a long time."[6]

Frustrated by the stylistic dominance of abstraction, gathers inspiration from artists like William T. Wiley, Alan Shields, and Jonathan Borofsky, who utilized representational imagery. Collages pictures of cowboys and images of the West; the paintings are summarily dismissed by his professors.

## 1972–73

Receives his BFA from CalArts in 1972 at the age of 23 and moves to Chicago. Works at the Museum of Contemporary Art as a guard and installation assistant. Meets artists and collectors, visits museums and galleries, and spends hours in the Art Institute of Chicago absorbing the way that painters capture the figure throughout art history.

The Hairy Who, including Jim Nutt and Ed Paschke, is the dominant school of painters in Chicago. They create brash, sexually charged, imagistic, neo-pop paintings. Experiments with the group's techniques but doesn't share their "perverse glee at the insanity of pop culture."[7] However, it does suggest a path other than abstraction.

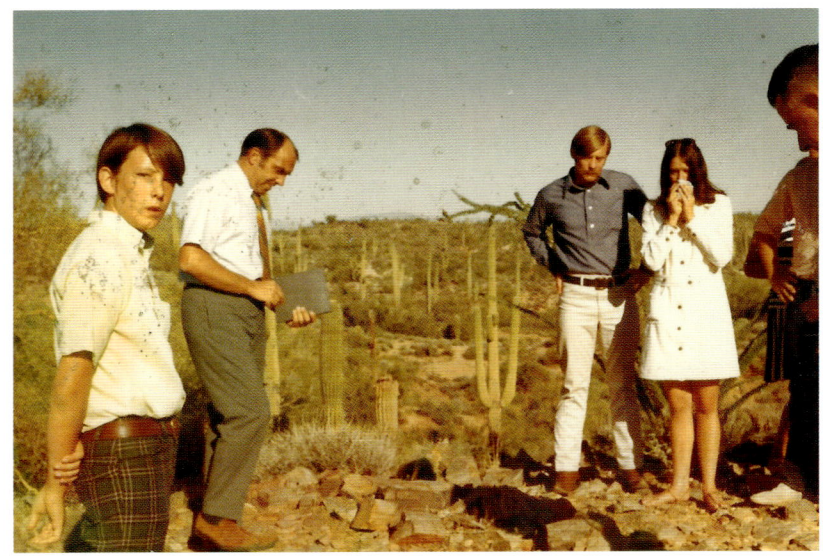

Janet Fischl's funeral in Phoenix, Arizona, 1970.

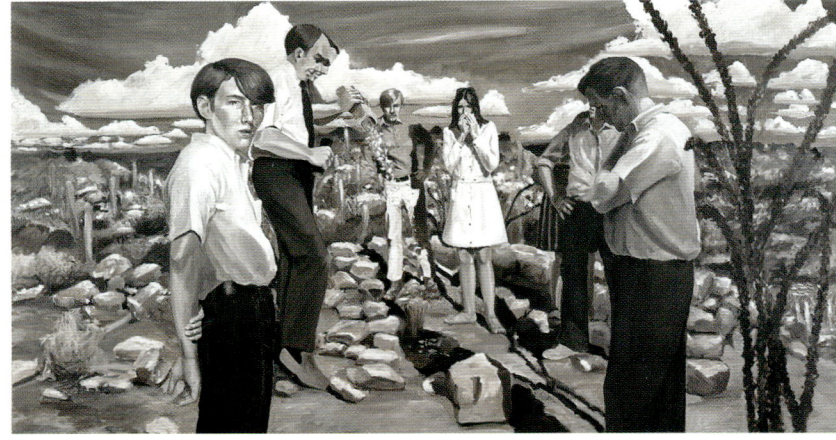

Eric Fischl, *The Funeral*, 1980. Oil on canvas. 55⅛ × 103⅛ in. (139.8 x 261.8 cm). Hirshhorn Museum and Sculpture Garden, Regents Collections Acquisition Program with Matching Funds from the Jerome L. Greene, Sydney and Frances Lewis, and Leonard C. Yaseen Purchase Fund, and the Joseph H. Hirshhorn Purchase Fund, 1990.

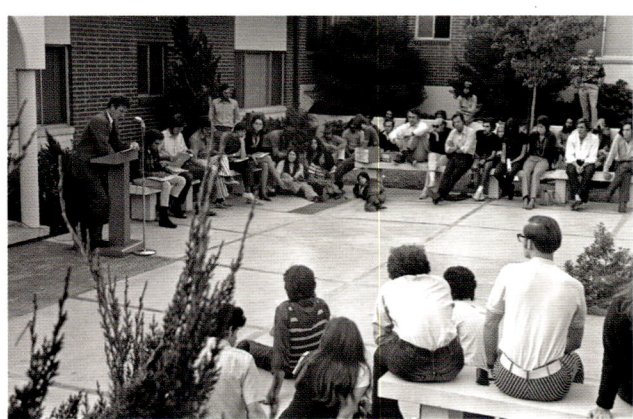

Opening day at CalArts interim Burbank campus, 1970.

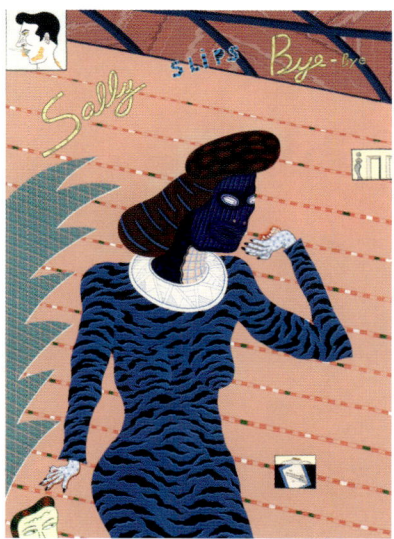

Jim Nutt (American, b. 1938), *Sally Slips Bye-Bye*, 1972. Acrylic on canvas. 42 × 31⅛ in. (106.7 × 79 cm). The Art Institute of Chicago, Gift of the Robert A. Lewis Fund in memory of William and Polly Levey, 1982.396.

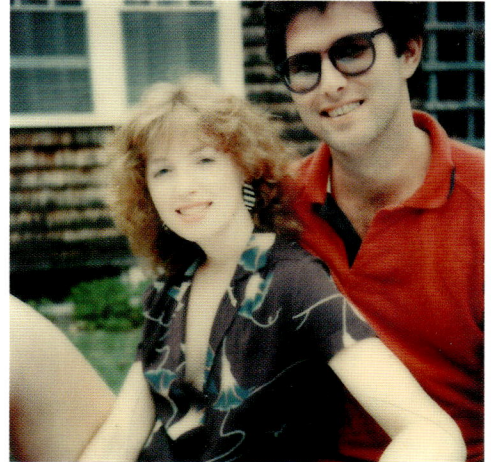

Fischl with April Gornik at the beginning of their relationship.

## 1974

Takes a teaching position at Nova Scotia College of Art and Design (NSCAD) in Halifax, Canada, regarded as one of the best art schools in North America. Like CalArts, it was focused on Minimalism and conceptual art and championed artists like Carl Andre, Lawrence Weiner, Vito Acconci, and Joseph Beuys. This proves to be a key period in his development as an artist as he struggles with his work and its relevance. Later recalls, "the trajectory of my life, my career and my achievements all have a direct relationship to NSCAD."[8]

Travels regularly to New York City to visit galleries and exhibitions.

## 1975

Promoted to assistant professor at NSCAD.

In October, *Bridge Shield Shelter*, curated by Bruce W. Ferguson at Dalhousie Art Gallery in Halifax, is his first solo exhibition. Features early abstract paintings and includes a catalog with texts by the artist.

Allan MacKay selects two of his abstract paintings for the exhibition *Canada Canvas* organized by Time-Life. Exhibition travels throughout Canada, and the Edmonton Art Gallery purchases a work—his first painting sale.

Begins a transition to figuration, taking on "the look and feel of the physical world. . . . I was starting to tell stories."[9] Draws from his coastal surroundings to paint an imaginary, archetypal nuclear family of fishers. Psychological tensions between the figures and their portentous objects, like a bathtub and chairs, are there from the start.

Swiss curator Jean-Christophe Ammann visits his studio and admires black-and-white images of houses, boats, bridges, sleds, furniture, fish, and human figures painted directly on the wall. Ammann selects four works, including two large murals on poster board, for a Kunsthalle Basel exhibition of promising young Canadian artists in 1978.

Meets April Gornik (b. 1953), originally from Cleveland, in her last year of the BFA program at NSCAD. Eventually she becomes his romantic partner, artist colleague, and lifelong muse (though not always recognizable or identified). Later compares his study of her form to that of nineteenth-century French painter Pierre Bonnard, who painted his wife, Marthe, throughout his career.

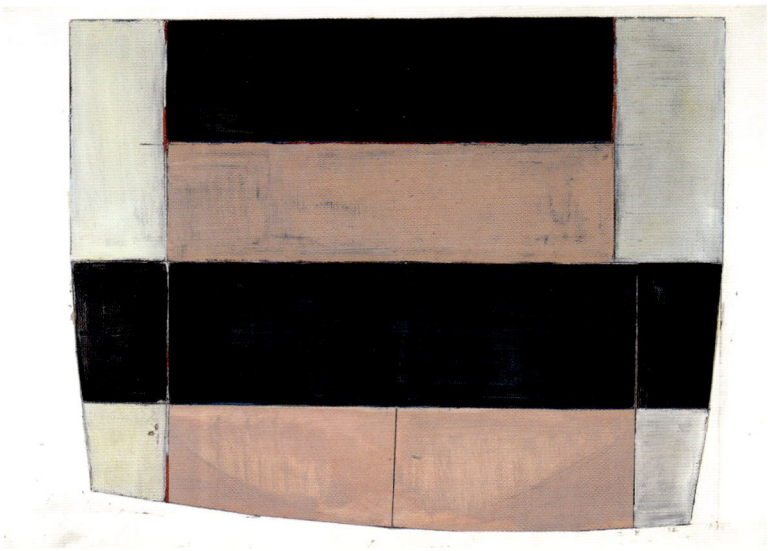

Eric Fischl, *Shield*, 1974. Oil and wax on paper. 21 × 29¾ in. (53.34 × 75.565 cm). Private Collection.

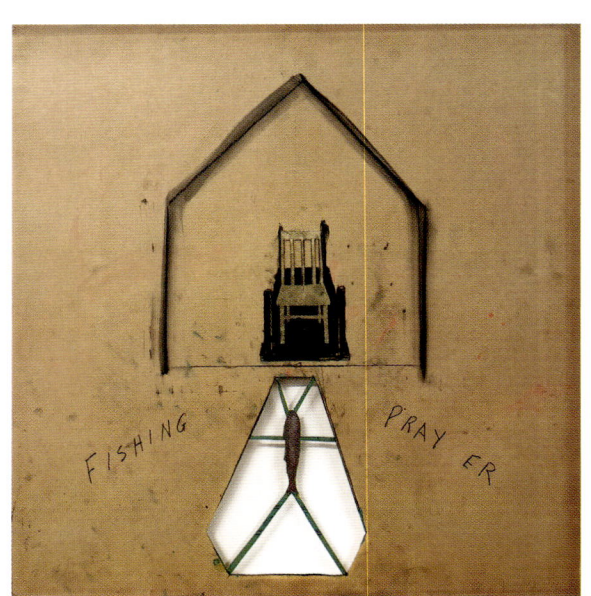

Eric Fischl, *Untitled (Fishing Prayer)*, 1976. Mixed media on paper. 21¾ × 21¾ in. (55.245 × 55.245 cm). Collection of the artist.

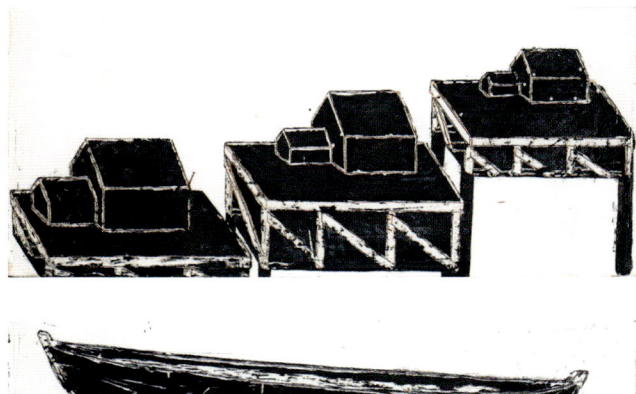

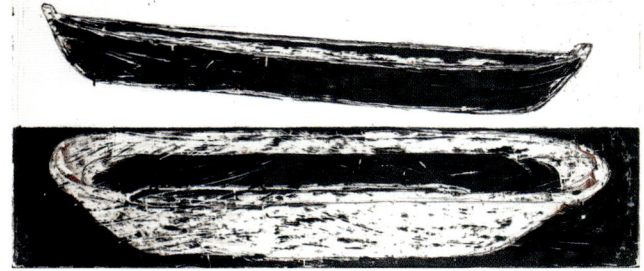

Eric Fischl, *Study for Boat and Tub*, maquette for mural (two-sided), 1976. Oil and beeswax on wood. 24 × 48 in. (60.96 × 121.92 cm). Collection of the artist.

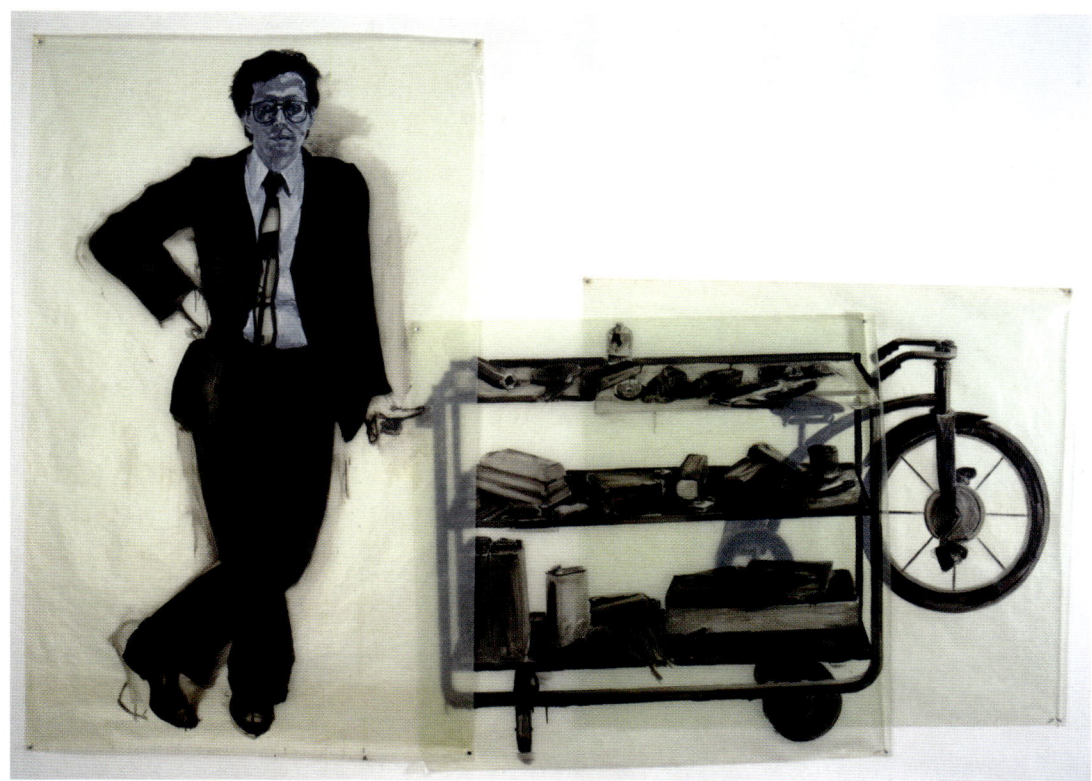

Eric Fischl, *Self Portrait*, 1980. Oil on glassine. 113 × 78½ in.
(287 × 199.4 cm). Private Collection.

## 1976

Begins painting in oil on glassine. The slick, forgiving
surface and large size (four-by-ten-foot rolls) allow
him to paint spontaneously with his whole arm. Its
transparency enables him to overlay figures and
objects in a manner that would unlock his later compositional process (PLATES 34, 41).

## 1977

With Gornik, travels to Europe for the first time. Visits
the Louvre in Paris, the Uffizi in Florence, and the
Prado in Madrid, gathering inspiration from the work
of Michelangelo, Donatello, Jean-Auguste-Dominique
Ingres, Jacques-Louis David, and Diego Velázquez,
among others. Begins to travel often to Europe, and
France in particular, to study figurative painting.

Stages a performance of the fisher family narrative
in three Canadian cities. Writes chants, which are
performed by a composer and singer while he draws
mural-sized images of the mother in a bathtub.
Experiments with painting, sculpture, collage, text,
and performance to represent and animate the lives
of this imaginary family.

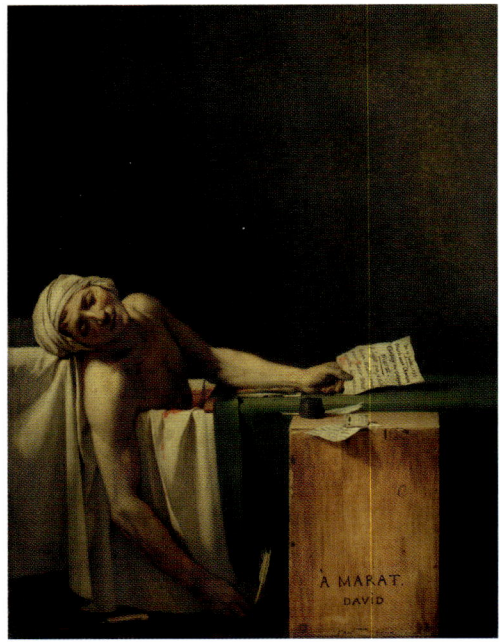

Jacques-Louis David (French, 1748–1825), *Marat assassiné (The Death of Marat)*, 1793. Oil on canvas. 70 × 50⅝ in. (165 × 128 cm). Musées Royaux des Beaux-Arts/Brussels/Belgium, Legs de M. Jules-David Chassagnol, Paris, 1886.

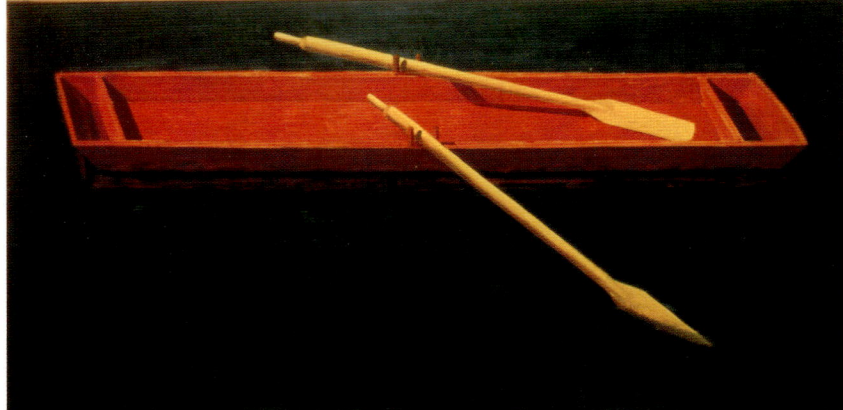

Eric Fischl, *Rowboat*, 1978. Oil on plywood. 48 × 96 in. (121.9 × 243.8 cm). Collection unknown.

## 1978

Artist Joseph Beuys is the commencement speaker at NSCAD.

The National Gallery of Canada, Ottawa, purchases six of Fischl's early paintings.

Paints his last artwork in Halifax. *Rowboat,* a full-color oil painting, signals a more developed style.

Resigns from his position at NSCAD, and Gornik graduates. Together, move to New York City, joining other CalArts alumni and friends, and quickly becoming part of a vibrant art and social scene which included artists of the Pictures Generation—Cindy Sherman, Robert Longo, Barbara Kruger, and Sherrie Levine—and artists soon to be associated with Neo-Expressionism, including Julian Schnabel and former studio-mate Salle. Both movements focus on a return to recognizable imagery in art.

Works as an art handler. In the studio, begins to transition to more complex, psychological narratives based upon his own experiences.

In December, the group exhibition *New Image Painting* opens at the Whitney Museum of American Art, New York. Curator Richard Marshall proposes that recognizable imagery is slinking back into painting and features work done within the last four years. Fischl particularly recalls the work of Susan Rothenberg and David True.

## 1979

Paints *Sleepwalker*, a large, startling painting of an adolescent boy either urinating or masturbating in a backyard kiddie pool (SEE FIG. 27). "I deliberately chose my subject because it was taboo. Like many of my peers, I was testing the bounds of propriety, both socially and artistically, trying to get people to notice my work." *Sleepwalker* lays the groundwork for themes that will continue throughout his career and quickly draws attention. Critic Donald Kuspit calls it Fischl's "first fully articulated statement of purpose."[10]

Increasingly looks at historic painters, including Édouard Manet, Edgar Degas, Winslow Homer, Pierre Bonnard, Max Beckmann, and Edward Hopper.

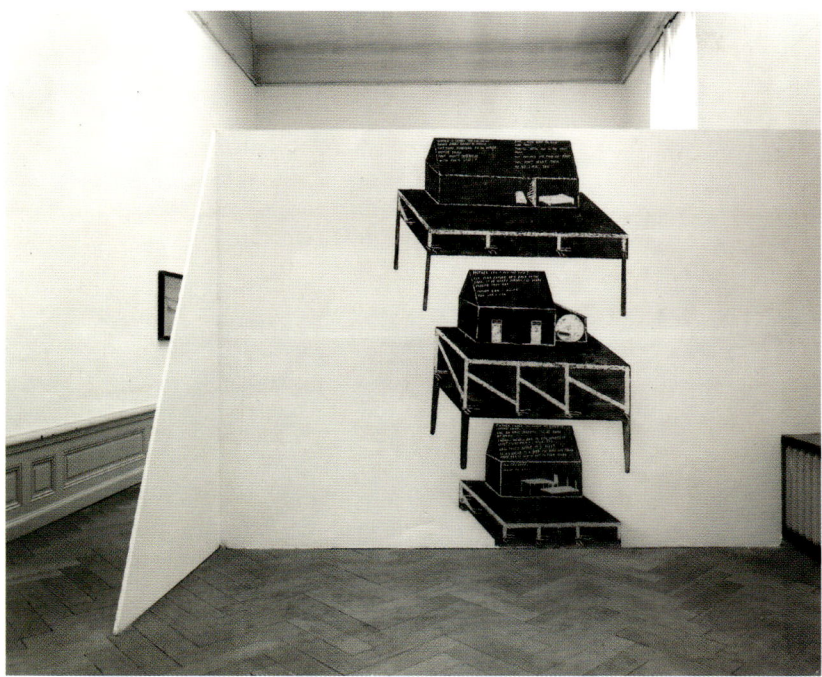

Eric Fischl, *Mural*, 1978. Oil and wax resist on plaster board. 96 × 144 in. (243.84 × 365.76 cm).

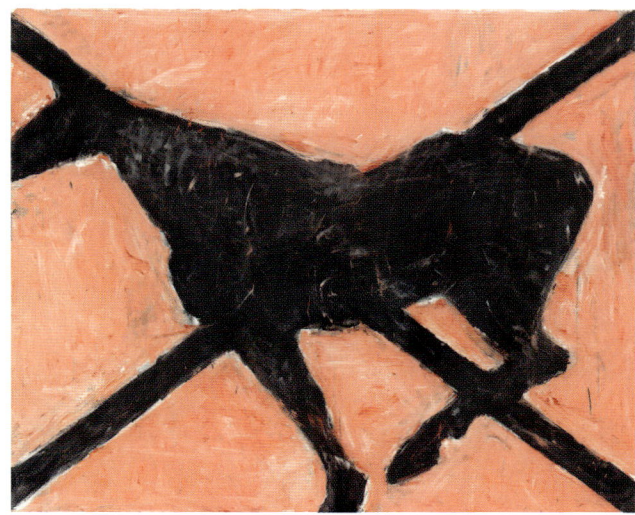

Susan Rothenberg (American, 1945–2020), *Butterfly*, 1976. Acrylic on canvas. 69½ × 83 in. (176.5 × 210.8 cm). Gift of Perry R. and Nancy Lee Bass. National Gallery of Art, Washington 1995.6.1.

On July 15, President Jimmy Carter delivers his "crisis of confidence" speech—or what his detractors call the "malaise" speech—addressing the energy crisis, unemployment, and inflation. Calls on Americans to face up to the crisis in their own values.

Mary Boone Gallery mounts a sold-out show of Schnabel's well-known plate paintings; Sherman presents her acclaimed *Untitled Film Stills* at the Metro Pictures gallery; and Gagosian Gallery presents a solo show with Salle. The exhibitions are another indication that artists, particularly in New York, are introducing recognizable figures and objects into their work with ambiguous, edgy, and discomfiting impact.

## 1980

Sells out his first solo exhibition at Edward Thorp Gallery. Critics identify his new paintings as commentaries on the crisis of American identity.

Captures the emotions and tension of his mother's burial a decade earlier in *A Funeral*.

Increasing pluralism in the art world and new voices rise, particularly women and artists of color, exploring the figure and identity politics.

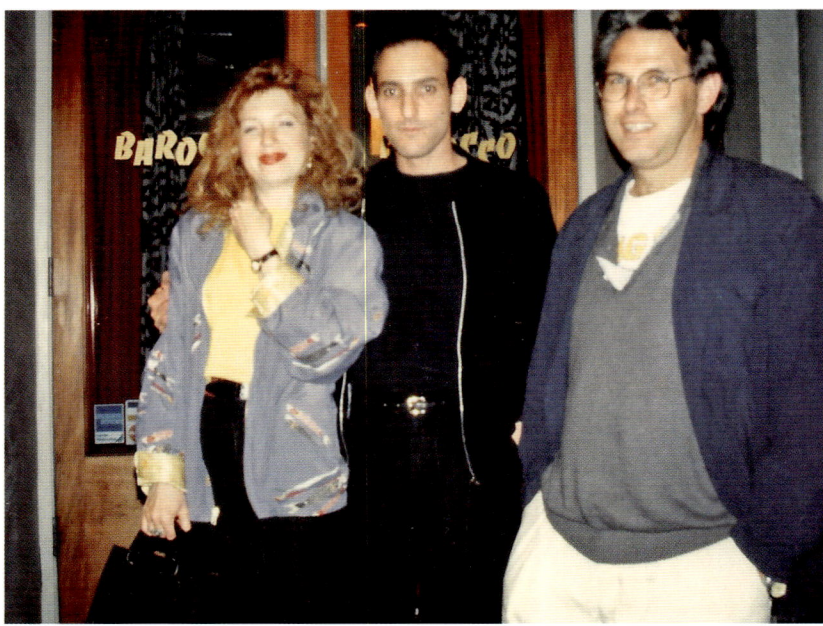

April Gornik, David Salle, and Fischl in New York, 1980s.

## 1981

Sable-Castelli Gallery in Toronto mounts an exhibition of his work. Receives an enthusiastic full-page review focusing on *A Woman Possessed,* an autobiographical work depicting a woman passed out on a driveway and being dragged away by an adolescent boy (PLATE 25). Shares the review with his father and siblings, who have mixed responses.

Neo-Expressionism in European and American contemporary painting is codified by a survey exhibition, *A New Spirit in Painting*, curated by Norman Rosenthal for the Royal Academy, London.

Paints *Bad Boy* (PLATE 15) and *Grief.* The ambiguity and psychological and sexual tension in the former, and the exploration of grief and death in the latter, become recurring themes. *Art in America* critic Peter Schjeldahl describes *Grief* as "Fischl's first completely masterful work."[11]

Works are included in numerous group exhibitions across the US exploring new realism and figuration.

## 1982

Ronald Reagan's presidency (1981–89) brings heightened social and economic conservatism. "Reaganomics" calls for corporate deregulation, reductions in government spending, and tax cuts. Materialism and consumerism are on the rise, cable networks like CNN and MTV emerge, blockbuster movies prevail, and the first IBM personal computer is introduced. Booming equities and real estate markets, fed by gentrification, characterize New York City.

Prosperous and heady time in the New York art world, with many new galleries and collectors. Quits his art handling job with increasing sales and critical acclaim. Life with Gornik includes exhibition openings, drug- and alcohol-fueled parties, and lavish restaurants, clubs, and travel.

Travels to Venice, Italy. Borrowing a friend's camera, starts photographing groups on the beaches at Lido. Begins using photographs more freely and actively in his compositional process. This allows him to capture animated bodies more quickly and spontaneously than sketching.

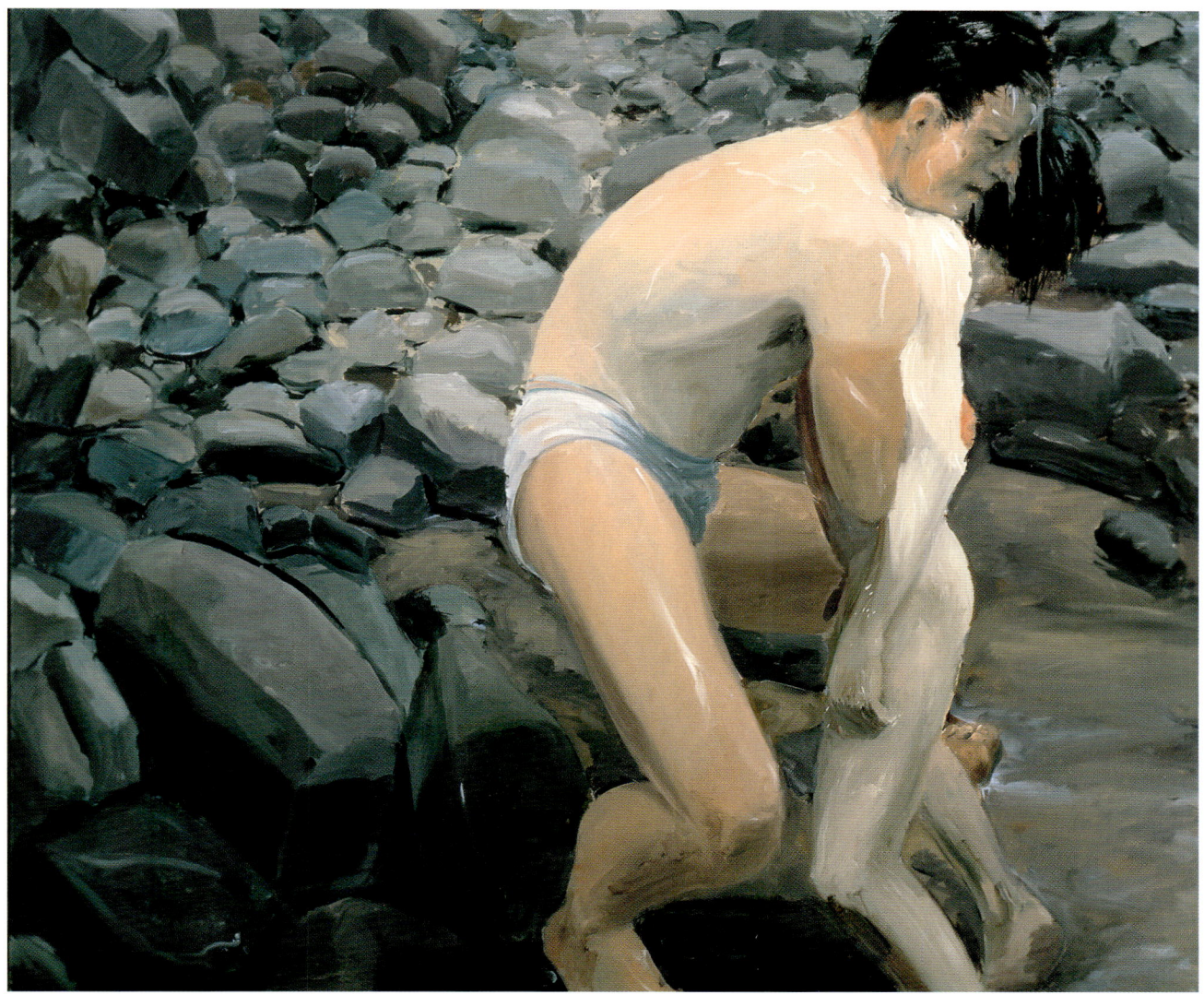

**Eric Fischl**, *Grief*, **1981**. Oil on canvas. 60 × 65 in. (152.4 × 165.1 cm).
Cincinnati Art Museum; Gift of RSM Co., 1986.1343.

*The Old Man's Boat and the Old Man's Dog* showcases an increasing ability to paint complex compositions (PLATE 35).

Works are included in *Focus on the Figure: Twenty Years* at the Whitney Museum, New York, and *American Still Life 1945–1983* at the Contemporary Arts Museum, Houston, which travels nationally. Other group exhibitions in Japan, Germany, Italy, and Spain.

In December and January of 1983, *Art in America* dedicates two issues to exploring "The Expressionism Question." Featured artists include Fischl, Salle, Schnabel, Rothenberg, Joan Snyder, and Pat Steir, among others.

# 1983

Receives first invitation to participate in the closely watched Whitney Biennial at the Whitney Museum. *Inside Out* and *The Old Man's Boat and Old Man's Dog* are included (SEE FIG. 26).

May and June spent in Saint-Tropez, France. Takes hundreds of pictures of bodies in motion on daily beach visits. Struck by the unselfconsciousness of nude French bathers of all ages. Paintings set at the beach recur throughout his career.

The diptych *A Visit to / A Visit From / The Island* contrasts a nude white family frolicking at a beach with a panel showing the desperation of Haitian refugees trying to come ashore in a storm with deadly consequences (see FIG. 23). Black and brown figures appear in Fischl's work with ambiguous intent: as participants in the privileged settings, threatening white privilege and assumptions, or pointedly exposing it.

Incorporates non-Western sculpture into many of his domestic settings, as in *Slumber Party* (PLATE 17). "I grew up in an environment where every house I went into had some object that was foreign. . . . It was meant to represent worldliness, but what it really highlighted was the smallness of their own reality set against this object they didn't really know anything about."[12]

Experiments with multipanel paintings to deconstruct narratives; compositions recall the paintings on glassine.

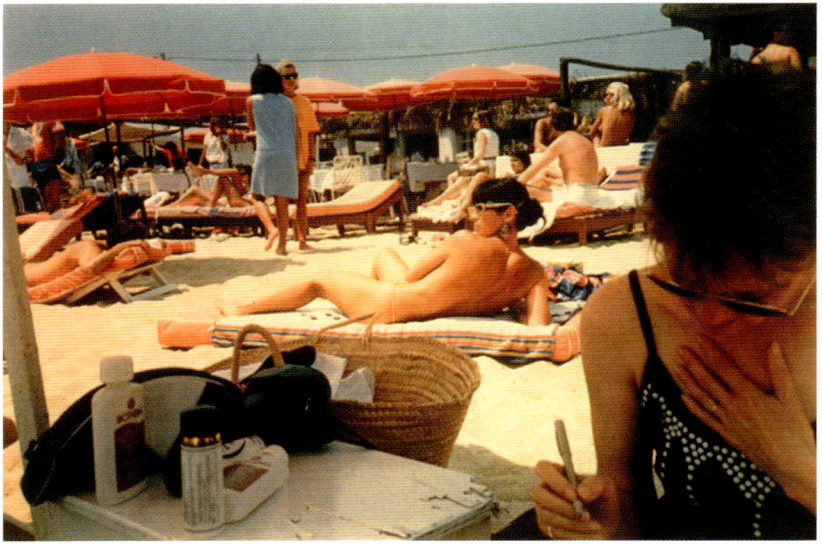

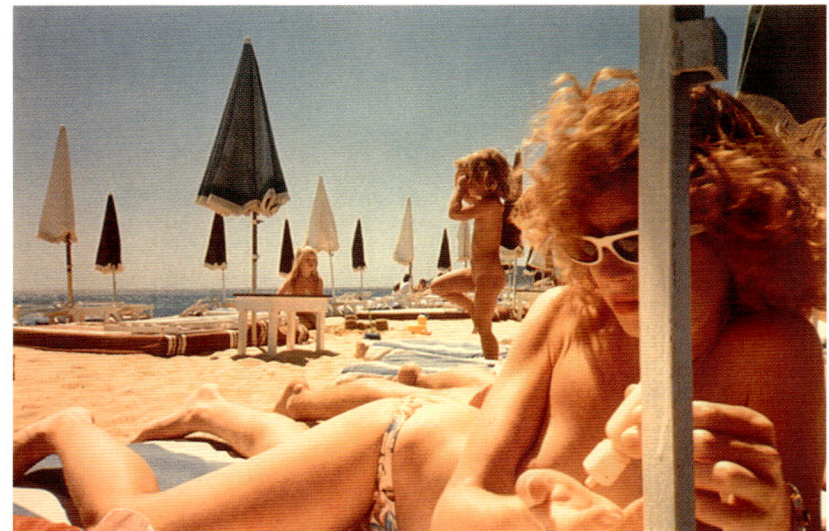

Fischl's photographs from Saint-Tropez, 1983.

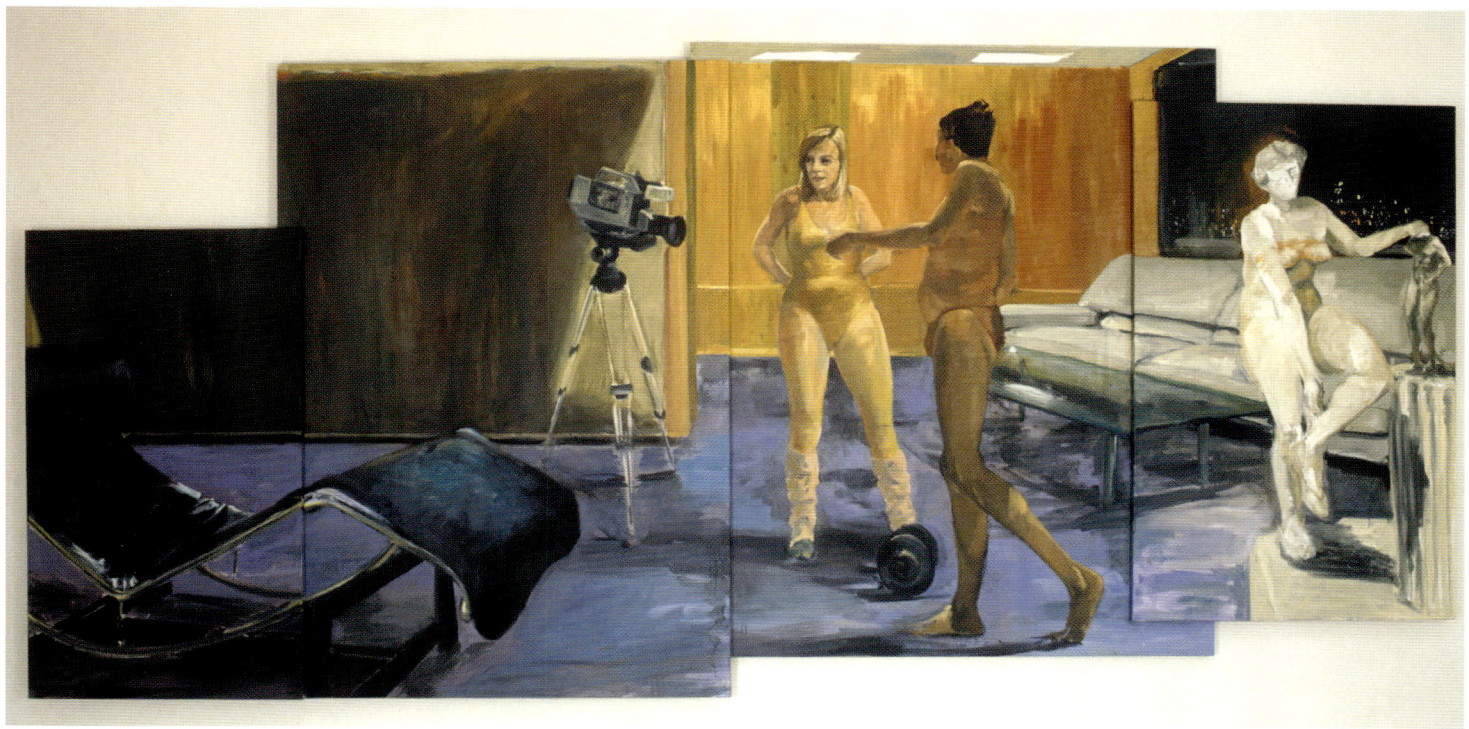

Eric Fischl, *Fort Worth*, 1985. Oil on canvas. 98 × 216 in.
(248.9 × 548.6 cm). The Broad Art Foundation.

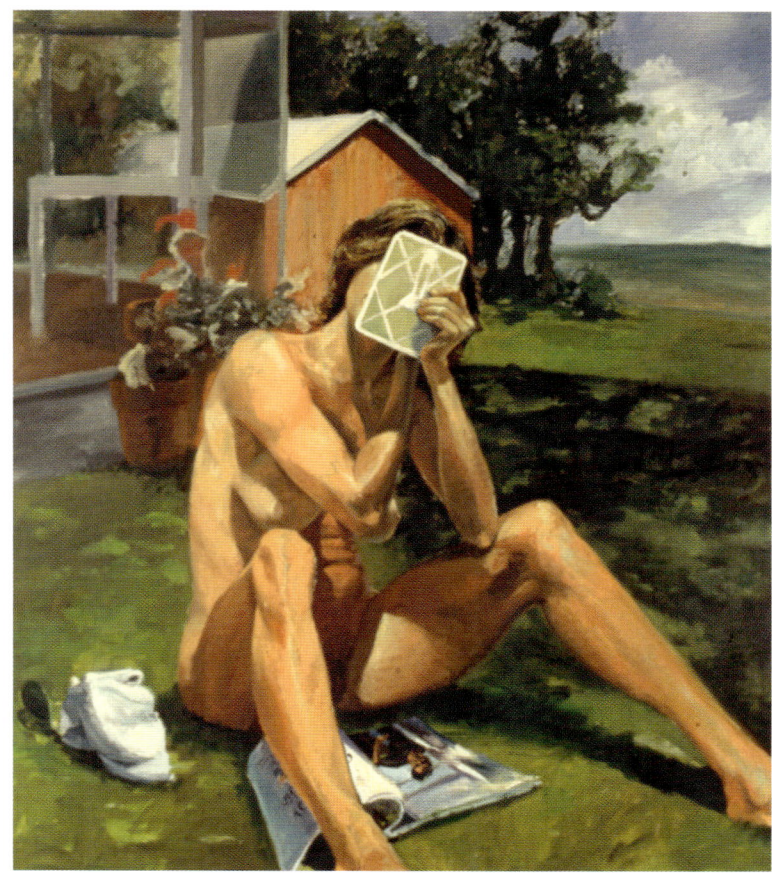

Eric Fischl, *Vanity*, 1984. Oil on canvas. 108 × 96 in. (274.3 × 243.8 cm).
Collection unknown.

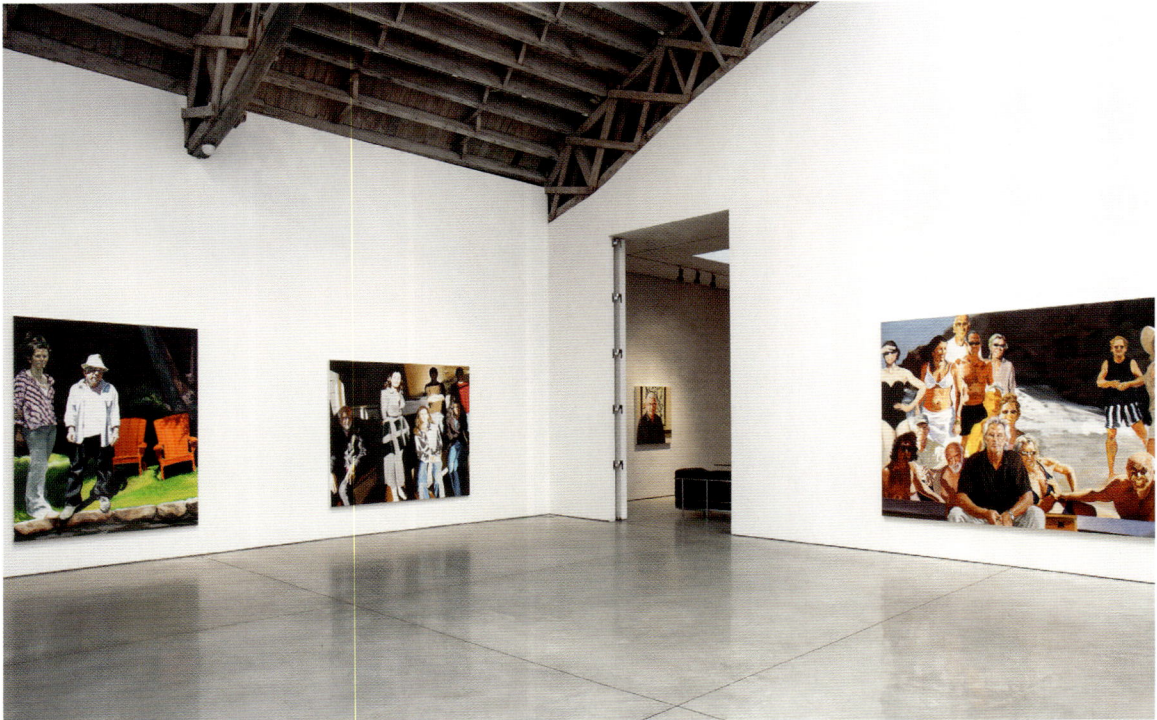

Installation view from *Eric Fischl Portraits* at Mary Boone Gallery (February 11–March 13, 2012), New York. From left to right: *Edie and Paul* (2010), *The Clemente Family* (2005), and *Self Portrait: An Unfinished Work* (2011).

# 1984

Included in *Paradise Lost/Paradise Regained: American Visions of the New Decade*, the group exhibition in the US Pavilion at the Venice Biennale organized by The New Museum of Contemporary Art, New York.

Six-page feature by Schjeldahl, "Bad Boy of Brilliance," in May issue of *Vanity Fair*. Paints *Vanity*, exploring the contradictions of celebrity.

Through an introduction from Salle, and after seeing the painting *St. Tropez*, Mary Boone agrees to represent him (PLATE 36). Sells out his first exhibition in October, with three paintings going to museums. Mary Boone Gallery presents regular exhibitions of his work into 2012.

Father takes him to a nudist colony in the south of France. Fischl describes the experience as both "ordinary and surreal" and "like one of my paintings come to life."[13] Paints *Portrait of the Artist as an Old Man* (SEE FIG. 19).

Included in *American Neo-Expressionists*, the first museum exhibition to fully address the loose movement, at the Aldrich Contemporary Art Museum, Ridgefield, Connecticut.

Included in more than fifteen other group exhibitions at US and international museums, including MoMA, San Francisco Museum of Modern Art, and Hirshhorn Museum and Sculpture Garden, Washington, DC. Exhibitions focus on new American painting, the New York scene, and figurative work.

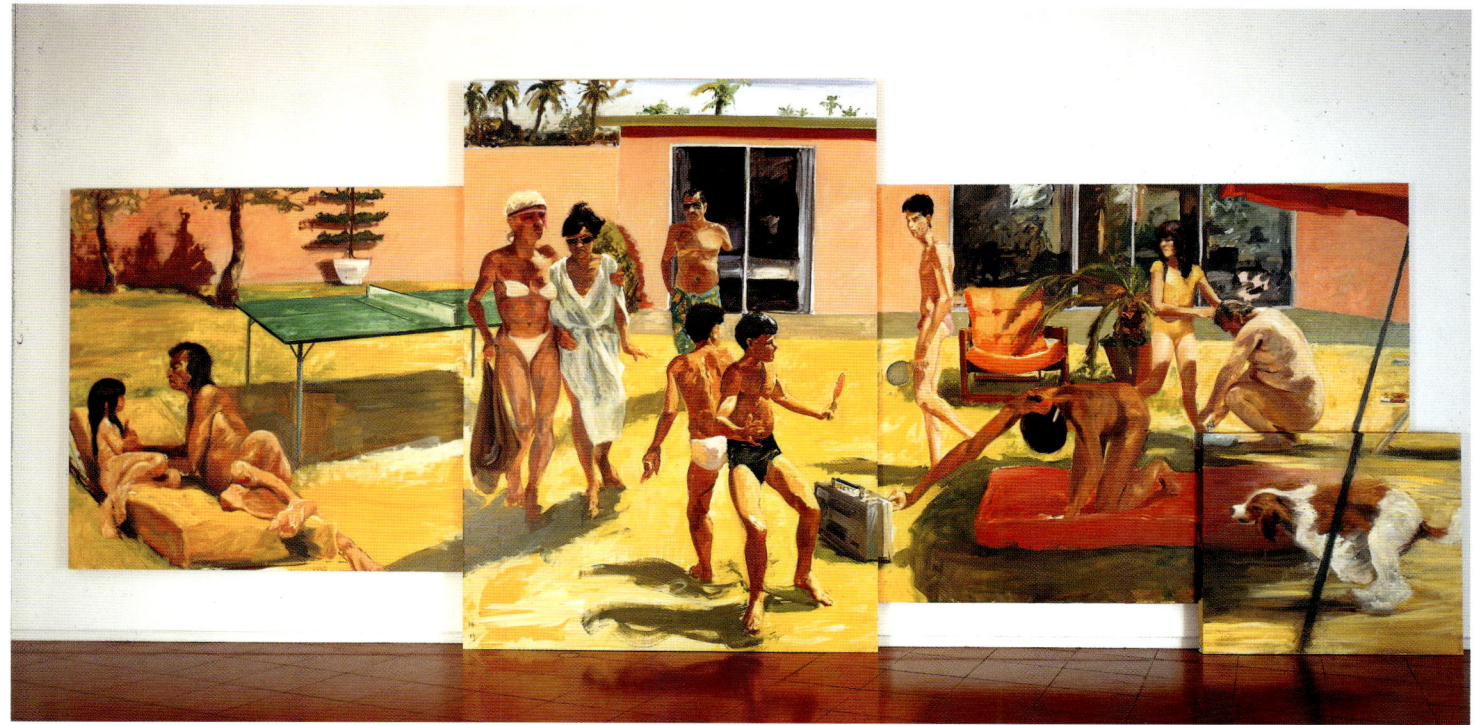

Eric Fischl, *Saigon Minnesota*, 1985. Oil on canvas. 120 × 296 in. (304.8 × 752 cm). National Gallery of Art, Robert and Jane Meyerhoff Collection (1992.28.71).

# 1985

Ferguson curates solo exhibition with catalog at Mendel Art Gallery in Saskatoon, Canada, which travels into 1986 to Van Abbemuseum, Eindhoven, the Netherlands; Kunsthalle Basel; the Institute of Contemporary Arts, London; the Art Gallery of Ontario, Toronto; and Museum of Contemporary Art, Chicago. An expanded version with twenty-eight paintings ends at the Whitney Museum. American art critic and philosopher Arthur C. Danto positively reviews the exhibition. In London, the exhibition is picketed by women against violence to women.

*Saigon Minnesota*, a four-panel painting, marks a shift to more specific references to current events. Asian American figures refer to the US involvement in Vietnam. It also draws on his horror over a report of child sexual abuse, child pornography, and murder in a small Minnesota town.

With Gornik, buys a small farmhouse in Sag Harbor, a historic whaling village on the East End of Long Island, New York. Split their time between New York City and Sag Harbor.

Experiments with different printing techniques including aquatint, etching, and monotypes.

The *Carnegie International*, at the Carnegie Museum of Art, Pittsburgh, includes *Dog Days* (1983), *Imitating the Dog (Mother and Daughter II)* (1984), and *A Brief History of North Africa* (1985).

Schjeldahl writes "Post-Innocence: Eric Fischl and the Social Fate of American Painting," for the international art magazine *Parkett*. Creates *Squatter,* an original etching, for the publication, which also includes an artist interview by Gerald Marzorati.

*Portrait of the Artist as an Old Man* and *The Power of Rock and Roll* included in the Whitney Biennial.

Eli and Edyth Broad acquire *Haircut* (1985) and go on to collect thirteen more paintings.

## 1986

Quits drinking and drugs after some concerning episodes and considering his family history.

*Eric Fischl: Scenes Before the Eye*, curated by Constance Glenn for University Art Museum, California State University, Long Beach, focuses on works on paper. Travels to the University Art Museum, University of California, Berkeley; Contemporary Arts Center, Honolulu; Baltimore Museum of Art; and Saint Louis Art Museum.

Collaborates with *Village Voice* art critic Jerry Saltz on the book *Sketchbook with Voices*.

Lectures at Yale School of Art. Women students give a forceful feminist critique of his work. Returns to Yale as a visiting artist in 2004–2005, 2008–2009, and 2013–14, and receives strikingly different responses from the students. "The first time, I was attacked by feminists. The second time, I was attacked by Marxists. The third time: 'Can you tell me who pays for framing?' So, business has entered the room."[14]

## 1987

In June, international exhibition *documenta 8* opens in Kassel, Germany, with a focus on the sociopolitical responsibility of art. Three multipanel paintings are featured: *Catboy* (1986), *Scarsdale* (1986), and *Portrait of a Dog* (1987).

Sees an exhibition of photographs by Pierre Bonnard at the Musee d'Orsay, Paris (October 1987–January 1988). Struck by their combination of domesticity, innocence, anxiety, and awkwardness.

On October 19, US stock market crashes, bringing economic instability and fears of a depression. The art market plateaus and New York galleries close, yet his prices continue to rise.

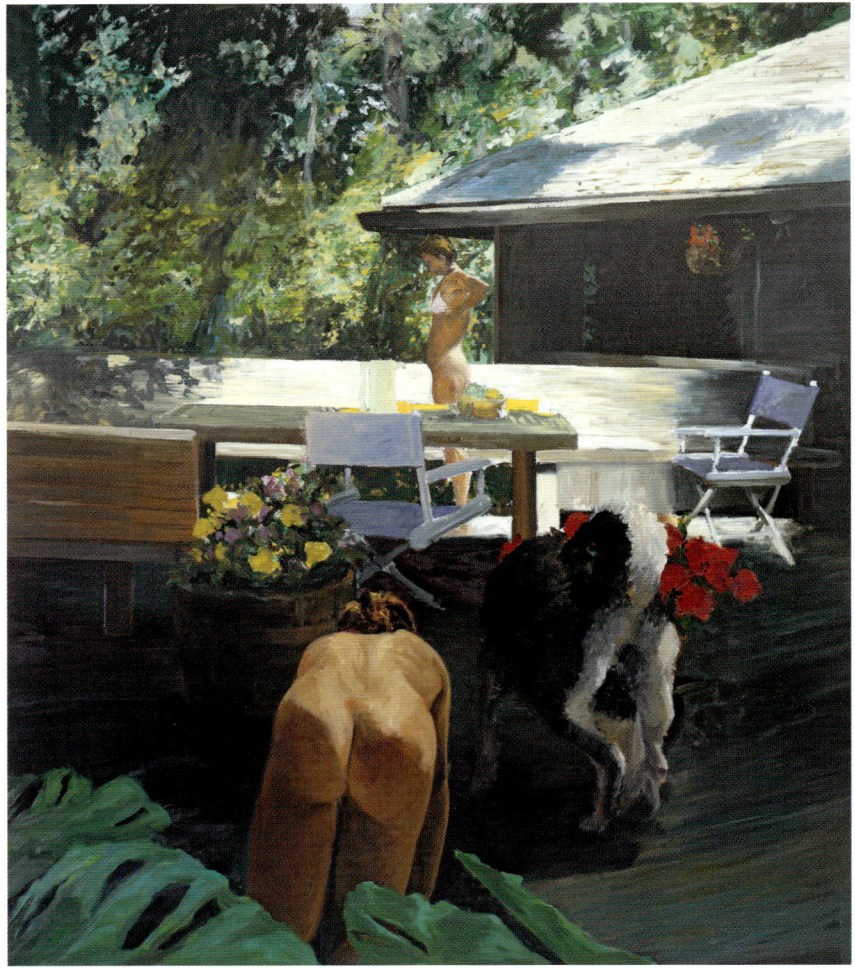

Eric Fischl, *Imitating the Dog (Mother and Daughter II)*, 1984. Oil on canvas. 96 × 84 in. (243.8 × 213.4 cm). Collection unknown.

Featured in group exhibitions at more than a dozen US and international museums, including *Avant-Garde in the Eighties*, Los Angeles County Museum of Art, and *Past/Imperfect: Eric Fischl, Vernon Fisher, Laurie Simmons*, Walker Art Center, Minneapolis, which travels nationally.

## 1988

After a fire in their New York apartment, lives for more than a year in Sag Harbor with Gornik. Time away from the pressure and scrutiny of the art world is liberating. Starts to "play" in the studio and makes a series of small clay maquettes, then photographs them in black and white to fully study the body.

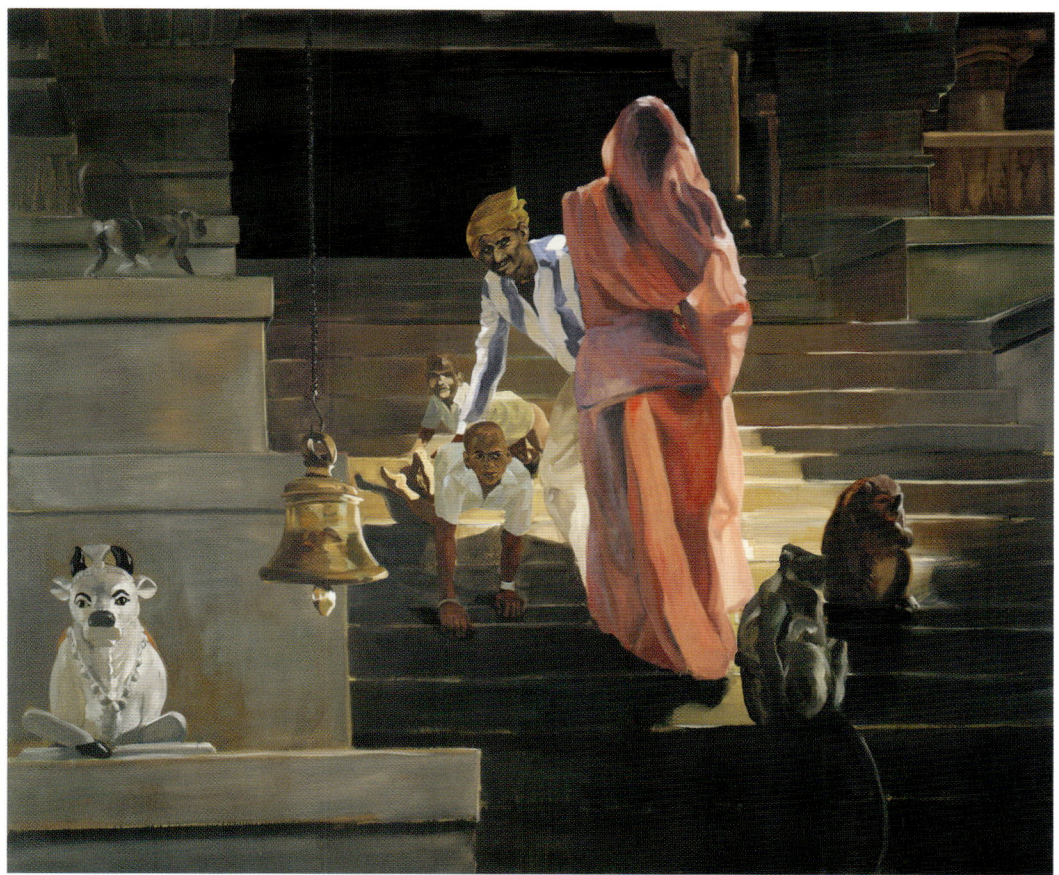

Eric Fischl, *On the Stairs of the Temple*, 1989. Oil on linen. 115 × 140 in. (292.1 × 355.6 cm). Collection of Neda Young.

Metropolitan Museum of Art, New York, presents *Degas*, the first large-scale retrospective exhibition of the work of Edgar Degas in more than fifty years.

Monograph *Eric Fischl* is published, including an essay by Schjeldahl, who calls Fischl "the first great painter of the United States in decline," and argues that no contemporary artist other than Anselm Kiefer "so illuminates (not just illustrates, not just symptomizes) civilization's current state."[15]

Philip Roth, American novelist and author of short stories known for his controversial explorations of American identity and masculinity, writes the catalog essay for Fischl's exhibition at Mary Boone Gallery and Galerie Michael Werner, Cologne, Germany. In *Time*, art critic Robert Hughes reviews the exhibition and calls Fischl "the painter laureate of American anxiety in the '80s."[16]

# 1989

Meets Irish-born British painter Francis Bacon, whom he considers a master of abstract figuration, at Fischl's exhibition at Waddington Galleries, London.

Spends a month in Ahmedabad, India, as an artist-in-residence with Gornik at Villa Sarabhai, a family estate designed by Swiss modernist architect Le Corbusier. The social settings, spaces, and lived experiences are strikingly different from his life to date. Returns with hundreds of photographs. Paints a series inspired by the residency, which debuts at Mary Boone Gallery in May 1990. For critics, collectors, and the public, they are a disconcerting change in subject matter.

*Birth of Love* (1981) is included in *Suburban Home Life: Tracking the American Dream*, curated by Miwon Kwon at the Whitney Museum.

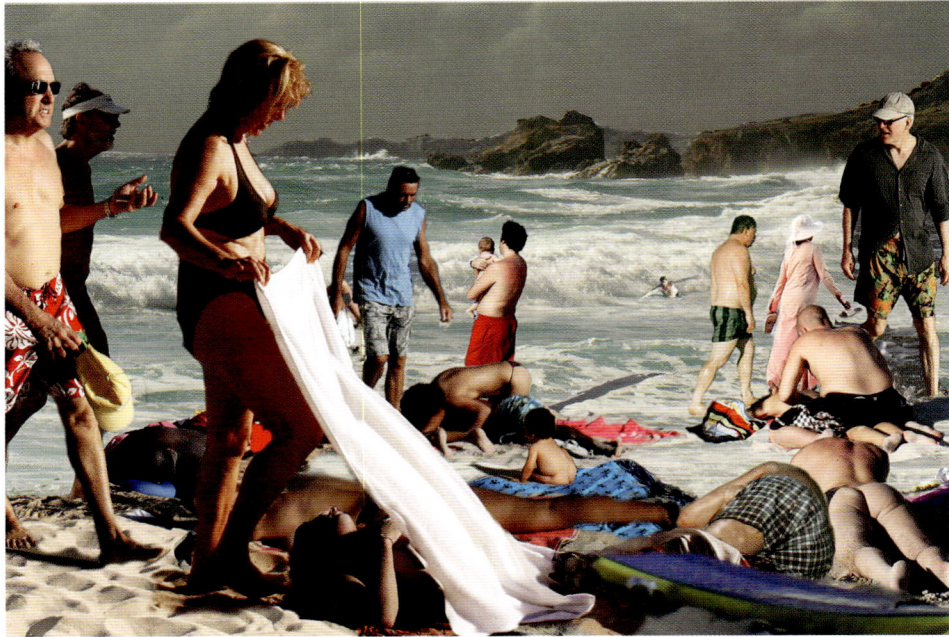

Eric Fischl, *Scenes From Late Paradise: Stupidity Study #1*, 2007. Digital collage. Collection of the artist.

## 1990

At the age of forty-two, grapples with his circle of artists and friends no longer dominating New York art world conversations, exhibitions, and galleries.

Photoshop is released and becomes a popular tool for editing and manipulating digital images. Fischl starts to collage his photographs digitally rather than physically or mentally. Inspires layered compositions like *The Call of the Ball* (1993; PLATE 37) and *What There Is Between You and Me* (1992).

Invited by publisher and gallerist Peter Blum to work on monotypes with lithographer Maurice Sanchez. The resulting *Scenes and Sequences* series is exhibited at the Grunwald Center for the Graphic Arts in Los Angeles and travels to Yale University Art Gallery, New Haven, Connecticut, and the Hood Museum of Art, Hanover, New Hampshire.

*Eric Fischl: Works in Progress* opens at the Walker Art Center. A solo exhibition is held at the Akademie der Bildenden Künste, Vienna, and Musée cantonal des Beaux-Arts, Lausanne, Switzerland.

## 1991

Solo exhibitions at Aarhus Kunstmuseum, Denmark; Louisiana Museum of Modern Art, Copenhagen; and Guild Hall, East Hampton, New York. The Milwaukee Art Museum organizes an exhibition of his drawings which travels to US museums.

Included in group exhibition *American Realism & Figurative Art: 1952–1990* which travels to museums throughout Japan. *On the Stairs of the Temple*, *The Tire Store*, and *In the Temple* (all 1989) are included in the Whitney Biennial.

## 1992

Meets acclaimed director Mike Nichols, whose films include *The Graduate* (1967), *Catch-22* (1970), and *Working Girl* (1988). American film becomes a major influence for Fischl as he and Nichols become close friends. In 1999, Fischl paints a portrait of Nichols (now in the collection of the Met).

Featured, with Gornik, in the exhibition *Four Friends* at the Aldrich Contemporary Art Museum. It travels to three other US museums.

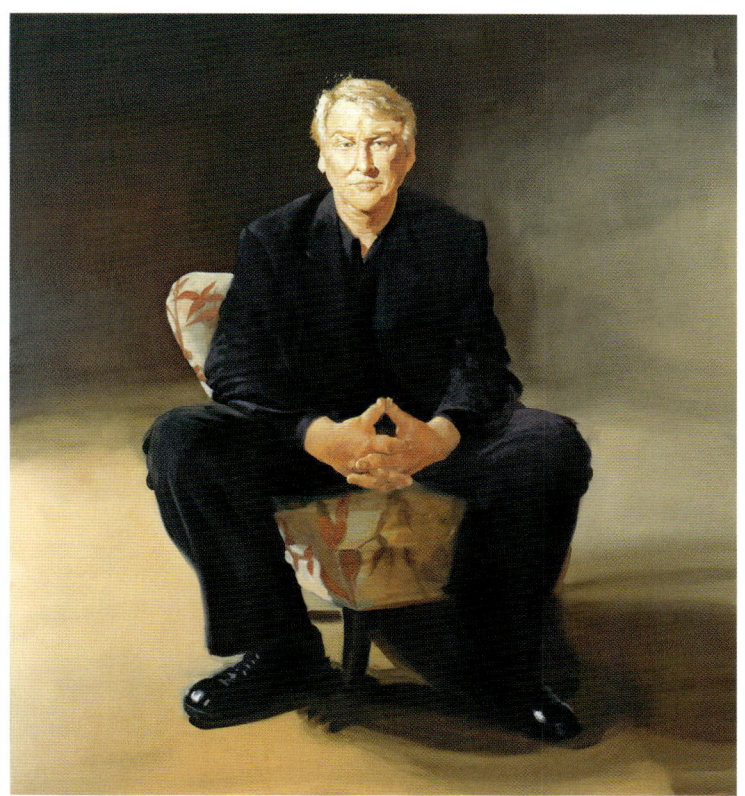

Eric Fischl, *Mike*, 1999. Oil on linen. 69 × 65.1 in. (175.3 × 165 cm). Metropolitan Museum of Art, Anonymous Gift, in honor of the artist, 2003 (2003.213).

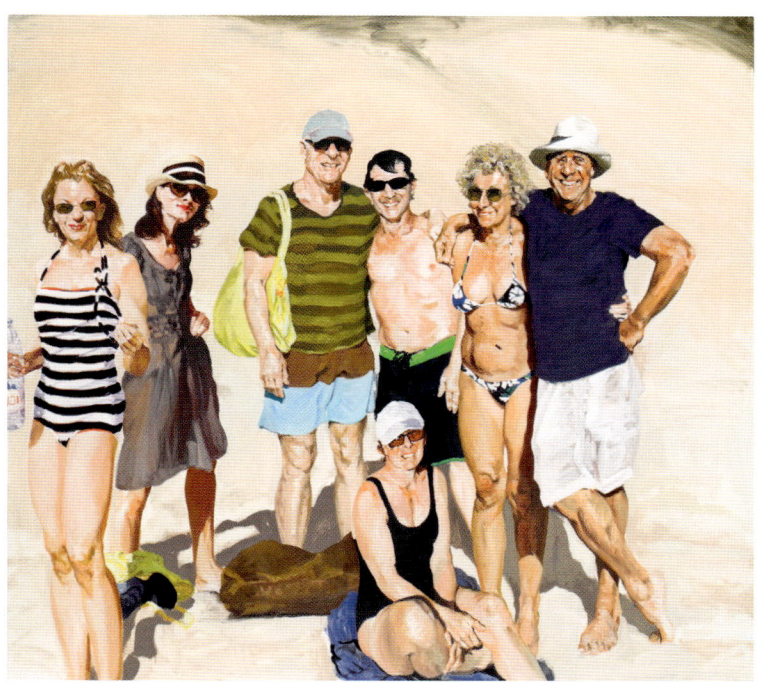

Eric Fischl, *Saint Barts: Ralph's 70th*, 2009. Oil on linen. 96 × 108 in. (243.8 × 274.3). Casa MER, Madrid/Segovia, Spain.

## 1993

Meets pathbreaking comedian, actor, writer, producer, and musician Steve Martin. Both had similar 1950s suburban childhoods with fraught family dynamics. They share a fascination with the American experience and a love of art history. With Gornik, visits Martin's home on St. Barts, which becomes an annual pilgrimage. Martin writes an essay focused on the painting *Barbeque*—which is part of his collection—for Fischl's monograph published in 2008.

## 1994

Paints *The Travel of Romance,* a five-painting sequence depicting the stages of a woman's life. A meditation on the theme of desire and aging, the series is rendered with dramatic use of light.

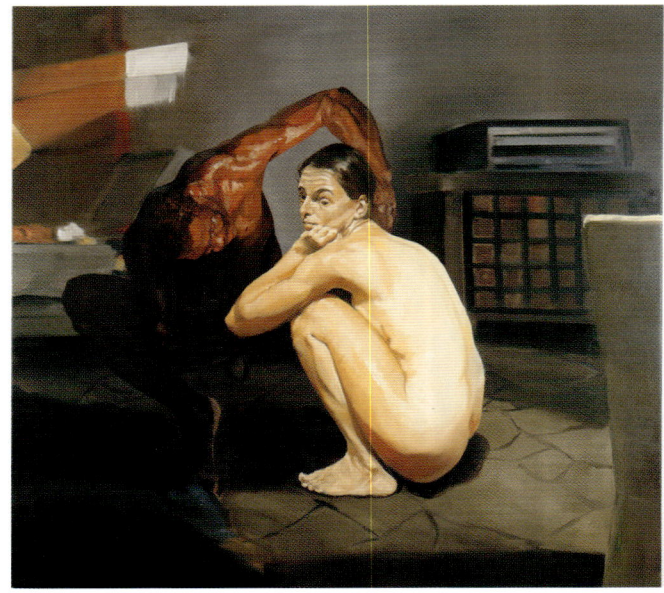

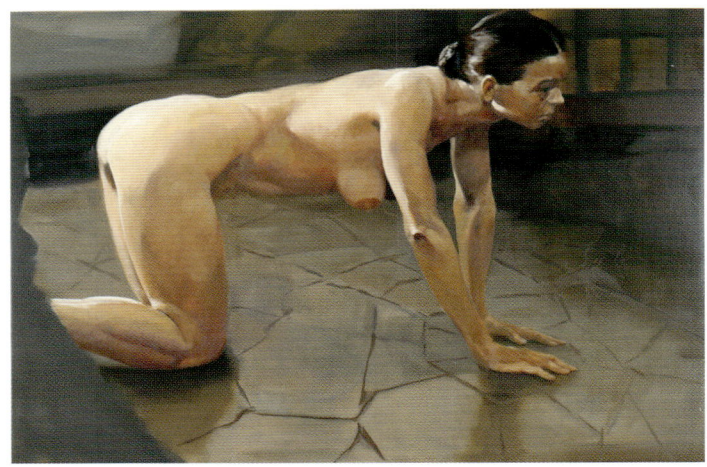

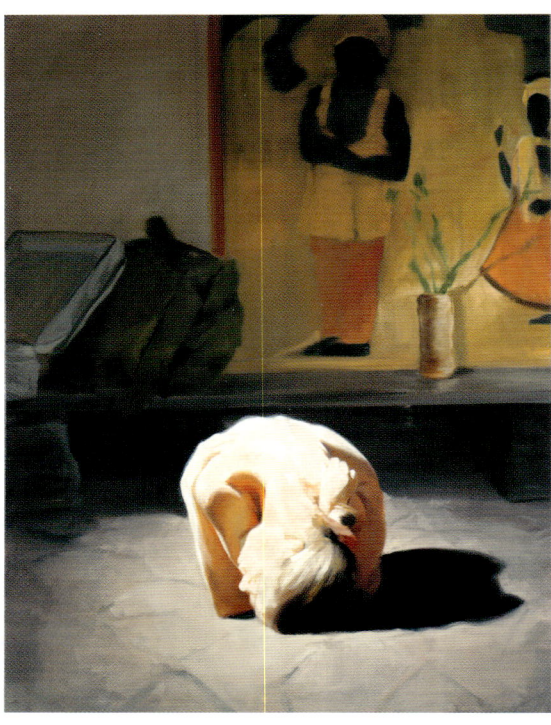

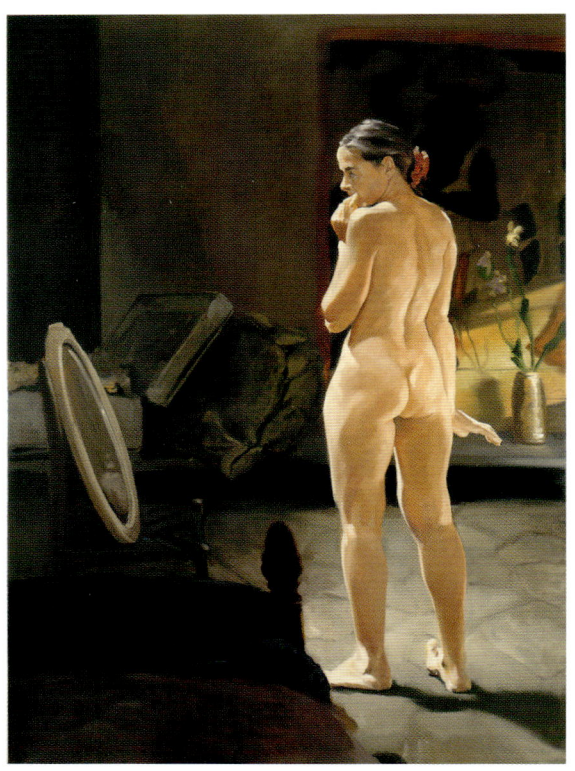

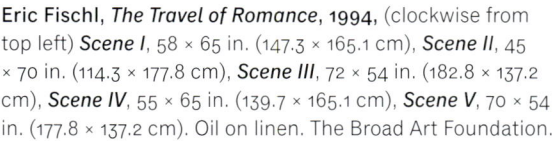

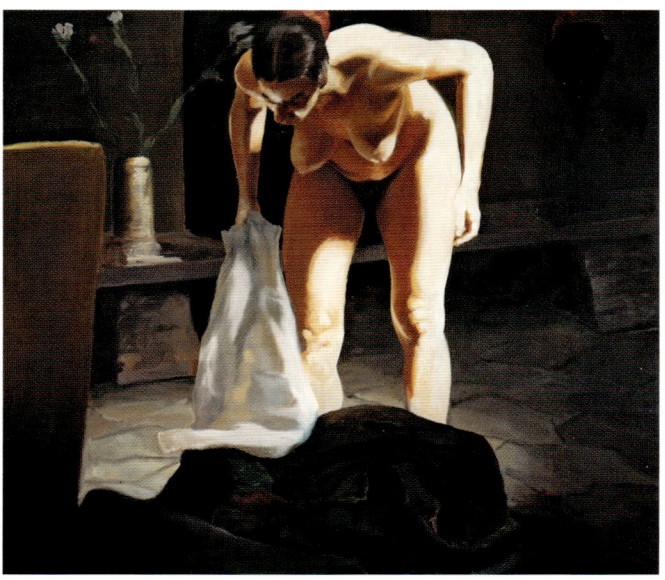

Eric Fischl, *The Travel of Romance*, 1994, (clockwise from top left) *Scene I*, 58 × 65 in. (147.3 × 165.1 cm), *Scene II*, 45 × 70 in. (114.3 × 177.8 cm), *Scene III*, 72 × 54 in. (182.8 × 137.2 cm), *Scene IV*, 55 × 65 in. (139.7 × 165.1 cm), *Scene V*, 70 × 54 in. (177.8 × 137.2 cm). Oil on linen. The Broad Art Foundation.

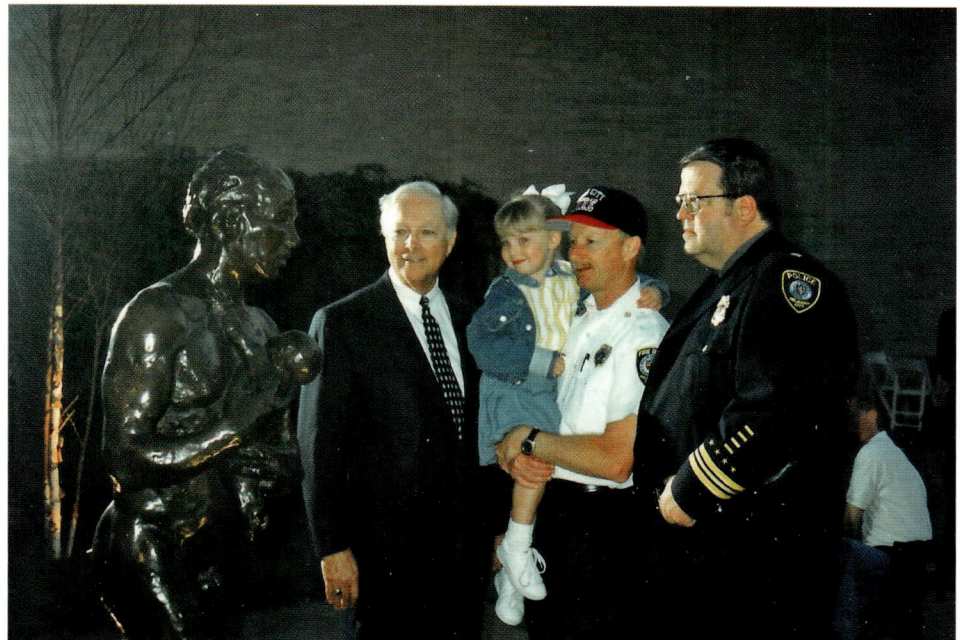

Installation of *Man with Child* sculpture at the Oklahoma City Museum of Art in Oklahoma City, Oklahoma, 1995.

## 1995

April 19, the Oklahoma City Federal Building is bombed by American terrorists, killing 168 people, including nineteen children. Donates his 1992 sculpture *Man with Child* as a memorial and is surprised when the nude figures are received without controversy. Local chief of police thanks him for creating a work that represents all (male) first responders.

## 1996

Father Karl dies in Phoenix. Preparing for the burial and memorial with his siblings, he is horrified by the distortion of values and the business of death in the US.

Grieves his father during a two-month stay as a fellow at the American Academy in Rome. He finds the city steeped in history, memory, and rituals. Paints a series addressing themes of grief, loss, aging, and death set in Roman cathedrals and ruins (SEE FIG. 14).

## 1997

Inspired by American realist painter Edward Hopper, works on a series of paintings with men and women in ambiguous relationships in the constricted space of a bedroom. The two artists share preoccupation with the contradictions of the American experience— alienation and loneliness combined with values of self-reliance and social mobility. Some are included in the group exhibition *Realism After Seven A.M.* at the Edward Hopper House, Nyack, New York.

## 1998

At the age of fifty, marries Gornik in Rome.

Paints *Portrait of the Artist* in response to Max Beckmann's 1927 *Self Portrait in Tuxedo*. Beckmann appears ready for Berlin nightlife; Fischl dons a ridiculous mask and Shriner's hat. "I so overexpose myself in my work that the idea of exposing myself further in a self-portrait seems absurd."[17]

Gagosian Gallery, New York, mounts a solo sculpture exhibition.

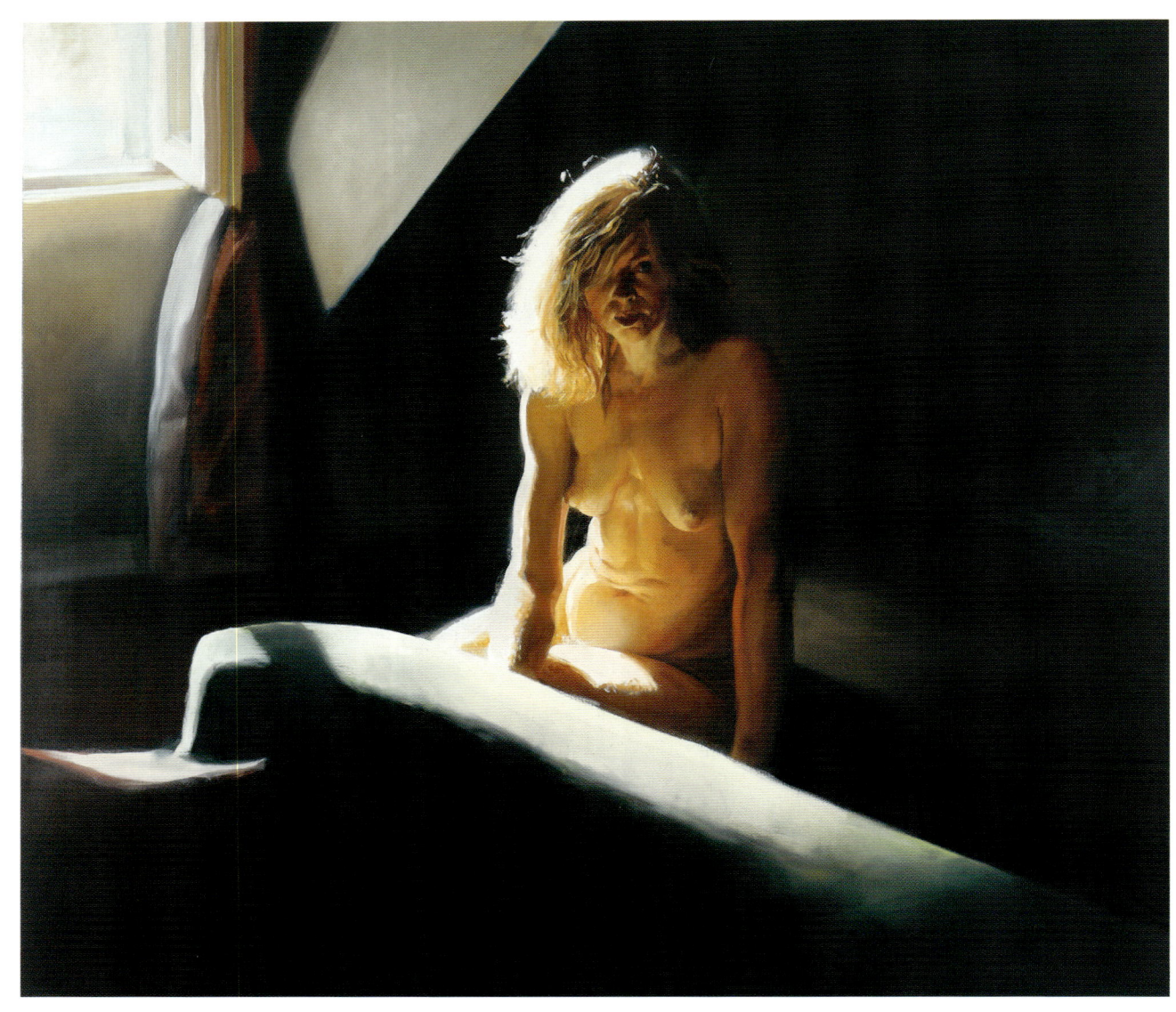

Eric Fischl, *April in Paris*, 1998. Oil on linen. 61 × 71 in.
(154.9 × 180.3 cm). Private Collection.

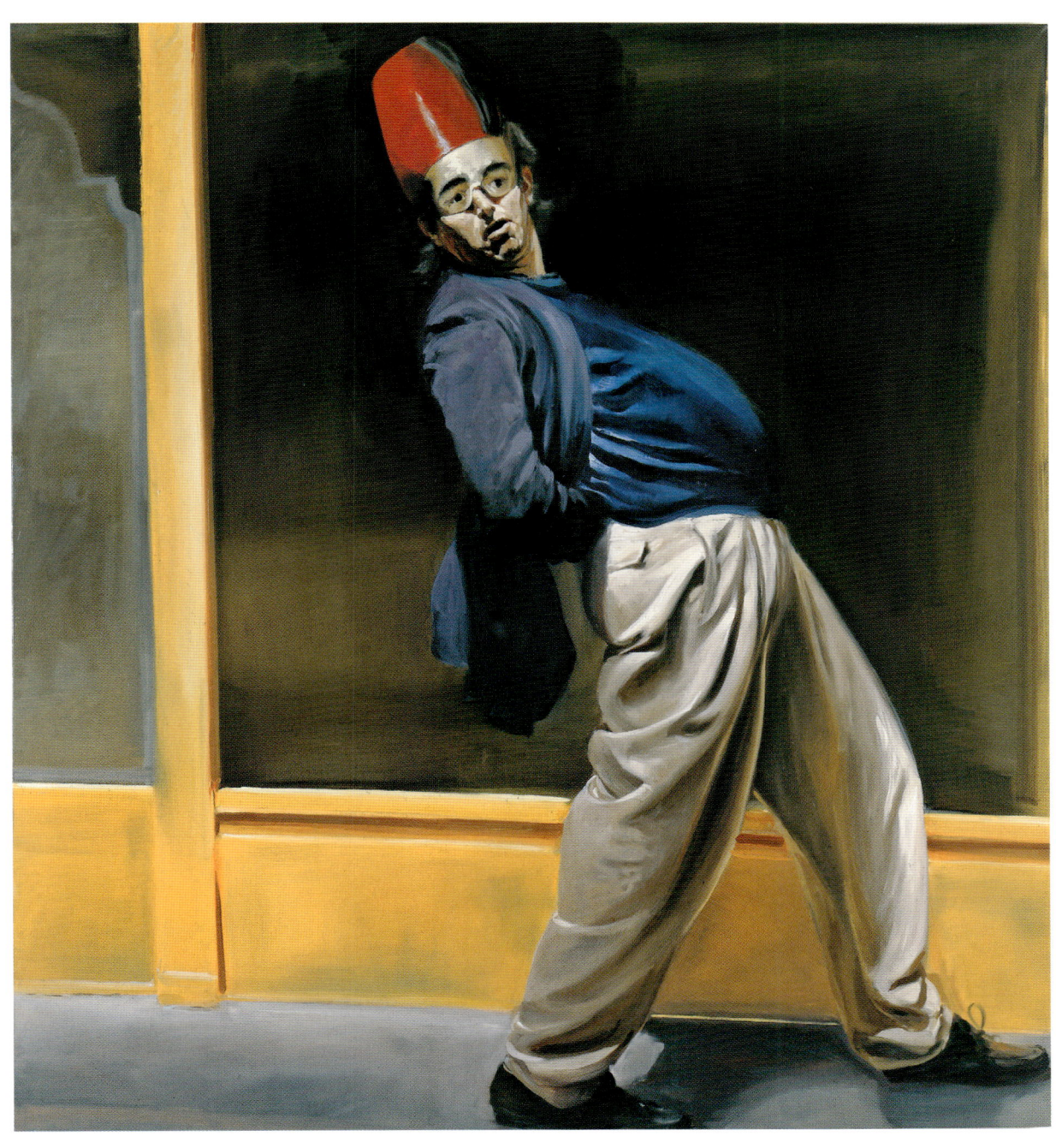

**Eric Fischl,** *Portrait of the Artist,* **1998.** Oil on linen. 72 × 68 in.
(182.9 × 172.7 cm). Collection unknown.

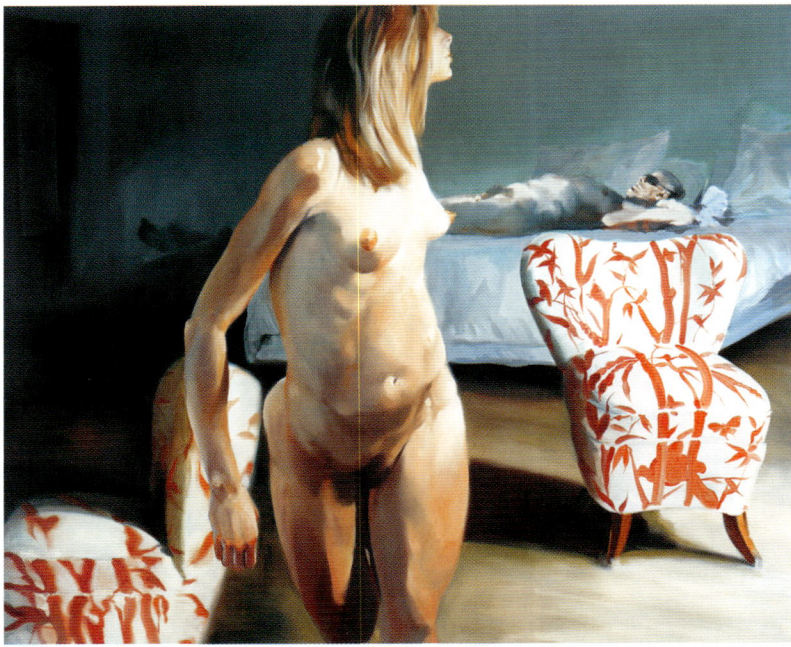

Eric Fischl, *The Bed, The Chair, Jet Lag*, 2000. Oil on linen. 85 × 105⅝ in. (215.9 × 268.3 cm). Private Collection.

## 1999

Work enters museum collections including Museum of Contemporary Art, Chicago; Seattle Art Museum; the Whitney Museum; and the Louisiana Museum of Modern Art.

Visits the YBA (Young British Artists) exhibition *Sensation*, drawn from the Saatchi Collection at the Brooklyn Museum, and is not a fan. YBA are a sensation on the international art scene with their openness to materials and processes, shock tactics, and entrepreneurial activity.

## 2000

In August, Arthur Ashe Commemorative Garden in Flushing Meadows Corona Park, New York, opens on the first day of the US Open. At the center is Fischl's *Soul in Flight*, a fourteen-foot-tall sculpture of a nude tennis player commissioned by the board of the US Tennis Association, including Ashe family members.

Monacelli Press publishes a major monograph covering his work from 1970 to 2000 with essays by Danto,

Martin, and Robert Enright. An update is published in 2008 including Fischl's work between 2000 and 2007.

## 2001

On September 11, terrorists attack the Twin Towers of the World Trade Center in Lower Manhattan. Close to 3,000 people are killed. The attack brings a profound new sense of vulnerability to Americans.

*Jasper Johns to Jeff Koons: Four Decades of Art from the Broad Collections* opens at the Los Angeles County Museum of Art with two paintings from the early 1980s. The show travels into 2003 to the Corcoran Gallery of Art, Washington, DC; the Museum of Fine Arts, Boston; and the Guggenheim Bilbao, Spain.

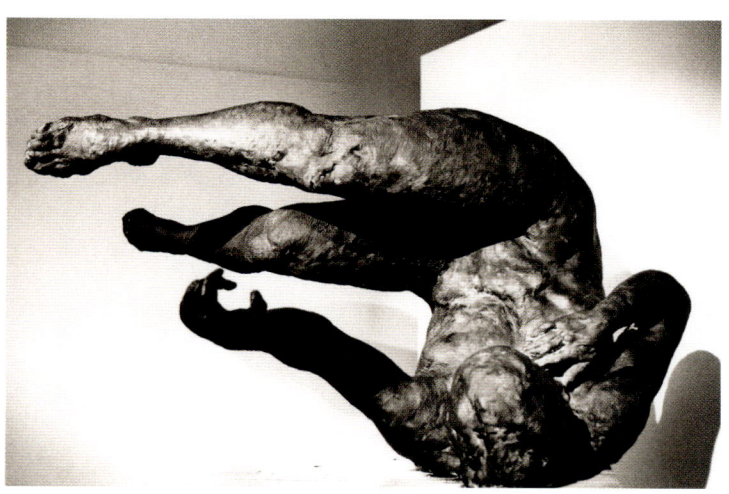

*Tumbling Woman* (2002; first of a series of five bronze sculptures) shown at Rockefeller Center in September 2002.

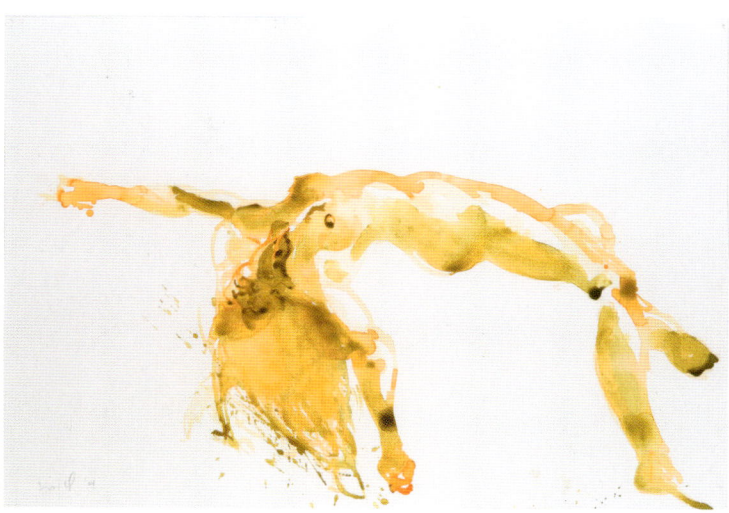

**Eric Fischl,** *Falling Figure #14*, **2001**. Watercolor on paper. 40 × 60 in. (101.6 × 152.4 cm). Collection of the artist.

## 2002

Invited by Martin Hentschel, director of the Kunstmuseen Krefeld, Germany, stages a series of paintings in Haus Esters, a private home designed by Mies van der Rohe in 1928. *Krefeld Project* and *Krefeld Redux* (through 2006) focus on an alienated couple in a tasteful mid-century modern domestic interior (PLATES 20, 21). The Kunstmuseen shows the work in Haus Esters in 2003.

With profound belief in the healing power of art and feeling a need to humanize the staggering number of deaths from the 9/11 attacks, creates his *Tumbling Woman* watercolors and life-size bronze sculpture. The sculpture is displayed at Rockefeller Center on the one-year anniversary and is received with shock by the public and criticism in the press. It is removed less than two weeks later.

Receives an honorary doctorate from NSCAD and gives the convocation address.

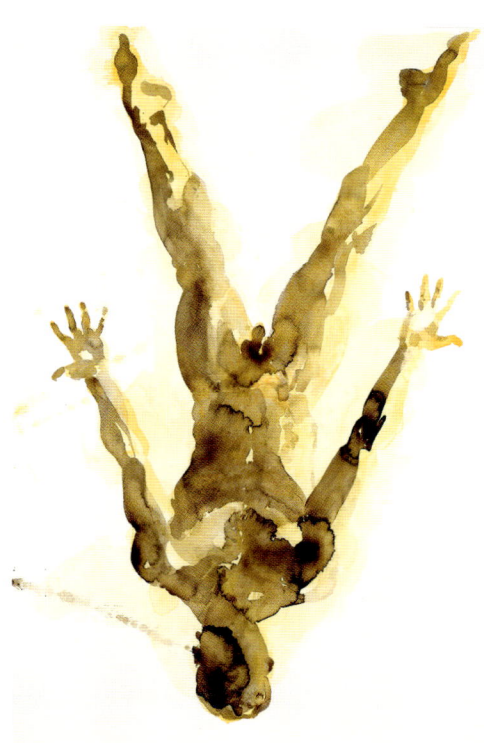

**Eric Fischl,** *Falling Figure #2*, **2001**. Watercolor on paper. 59¾ × 40¼ in. (151.2 × 102.2 cm). Collection of the artist.

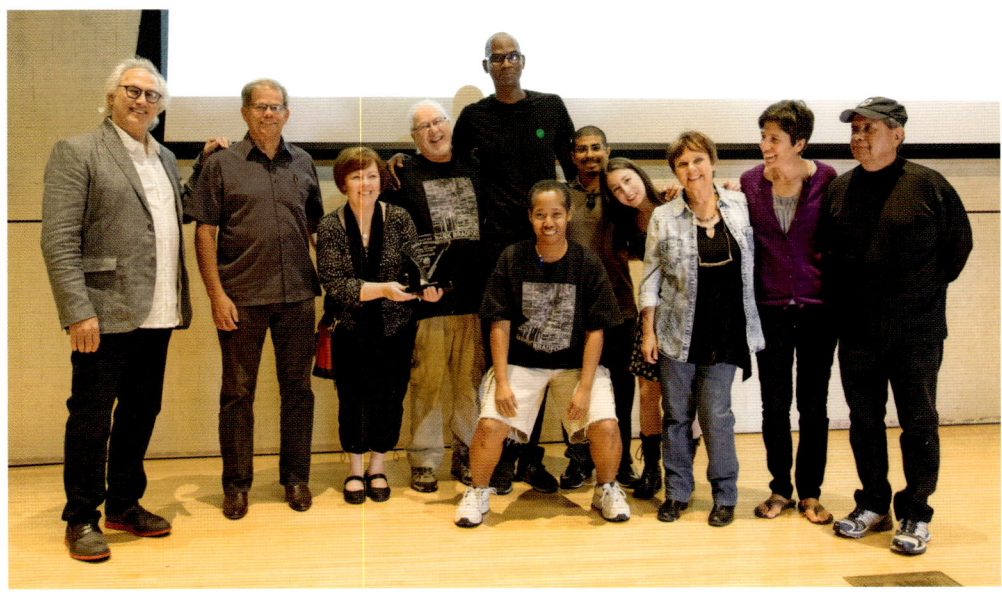

Fischl and artist Mark Bradford with Phoenix College Vanguard Award winners at Phoenix Art Museum, 2015.

## 2003

Opening in September, the Kunstmuseum Wolfsburg, Germany, presents a solo exhibition of nearly eighty paintings and drawings from 1979 to 2001.

## 2004

With Gornik, moves to Sag Harbor full time.

## 2005

Initiates and funds an annual series of visiting artist critiques and student awards at Phoenix College to support emerging artists. After a few years, the awards are presented at Phoenix Art Museum before a public lecture by the visiting artist. Artists have included Gornik, Salle, Andres Serrano, Mark Bradford, Njideka Akunyili Crosby, and Caroll Dunham.

## 2006

Elected fellow at the American Academy of Arts and Letters. Fischl's work was acquired and exhibited by the Academy beginning in 1989.

## 2007

Contributes the powerful essay "A Meditation on the Death of Painting" to the Parrish Art Museum's exhibition catalog for *All the More Real: Portrayals of Intimacy and Empathy* in Southampton, New York.

Invited by German art dealer Rafael Jablonka to make a series after attending a bullfight near Málaga, Spain. The eight paintings are another take on his ongoing exploration of male identity, death, and ritual. Exhibited in his first solo exhibition at a Spanish museum, the Centro de Arte Contemporáneo de Málaga.

## 2008

The Musée National d'Art Moderne, Centre Georges Pompidou, Paris, acquires *Strange Place to Park No. 2* (1992).

The Frist Center for the Visual Arts includes Fischl in a group exhibition, *Paint Made Flesh*, in 2009. The exhibition includes European and American painting since the 1950s. Travels to Phillips Collection, Washington, DC, and Memorial Art Gallery, Rochester, New York.

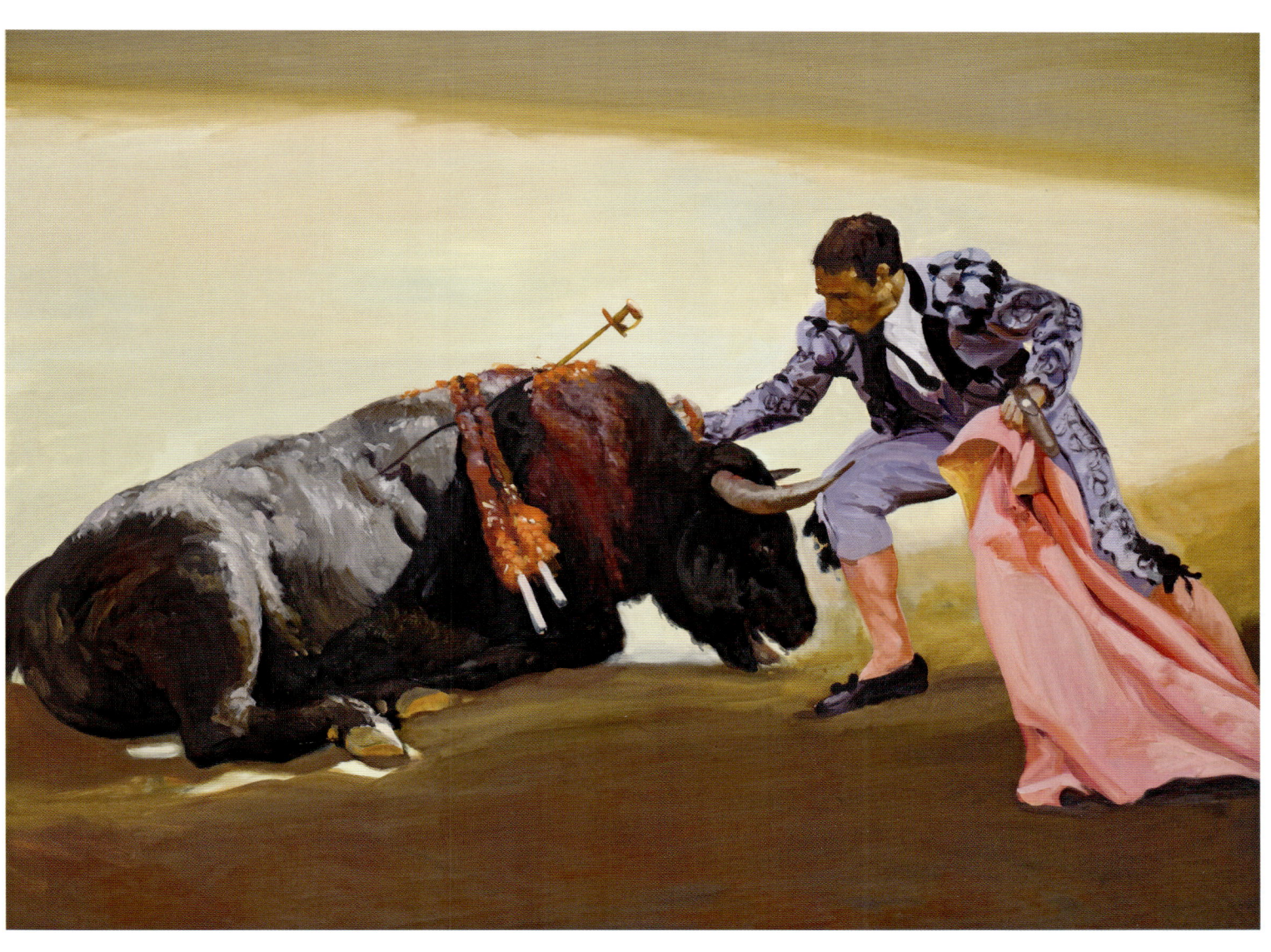

Eric Fischl, *Corrida in Ronda #1*, 2008. Oil on linen. 77 × 108 in.
(195.6 × 274.3 cm). Private Collection.

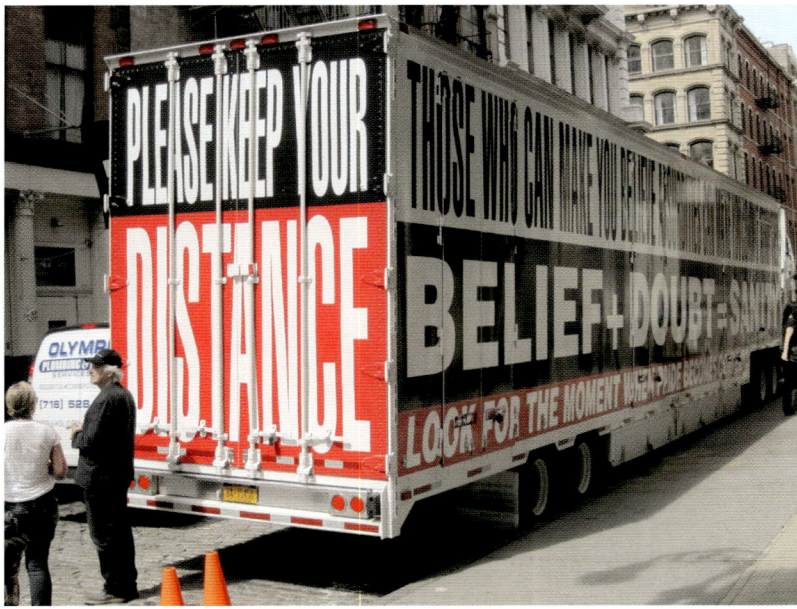

Fischl with the *America Now and Here* truck, wrapped in a vinyl truck wrap by Barbara Kruger (American, b. 1945), *Untitled (Truck)*, 2011.

## 2011

Skartstedt Gallery in New York presents its first exhibition of his work focused on early paintings. Shows regularly at branches in London, Paris, and New York through today.

Aligning with his desire to increase the relevancy of art and heal a polarized, post-9/11 nation, launches *America: Now and Here.* The traveling exhibition features artists from various disciplines in public spaces and strives to encourage dialogue about American identity. Works on the project for several years as founder and lead curator, debuting the project in Kansas City before traveling to Detroit and Chicago. Later, fundraising challenges put the project on hold.

## 2012

*Dive Deep: Eric Fischl and the Process of Painting* organized by the Pennsylvania Academy of Fine Arts (PAFA), Philadelphia, and the San Jose Museum of Art, California. At the opening, meets Arcmanoro Niles, who is pursuing his undergraduate degree at PAFA.

Receives honorary degree from the School of the Art Institute of Chicago.

Writes *Bad Boy: My Life On and Off the Canvas* with journalist and friend Michael Stone, published by Crown. *The New York Times* cultural critic Laura Kipnis writes, "the same observational frankness that imbues his paintings makes this a brave and candid book." *The Guardian* art critic Andrew Russeth calls it "a clear-eyed account of the art world's profound transformations over the past thirty or so years."[18]

## 2013

Starts a series of paintings set at international art fairs replete with dark-suited dealers, art stars, and collectors clutching cell phones and glasses of champagne in booths packed with art. First exhibited at Victoria Miro Gallery, London, in 2014.

Receives honorary doctorate from CalArts.

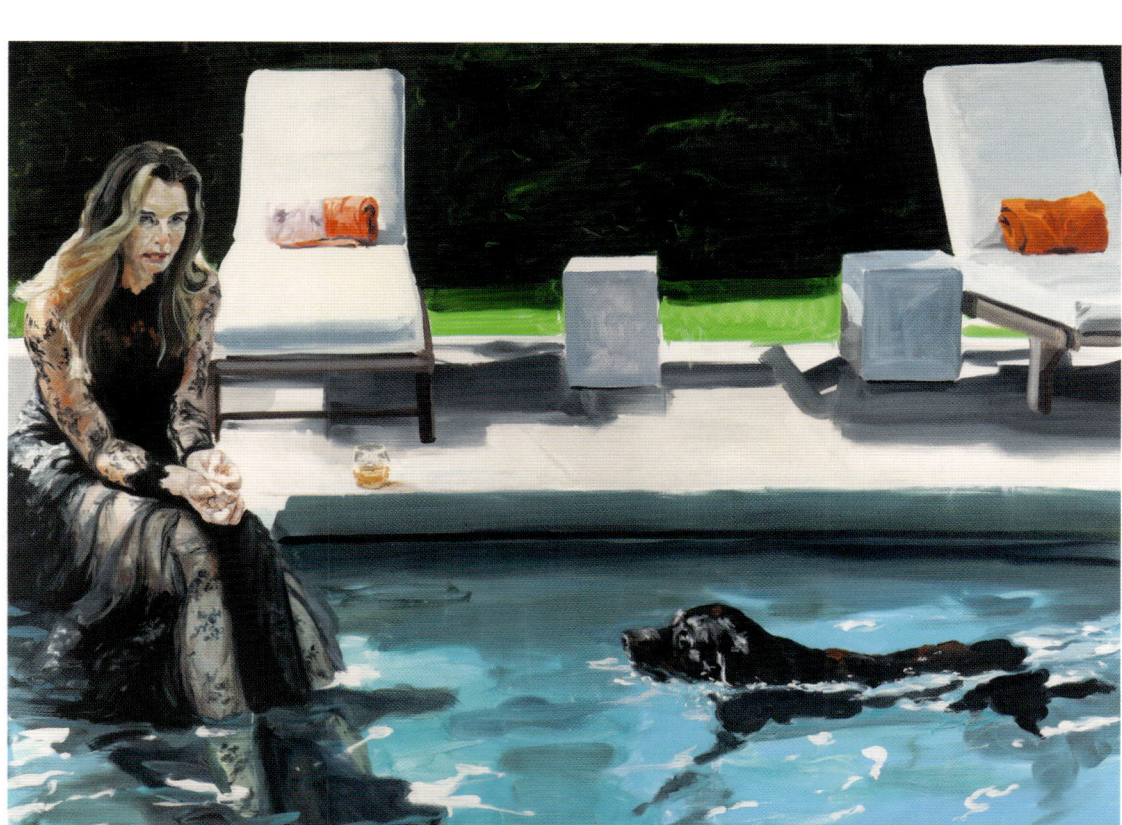

Eric Fischl, *Daddy's Gone Girl*, 2016. Oil on linen. 78 × 107 in.
(198.1 × 271.8 cm). Private Collection.

## 2014

The Albertina Museum, Vienna, presents *Eric Fischl:
Friends, Lovers and other Constellations*, February
13–May 18. The catalog for the exhibition of works on
paper and sculptures includes a dynamic conversation with artist Lawrence Weschler.

Curates *Disturbing Innocence* for the FLAG Art
Foundation in the Chelsea Arts Tower, New York.
Features fifty-eight historic and contemporary artists
who utilize images of dolls, toys, robots, and manne-
quins to trace "a subversive and escapist world at odds
with the values and pretensions of polite society."[19]

## 2015

*Slumber Party* (1983) is given to the Art Institute of
Chicago as part of the Edlis/Neeson Collection. It
goes on display with the rest of the collection for the
next fifty years.

## 2016

Paints a new series, *Late America*, during Donald
Trump's first presidential campaign and continuing
through his inauguration in January 2017. Set primarily in backyards and pools of the affluent, the large
paintings are allegories for the state of America (PLATE
28). "At first I (painted) in anger towards privilege and
towards the isolation of privilege, but anger alone
didn't explain to me how I was feeling, because it
didn't bring the fear into it, didn't bring the feeling
of helplessness into it. . . . Where we are is more the
pure state of vulnerability, [it is] collapse."[20] The series
premiers at Skarstedt Gallery, is featured on CNN, and
is discussed by Jerry Saltz in *New York Magazine*.

*Tumbling Woman* (2002), which caused such a furor
when it was first exhibited, is included in the group
show *Rendering the Unthinkable: Artists Respond to 9/11*
at the 9/11 Memorial and Museum, New York.

## 2017

Curates the exhibition *Hope and Hazard: A Comedy of Eros* for the Hall Art Foundation, Reading, Vermont. More than eighty works from the Foundation's collection explore "the absurd extremes associated with romantic and sexual love. Desire, passion, vulnerability, disappointment, pleasure, and torment."[21] Artists include Dunham, Nutt, and Salle as well as Robert Arneson, Georg Baselitz, Tracey Emin, Nicole Eisenman, Lee Friedlander, Jeff Koons, Robert Mapplethorpe, and Tom Wesselmann.

With Gornik, purchases a deconsecrated 1835 Methodist church in Sag Harbor. They thoughtfully transform it into The Church, a creative community center with diverse offerings including exhibitions, performances, lectures, and literary events.

Continues his exploration of Trump-era America with the series *Presence of an Absence*. Receives significant attention in the press, including articles and reviews by Adam Lehrer in *Forbes* and Roberta Smith in *The New York Times*.

In November, the Belvedere Museum in Vienna opens *Aging Pride*, an exhibition exploring the realities of aging in our time. *Frailty is a Moment of Self-Reflection* (1996) is included (PLATE 7).

## 2018

*Scenes From Late Paradise: Stupidity* (2007; PLATE 8) and *Late America* (2016) appear in a collection of short stories titled *It Occurs to Me That I Am America: New Stories and Art,* published in January, a year into the first Trump presidency. Authors include Alice Hoffman, Joyce Carol Oates, Richard Russo, Alice Walker, and Pulitzer Prize–winning Viet Thanh Nguyen.

The Dallas Contemporary in Texas mounts the exhibition *Eric Fischl: If Art Could Talk*, curated by Peter Doroshenko, from April to August. The thirty-two works look at his recent art fair paintings against the backdrop of his career-long interest in the history of art.

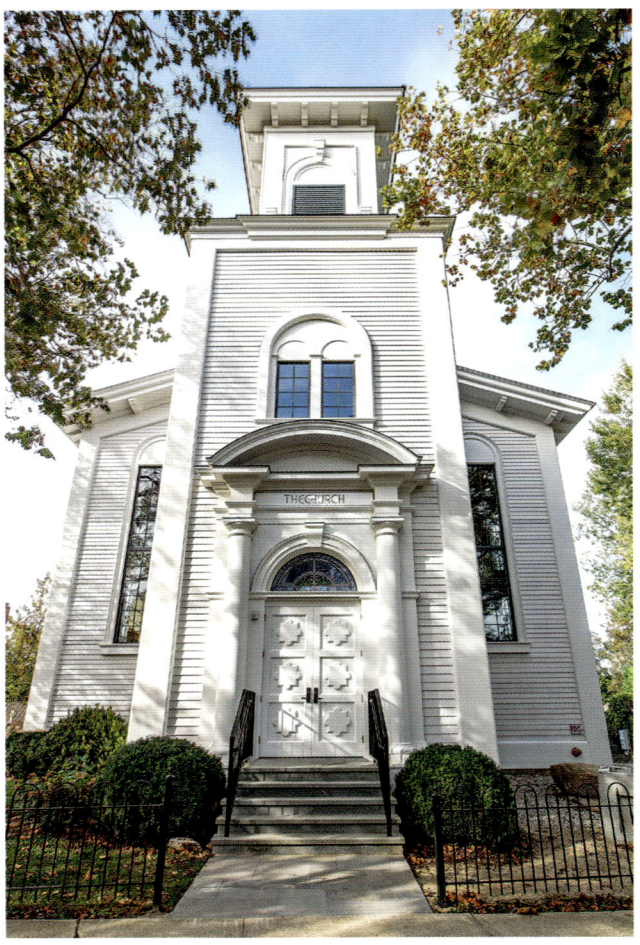

The Church, Sag Harbor, New York, 2020.

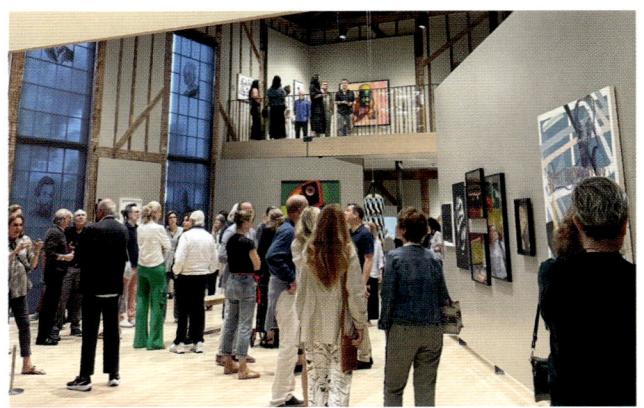

Opening reception of *Strike Fast, Dance Lightly: Artists on Boxing* at The Church in Sag Harbor, New York, 2023.

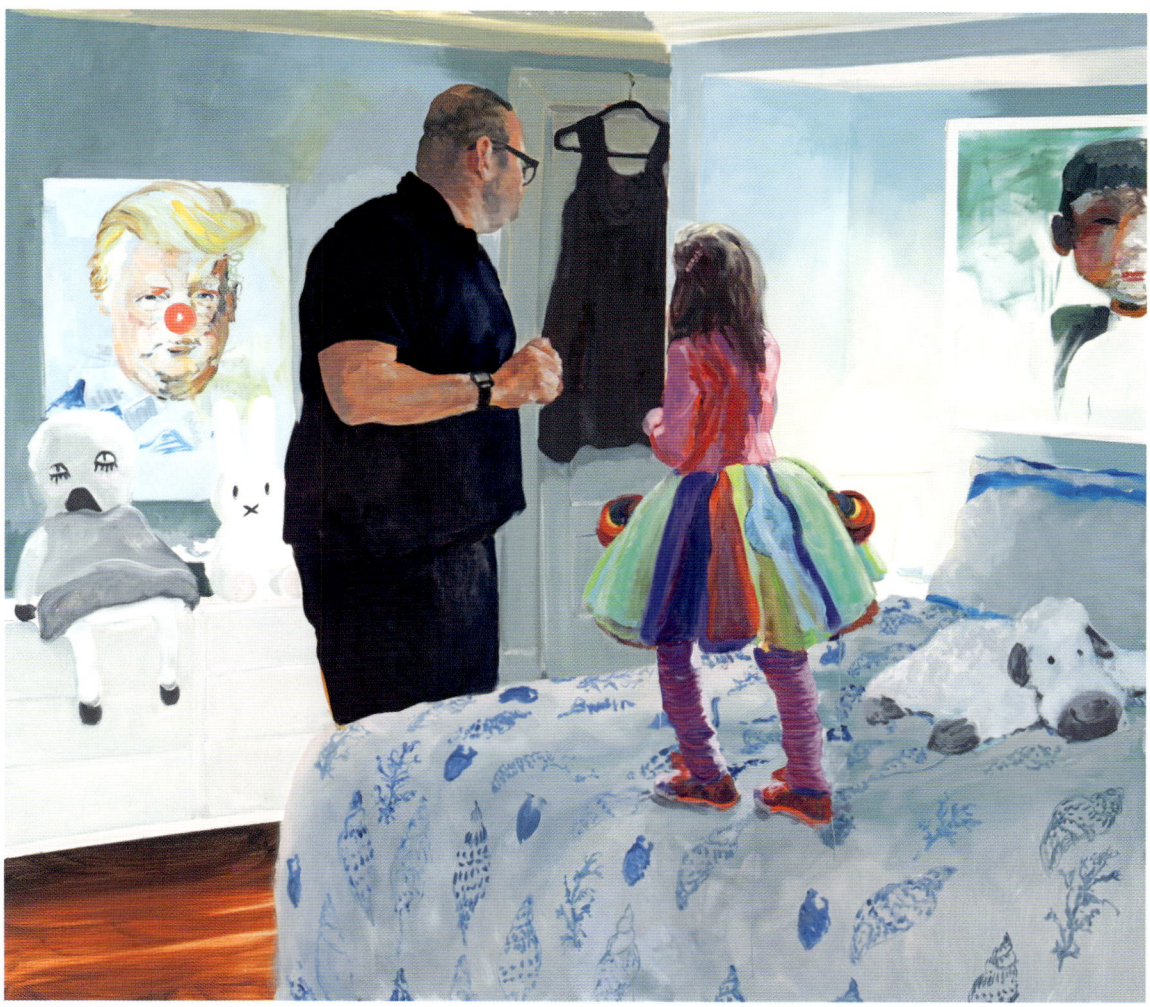

Eric Fischl, *Worry*, 2017. Oil on linen. 78 × 90 in. (198.12 × 228.6 cm).
Private Collection.

## 2019

New series *Complications From An Already Unfulfilled Life* is presented at Sprüth Magers Gallery, Los Angeles, in the summer.

## 2020–21

Spurred by the uncertainty of the global COVID-19 pandemic, starts painting in acrylic to work in a more improvisational manner and produces the new series *Meditations on Melancholia* (a mix of oil and acrylic) and *My Old Neighborhood* (2021; all acrylic).

Salle writes an essay for the Skarstedt Gallery catalog for *My Old Neighborhood* focusing on Fischl's intuitive process and the emotional content of the new paintings (PLATES 32, 33). Interviewed by Matt Lippiatt for *Turps Magazine*.

## 2022

Included in *We Are Family* exhibition at the New York Academy of Art.

Skarstedt Gallery presents the new series *Towards the End of an Astonishing Beauty: An Elegy to Sag Harbor, and Thus America* in the fall, including the painting, *The Parade Returns* (PLATE 39).

## 2023

*Woman*, an exhibition of paintings and sculpture, is held at Böhm Chapel, Jablonka Foundation, outside of Cologne, Germany.

## 2024

In January, gives a public lecture on Pierre Bonnard at Norton Museum of Art, West Palm Beach, Florida.

Skarstedt Gallery presents nine new paintings, *Hotel Stories*, in the spring (PLATE 9).

Victoria Miro Gallery, Venice, Italy, presents five large-scale, hand-painted bronze reliefs derived from Fischl's virtual paintings.

## 2025

Donald Trump is inaugurated for a second term in office.

Phoenix Art Museum presents *Eric Fischl: Stories Told* and accompanying volume.

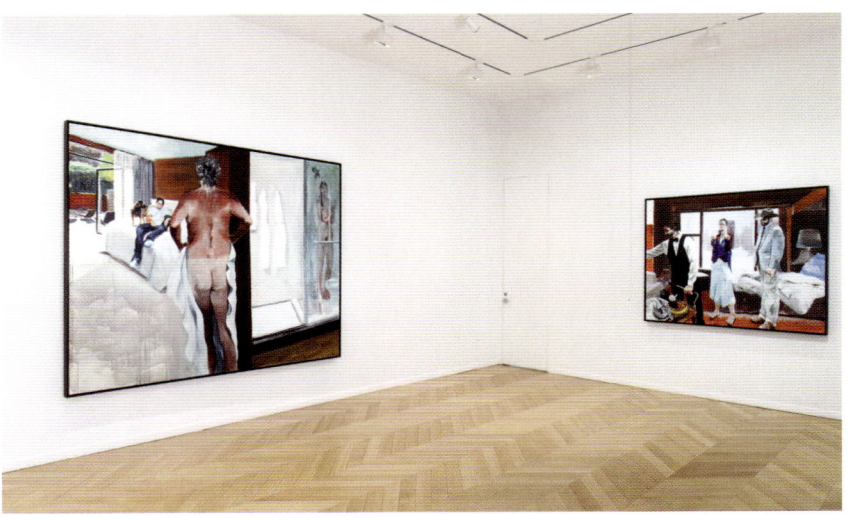

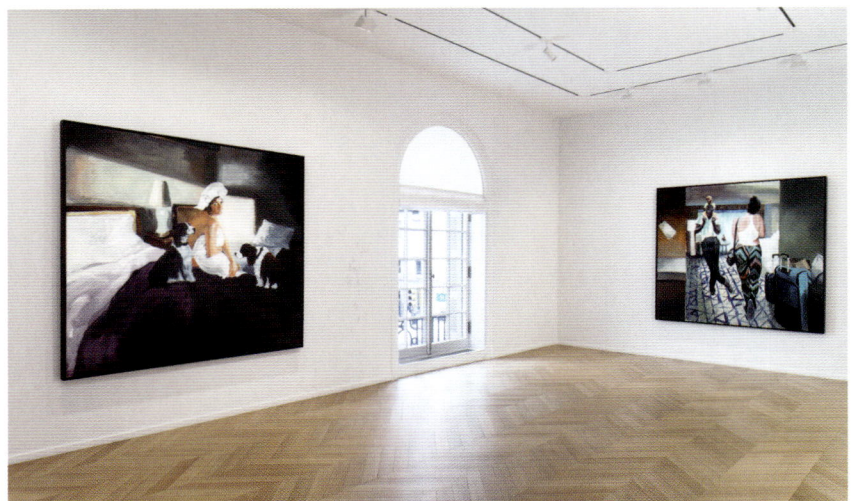

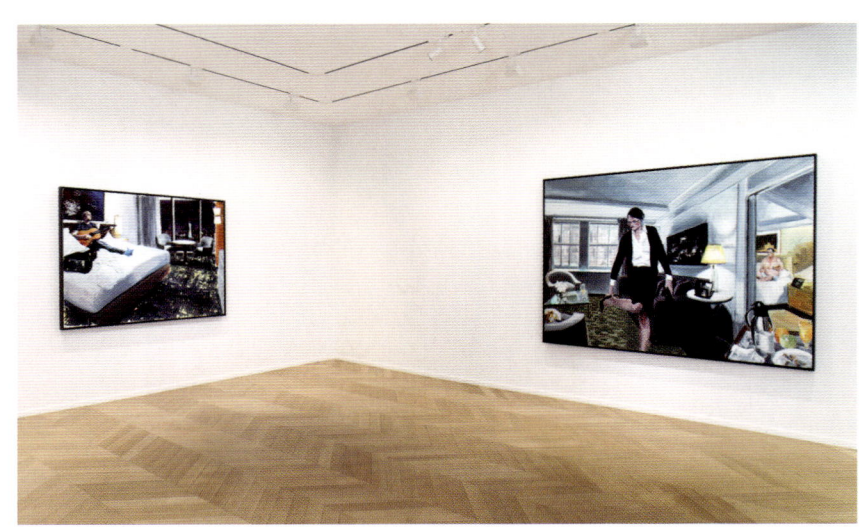

Installation views from *Hotel Stories* at Skarstedt Gallery, New York, March 14–May 4, 2024.

(top) From left: *Standoff* (2024) and *Hotel Service* (2023).

(middle) From left: *Untitled* (2023) and *October 8: Heading Home* (2023).

(below) From left: *King's Highway: Killing Time* (2024) and *Breakfast Begins the Day or Ends the Evening* (2023).

## Notes

1  Eric Fischl and Michael Stone, *Bad Boy: My Life On and Off the Canvas* (Crown, 2012), p. 10.

2  Fischl and Stone, *Bad Boy*, 33.

3  Fischl and Stone, *Bad Boy*, 34.

4  Eric Fischl quoted in Robert Enright, "Fischl on Fischl," in Arthur C. Danto, Robert Enright, and Steve Martin, *Eric Fischl 1970–2000* (Monacelli, 2000), p. 38.

5  Fischl and Stone, *Bad Boy*, 54.

6  Fischl and Stone, *Bad Boy*, 62.

7  Fischl and Stone, *Bad Boy*, 76.

8  Eric Fischl, "NSCAD Convocation Address of Dr. Eric Fischl," April 20, 2002, Halifax, Nova Scotia, transcript, https://nscad .ca/nscad-convocation-address-of-dr-eric-fischl/.

9  Fischl and Stone, *Bad Boy*, 86.

10  Fischl and Stone, *Bad Boy*, 118. Donald Kuspit, *Fischl* (Vintage, 1987), p. 3.

11  Peter Schjeldahl, "Witness," *Art in America*, 1988, quoted in Peter Schjeldahl, *Eric Fischl*, ed. David Whitney (Stewart Tabori & Chang, 1988), p. 20.

12  Enright, "Fischl on Fischl," 68.

13  Fischl and Stone, *Bad Boy*, 286.

14  Eric Fischl, conversation with Robert Berlind, *The Brooklyn Rail*, July/August 2014, https://brooklynrail.org/2014/07/art /eric-fischl-with-robert-berlind/.

15  Schjeldahl, *Fischl*, 11.

16  Robert Hughes, "Art: Discontents of The White Tribe," *Time*, May 30, 1988, https://time.com/archive/6712337 /art-discontents-of-the-white-tribe/.

17  Enright, "Fischl on Fischl," 268.

18  Laura Kipnis, "Charged Images," *New York Times*, June 23, 2013. Andrew Russeth, "To the Bone: In New Book, Eric Fischl Talks Painting, Drinking, Snorting," *Observer*, May 7, 2013.

19  *Disturbing Innocence*, exhibition at the FLAG Art Foundation, New York, October 25, 2015–January 31, 2016, https://www .flagartfoundation.org/exhibitions/disturbing-innocence-2/.

20  Julie L. Belcove, "Mourning in America," in *Late America* (Skarstedt Gallery, 2017), p. 8.

21  *Hope and Hazard: A Comedy of Eros*, Hall Art Foundation, Reading, VT, May 6, 2017–November 15, 2018, http://www .hallartfoundation.org/exhibition/hope-and-hazard -a-comedy-of-eros/information.

# PLATE LIST

PLATE 1
*Broken Hallelujah*
2023
Acrylic on linen
68 × 96 in. (172.7 × 243.8 cm)
Arora Collection, UK

## SINGLE & ALONE

PLATE 2
*Best Western*
1983
Oil on canvas
108 × 78 in. (274.3 × 198.1 cm)
Private Collection

PLATE 3
*The Sheer Weight of History*
1982
Oil on canvas
60 × 60 in. (152.4 × 152.4 cm)
Private Collection

PLATE 4
*New House*
1982
Oil on linen
67¼ × 96¼ in. (172.7 × 244.5 cm)
Collection Museum of Contemporary Art Chicago, Gift of
Stefan T. Edlis and Gael Neeson in honor of the MCA's
40th anniversary, 2007.14

PLATE 5
*Master Bedroom (Her Master's Voice)*
1983
Oil on canvas
84 × 108 in. (213.4 × 274.3 cm)
The Museum of Contemporary Art, Los Angeles. The Barry
Lowen Collection

PLATE 6
*Scarsdale*
1986
Oil on linen
96 × 93¼ in. (244 × 237 cm)
Private Collection

PLATE 7
*Frailty is a Moment of Self-Reflection*
1996
Oil on linen
68 × 58 in. (172.7 × 147.3 cm)
Private Collection

PLATE 8
*Scenes From Late Paradise: Stupidity*
2007
Oil on linen
84 × 108 in. (213.4 × 274.3 cm)
Hall Art Foundation

PLATE 9
*October 7: Heading Out*
2023
Acrylic on linen
62 × 72 in. (157.5 × 182.9 cm)
Private Collection

PLATE 10
*Scenes and Sequences: Man*
1986
Monotype
25¼ × 22½ in. (64.1 × 57.1 cm)
Collection of the artist

PLATE 11
*Study for Portrait of the Artist as an Old Man*
1985
Oil on chromecoat
16 × 11 in. (40.6 × 27.9 cm)
Collection of the artist

PLATE 12
*Untitled*
1989
Watercolor on paper
12½ × 9½ in. (31.8 × 24.1 cm)
Collection of the artist

PLATE 13
*Falling Figure #6*
2001
Watercolor on paper
59¾ × 40¼ in. (151.77 × 102.24 cm)
Collection of the artist

PLATE 14
*Falling Figure #7*
2001
Watercolor on paper
59¾ × 40¼ in. (151.8 × 102.2 cm)
Collection of the artist

## COUPLES & PAIRS

PLATE 15
*Bad Boy*
1981
Oil on canvas
66 × 96 in. (167.6 × 243.8 cm)
Private Collection

PLATE 16
*Untitled*
1982
Oil on canvas
84 × 84 in. (213.4 × 213.4 cm)
The Broad Art Foundation

PLATE 17
*Slumber Party*
1983
Oil on canvas
84 × 108 in. (213.4 × 274.3 cm)
The Art Institute of Chicago, gift of Edlis Neeson Collection, 2015.145

PLATE 18
*The Bed, The Chair, The Sitter*
1999
Oil on linen
78 × 93 in. (198.1 × 236.2 cm)
Private Collection, New York

PLATE 19
*The Bed, The Chair, Dancing, Watching*
2000
Oil on linen
69 × 78 in. (175.3 × 198.1 cm)
Private Collection, courtesy of Skarstedt Gallery

PLATE 20
*Bedroom, Scene #3, Mistakes Mistakes! Everything Shakes from All the Mistakes*
2004
Oil on linen
87 × 113 in. (221 × 287 cm)
Private Collection

PLATE 21
*Krefeld Project; Dining Room, Scene #2*
2003
Oil on linen
89 × 124 in. (226 × 315 cm)
Seattle Art Museum, 2014.25.19. Gift of the Virginia and Bagley Wright Collection, in honor of the 75th Anniversary of the Seattle Art Museum

PLATE 22
*Swimming Lovers*
1984
Oil on chromecoat
11 × 16 in. (27.9 × 40.6 cm)
Collection of the artist

PLATE 23
*Untitled (Two Figures)*
2006
Solar etching
45 × 32 in. (114.3 × 81.3 cm)
Collection of the artist

## FAMILIES & CARETAKERS

PLATE 24
*Time for Bed*
1980
Oil on canvas
72 × 96 in. (182.9 × 243.8 cm)
Private collection of David Geffen, Los Angeles

PLATE 25
*A Woman Possessed*
1981
Oil on canvas
68 × 96 in. (172.7 × 243.8 cm)
The Metropolitan Museum of Art, Gift of Per Skarstedt, 2024 (2024.616)

PLATE 26
*Barbeque*
1982
Oil on canvas
65 × 100 in. (165.1 × 254 cm)
Steve Martin and Anne Stringfield

PLATE 27
*Squirt*
1982
Oil on canvas
68 × 96 in. (172.7 × 243.8 cm)
Private Collection

PLATE 28
*Late America*
2016
Oil on linen
80 × 98 in. (203.2 × 248.9 cm)
Private Collection

PLATE 29
*Late America 2*
2020
Acrylic and oil on linen
78 × 110 in. (198.1 × 279.4 cm)
Forman Family Collection

PLATE 30
*Daddy's Girl Age 11*
2017
Oil on linen
84 × 108 in. (213.4 × 274.32 cm)
Skarstedt, New York

PLATE 31
*Island of the Cyclops: The Early Years*
2018
Oil on linen
80 × 98 in. (203.2 × 248.9 cm)
Lenhardt Collection

PLATE 32
*My Old Neighborhood: Red Balloon*
2021
Acrylic on linen
68 × 96 in. (172.7 × 243.8 cm)
Private Collection, New York

PLATE 33
*My Old Neighborhood: Private Property*
2021
Acrylic on linen
68 × 96 in. (172.7 × 243.8 cm)
Private Collection

PLATE 34
*Life Saver/ Life Preserver*
1979
Oil on glassine
65 × 84 in. (165.1 × 213.4 cm)
Private Collection

## CROWDS & PARADES

PLATE 35
*The Old Man's Boat and the Old Man's Dog*
1982
Oil on canvas
84 × 84 in. (213.4 × 213.4 cm)
Courtesy The Brant Foundation, Greenwich, CT, USA

PLATE 36
*St. Tropez*
1982
Oil on canvas
84 × 84 in. (213.4 × 213.4 cm)
Private Collection

PLATE 37
*The Call of the Ball*
1993
Oil on linen
65 × 50 in. (165.1 × 127 cm)
The Broad Art Foundation

PLATE 38
*Rift/Raft*
2016
Oil on linen
98 × 220 in. (248.9 × 558.8 cm)
Private Collection

PLATE 39
*The Parade Returns*
2022
Acrylic on linen
68 × 96 in. (172.7 × 243.8 cm)
Collection of Lise and Michael Evans

PLATE 40
*You Don't Need a Weatherman...*
2022
Acrylic on linen
75 × 65 in. (190.5 × 165.1 cm)
Courtesy of the artist and Skarstedt, New York

PLATE 41
*The Critics*
1979
Oil on glassine
72 × 121 in. (182.9 × 307.3 cm)
Private Collection

PLATE 42
*Scenes and Sequences: Fable*
1986
Monotype
25 × 34½ in. (63.5 × 87.6 cm)
Collection of the artist

PLATE 43
*Year of the Drowned Dog*
1983
Color etchings with aquatint, drypoint, and scraping printed
on six sheets of Zerkall paper
Printed by Peter Kneubuhler, Zurich
Published by Peter Blum Edition
22 × 69 in. (56 × 175.3 cm)
Collection of the artist

**DAWN BERG** is curatorial specialist at Phoenix Art Museum, where she coordinates the institution's publications. Previously, she managed the Museum's family programs connecting intergenerational audiences with the collection and special exhibitions.

**DR. KATHRYN BROWN** is reader in Art Histories, Markets, and Digital Heritage at Loughborough University (UK). Her books include *Women Readers in French Painting 1870–1890* (2012), *Matisse's Poets: Critical Performance in the Artist's Book* (2017), *Henri Matisse* (2021), *Dialogues with Degas: Influence and Antagonism in Contemporary Art* (2023), and *Art Auctions: Spectacle and Value in the 21st Century* (2024).

**ELEANOR HEARTNEY** is a New York–based art writer. Her numerous books on contemporary art include *Critical Condition: American Culture at the Crossroads* (1997), *Postmodernism* (2001), *Art and Today* (2013), *Postmodern Heretics: The Catholic Imagination in Contemporary Art* (2018), and *Doomsday Dreams: the Apocalyptic Imagination in Contemporary Art* (2019).

**HEATHER SEALY LINEBERRY** is curator emeritus at the Arizona State University (ASU) Art Museum, faculty associate in the ASU School of Art Museum Studies program, and guest curator at the Phoenix Art Museum. Recent exhibitions include *Energy Charge: Connecting to Ana Mendieta* (2016), cocurated with artist and curator Julio César Morales, and *New Earthworks* (2022), cocurated with artist Mark Dion.

**ELEANOR NAIRNE** is the Keith L. and Katherine Sachs Curator and Head of Modern and Contemporary Art at the Philadelphia Museum of Art. Previously, she was the Senior Curator at the Barbican Art Gallery, London, where her exhibitions included *Basquiat: Boom for Real* (2017), *Lee Krasner: Living Colour* (2019), *Jean Dubuffet: Brutal Beauty* (2021), *Soheila Sokhanvari: Rebel Rebel* (2022), *Alice Neel: Hot Off The Griddle* (2023), and *Julianknxx: Chorus in Rememory of Flight* (2023).

**ARCMANORO NILES** is a New York-based contemporary artist. A classically trained figurative painter known for his highly saturated portraits within domestic settings, Niles's work has been featured in recent group exhibitions at the Institute of Contemporary Art, Boston; Philbrook Museum of Art, Tulsa, Oklahoma; Wadsworth Atheneum Museum of Art, Hartford, Connecticut; and The MAC Belfast, Northern Ireland.

# ACKNOWLEDGMENTS

As the chronology in this volume makes clear, Eric Fischl's work has been actively presented in exhibitions and catalogs since the early 1980s. His first solo museum exhibition of figurative paintings toured internationally and concluded at the Whitney Museum in New York in 1985. At the outset of this project, forty years later, we were determined to build upon this substantial corpus by bringing fresh voices and current perspectives to a reconsideration of Fischl's career.

I would like to start by thanking the generous funders and supporters of the exhibition and accompanying publication, particularly Men's Arts Council, the Margaret T. Morris Foundation, and Steve Martin and Anne Stringfield. Thank you also to the lenders to the exhibition, as well as the individuals and institutions who shared works from their collections for this publication. They are private collectors, museums, foundations, and galleries from across the country and in Europe.

In early 2024 while we were working on this publication, Fischl's newest series of paintings, *Hotel Stories*, debuted at the New York-based Skarstedt Gallery. The staff of Skarstedt Gallery, which represents Fischl, assisted with locating many of the works and lenders, helped with the myriad project details, and welcomed several PhxArt and Scala staff members to the gallery. I want to particularly thank Per Skarstedt, Alison Ward, Manuela Hansen, Emma Laramie, and Emma Winder and recognize the gallery's generous support of the publication.

Catherine Tafur, Fischl studio manager, deftly oversees the artist's archive and responded to numerous requests for information and images. She also drove me several hours in a day to visit an art storage facility, sharing her experience of the work on our journey.

I am deeply grateful to the book's contributors—Dr. Kathryn Brown, Eleanor Heartney, Eleanor Nairne, and Arcmanoro Niles—who all responded to my request with enthusiasm and a wealth of ideas. They were a pleasure to work with through the editorial process. Together they provide a valuable reconsideration of an important, much-written about and much-exhibited American painter.

The Scala Arts Publishers crew were our partners throughout the book project and include Jennifer Norman, director of publications (New York); Claire Young, managing editor (London); and Morna McPherson, head of production (London). We are particularly grateful to designer Phil Kovacevich (New York), already a fan of Fischl's work, which comes through in his dynamic design, and Kati Woock, editor and project manager (Detroit), who carefully edited and shepherded texts and images.

Many PhxArt staff members and departments were involved in the production of this volume and will be intimately involved with the presentation of the exhibition. At this point, I would like to thank the exhibition team including Holly Mutascio, for early conversations on exhibition design, and Charlotte Quinney, interpretation manager, for copy editing; the registrar's office, including Laura Wenzel, senior director of collections and exhibitions; Kari Walters, registrar; and particularly Katie Jones-Weinert, digital assets manager, for all of her work with rights and reproductions; the development team led by Nikki DeLeon-Martin, deputy director and chief advancement officer; Sam Andreacchi, senior director of external affairs, for early marketing efforts; Executive

Assistant Ozzy Ledezma and Curatorial Administrator Indya Stewart, for all their behind-the-scenes work; and the Sybil Harrington Director and CEO Jeremy Mikolajczak, for his ongoing support and enthusiasm. Olga Viso, Selig Family Chief Curator and Director of Curatorial Affairs, has been a thoughtful, smart, and generous advisor and supervisor throughout the development of the curatorial thesis for the exhibition, the book conceptualization, and my introductory essay. I would like to sincerely thank Dawn Berg, curatorial specialist, who managed the book project for the museum with her considerable organizational skills. She also coauthored the chronology and, in that process, became a regular and valued conversant on Fischl's oeuvre and history.

I have known Eric Fischl for several years through his visits to present his student awards at Phoenix College, which have had a significant impact on young and emerging artists in our community. Of course, I knew Eric's work much earlier, when I was in undergraduate and graduate school in the early to mid-1980s, watching his paintings break on the scene to much acclaim and notoriety. It has been exciting and challenging to consider the entirety of his career and to revisit his work from today's perspective. He has been unfailingly responsive, collaborative, and generous throughout, sharing his time, thoughts, and work.

**HEATHER SEALY LINEBERRY**
Curator

# ILLUSTRATION CREDITS

Unless otherwise noted, all digital images were provided by Fischl Studio.

**Hello from Late America**
Courtesy Paula Cooper Gallery, New York, and the Estate of Elizabeth Murray (fig. 2); photo © Fine Art Images / Bridgeman Images (fig. 5).

**Navigating the Weight of History**
Photo Courtesy The Metropolitan Museum of Art, New York (fig. 10); Max Beckmann © 2025 Artists Rights Society (ARS), New York, digital image © The Museum of Modern Art/Licensed by SCALA / Art Resource, NY (fig. 12); photo licensed by SCALA / Art Resource, NY (fig. 13); photo G. Dagli Orti / ©NPL – DeA Picture Library / Bridgeman Images (fig. 15); Pierre Bonnard © 2025 Artists Rights Society (ARS), New York, photo ©RMN-Grand Palais / Art Resource, NY, photo: Agence Bulloz (fig. 16); photo Courtesy National Gallery of Art, Washington, DC (fig. 18); Image courtesy of Skarstedt Gallery, New York (fig. 19).

**To Sing the Body Electric**
Images courtesy of Skarstedt Gallery, New York (figs. 24, 26, 28); © The Estate of Alice Neel, Courtesy The Estate of Alice Neel and David Zwirner (fig. 25).

**Plates**
Image courtesy of Skarstedt Gallery, New York (2, 25, 30, 39, 40); Photo: Nathaniel Wilson (21).

**Paint What You Know?**
Photo: Katie Jones-Weinert (fig. 30); photo © Raffaello Bencini / Bridgeman Images (fig. 31); © Arcmanoro Niles. Courtesy the artist and Lehmann Maupin, New York, Seoul, and London (fig. 32).

**Artist Chronology**
Frank Stella ©2025 Frank Stella / Artists Rights Society (ARS), New York, digital image © The Museum of Modern Art /Licensed by SCALA / Art Resource, NY (p. 118); image Hirshhorn Museum and Sculpture Garden, provided by Fischl Studio (p. 120); The California Institute of the Arts Photographic Materials Collection. Courtesy of California Institute of the Arts Library & Institute Archives (p. 120); ©Jim Nutt, The Art Institute of Chicago / Art Resource, NY (p. 121); HIP / Art Resource, NY (p. 124); Susan Rothenberg ©2024 The Estate of Susan Rothenberg / Artists Rights Society (ARS), New York (p. 125); Courtesy of Mary Boone Gallery (p. 130); Courtesy of Eric Fischl Gallery (p. 142); Courtesy the artist and Sprüth Magers (p. 144); photo: Michael Heller (p. 146 top); photo: Kristen Santori (p. 146 bottom); Images courtesy of Skarstedt Gallery, New York. photos: John Berens (p. 148).

# INDEX

Page numbers in *italics* refer to illustrations.

Published on the occasion of the exhibition *Eric Fischl: Stories Told*, November 7, 2025–April 12, 2026. Organized by Phoenix Art Museum and curated by Heather Sealy Lineberry. © 2025 Phoenix Art Museum. All rights reserved.

*Eric Fischl: Stories Told* is made possible by Men's Arts Council, Margaret T. Morris Foundation, Steve Martin and Anne Stringfield, James and Janet Dicke, Bruce and Suzie Kovner and DL Winters Foundation.

Additional support provided by Rafael Jablonka and Erica Samuels.

The catalog is made possible through the generous support of Skarstedt Gallery.

All exhibitions at Phoenix Art Museum are underwritten by the Phoenix Art Museum Exhibition Excellence Fund, founded by The Opatrny Family Foundation with additional major support provided by Joan Cremin.

Book Copyright © 2025 Scala Arts Publishers, Inc.
First published in 2025 by Scala Arts Publishers, Inc.
1301 Avenue of the Americas
10th Floor
New York, NY 10019, USA
www.scalapublishers.com
An imprint of B. T. Batsford Holdings Ltd

ISBN 978-1-78551-593-4

Managing Editor at Scala Arts Publishers, Inc: Claire Young
Editor: Kati Woock
Design: Phil Kovacevich
Printed in China

Phoenix Art Museum
Catalog Coordinator: Dawn Berg
Rights and Reproductions: Katie Jones-Weinert and
    Kathy L. Borgogno
Copyediting: Charlotte Quinney

10 9 8 7 6 5 4 3 2 1

Library of Congress Cataloging-in-Publication Data: Names: Heather Sealy Lineberry with Dr. Kathryn Brown, Eleanor Heartney, Eleanor Nairne, Dawn Berg, Arcmanoro Niles, and Eric Fischl I Title: Eric Fischl: Late America I Phoenix Art Museum in association with Scala Arts Publishers, Inc,. New York I Description: Exhibition catalog at the Phoenix Art Museum, 2025 to 2026 I Identifiers: LCCN 2025936433 I ISBN 9781785515934 (hbk.) I Subjects: Painting | American art | Museums | Modern art

Cover: Eric Fischl, *Barbeque*, 1982. Oil on canvas. 65 × 100 in. (165.1 × 254 cm). Steve Martin and Anne Stringfield. Image courtesy of the artist. © 2025 Eric Fischl / Artists Rights Society (ARS), NY
Frontispiece: Eric Fischl, *Late America*, 2016. Oil on linen. 80 × 98 in. (203.2 × 248.9 cm). Private Collection. Image courtesy of the artist. © 2025 Eric Fischl / Artists Rights Society (ARS), NY
Page 4: Eric Fischl, *The Philosopher's Chair,* 1999. Oil on linen. 75 × 86 in. (190.5 × 218.4 cm). Collezione Maramotti, Reggio Emilia, photo: Carlo Vannini. Image courtesy of the artist. © 2025 Eric Fischl / Artists Rights Society (ARS), NY

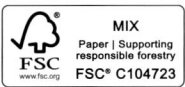